William Dean Howells
Second Edition

Twayne's United States Authors Series

David J. Nordloh, Editor

Indiana University, Bloomington

TUSAS 16

WILLIAM DEAN HOWELLS
(1837–1920)

William Dean Howells
Second Edition

By Kenneth E. Eble
University of Utah

Twayne Publishers • *Boston*

William Dean Howells, Second Edition

Kenneth E. Eble

Copyright © 1982 by G. K. Hall & Company
All Rights Reserved
Published by Twayne Publishers
A Division of G. K. Hall & Company
70 Lincoln Street
Boston, Massachusetts 02111

Book Production by Marne B. Sultz
Book Design by Barbara Anderson

Printed on permanent/durable acid-free
paper and bound in the United States
of America.

Library of Congress Cataloging in Publication Data

Eble, Kenneth Eugene.
   William Dean Howells.

   (Twayne's United States authors series:
TUSAS 16)
   Bibliography: p. 204
   Includes index.
   1. Howells, William Dean, 1837-1920
—Criticism and interpretation.
I. Title.   II. Series.
PS2034.E24   1982   818'.409   82-11876
ISBN 0-8057-7372-X

To George, both brother
and father

Contents

Contents

About the Author

Kenneth Eble, a professor of English at the University of Utah, specializes in the humanities and American literature. He received his M.A. degree from the University of Iowa and his Ph.D. from Columbia University in 1956 with a dissertation on William Dean Howells. He is the author of *F. Scott Fitzgerald* in this series, revised edition 1977, and has published widely on literary subjects.

Professor Eble has had an equally distinguished career as a writer and scholar active in support of higher education. His books include *The Profane Comedy: American Higher Education in the Sixties* and *A Perfect Education*, both for Macmillan, and *Professors as Teachers, The Craft of Teaching*, and *The Art of Administration* for Jossey-Bass Publishing Company. He was chairman of Committee C on Research, Teaching and Publication of the American Association of University Professors from 1970 to 1976, and director of the Project to Improve College Teaching for the AAUP and the Association of American Colleges from 1969 to 1971.

Professor Eble served as chairman of the Department of English at the University of Utah from 1964 to 1969, and he was the first faculty member to be named to the position of University Professor at Utah for 1976–77. He lives with his wife and three children in Salt Lake City, Utah.

Preface

William Dean Howells constitutes a curious case in American literature, and that literature, like any national literature if closely examined, has a good many curious cases: Emily Dickinson writing those little packets of poems, Walt Whitman that big packet, Herman Melville and his whale and his abandoning of fiction, Hawthorne and his secluded years. Howells's curious place is that of an author whose presence loomed very large during most of his lifetime and who was quickly forgotten after his death. Every literature has its popular successes whose names are forgotten within a generation or less. Who remembers Henry Cuyler Bunner or William C. Brownell or Hamilton Wright Mabie?

Yet, there are differences between Howells and these and any other examples that might be brought forth. One difference is in the sheer volume and variety of Howells's work: 137 volumes of one sort and another, thirty-five novels in all, his name in leading periodicals issue after issue for some forty years. Another difference is how high he stood in his time, the foremost critic and editor in America, and a fiction writer placed with those two *un*forgotten American writers, Mark Twain and Henry James. A third difference is that among academic scholars, Howells is still regarded as a major writer, notwithstanding his neglect by the common reader.

Knowledgeable readers who are concerned with the course of American literature, the nature of American society and culture, apparently see more in Howells than do others. And conversely, Howells, even strongly supported by academicians, has never since his death experienced a revival of interest that would bring him to the attention of a wide audience.

A main purpose of this book, then, is to furnish an acquaintance with Howells which may lead readers to read his works. In writing the book, I have reread most of Howells's work and have tried to be fair and honest about my reactions, not only from this reading but from an acquaintance which goes back thirty years. I have read most of the critical books and articles as they have appeared, and annotations of major books and of periodical articles of importance are included in the bibliography.

Two books—Edwin H. Cady's two-volume biography (1956) and Kenneth Lynn's *William Dean Howells: An American Life* (1971)—have been as important to me in this study as they have been to other scholars. The contribution of this present book is that it has drawn upon the full range of Howells materials, a large part of which was under family restrictions in the Houghton Library collection until 1972. It has also had the advantage of drawing upon the work of those many scholars engaged in preparing the various volumes in the CEAA Edition of Howells's works. It casts no reflection on the scholarship of Clara and Rudolf Kirk that a new and independent book is taking the place of their volume (1962) in the Twayne series. Their work, like that of many other Howells scholars, is hereby gratefully acknowledged.

I hope this book will bring some readers to Howells with a sense of discovery, of inviting them to become better acquainted with a writer who resembles, more than most authors, our own selves, a good but erring man who happened to write for a living, and whose writing helps us see ourselves more clearly. He can aptly be called the father of us all, father in the sense that the family occupies such a central place in his fiction, father in the sense that even as he worked through being a dutiful son, it was toward becoming a responsible father, and father in the sense that the late nineteenth century is father to the twentieth despite its efforts to disavow that paternity.

The design of this book needs no great explaining. The order is chronological, and the books Howells wrote are taken up and discussed pretty much in the order of their appearance. Since his own autobiographical writings give us much information about his early life, they will be drawn on in the early chapters and related to his other works later in the study. Specific acknowledgment of facts relating to Howells will be made in the text and in footnotes, but the general indebtedness to other writers is as broad as indicated in the citations and bibliography. In the final chapter, I will try to assess Howells's stature as reflected in the rise and fall of his literary reputation, and will call attention to major criticism and scholarship during and after his life.

I wish to acknowledge with thanks permission to use materials from the Houghton Library, Harvard University, and the assistance of David Nordloh and Christoph Lohmann, editors of *A Selected Edition of W. D. Howells*, in working with materials in the Howells Center at Indiana University. Thanks, too, to John N. M. and William W. Howells for conversation and correspondence with them. I wish also to acknowledge with thanks permission from the following publishers and publications: Doubleday for material from *Life and Letters of William Dean Howells*, Belknap Press of Harvard University Press for material from Mark Twain-Howells Letters, Indiana University Press for material from various volumes of A Selected Edition of W. D. Howells, and Twayne Publishers for material from *Selected Letters of W. D. Howells*. The photograph of Howells is from *Brahmins & Bullyboys: G. Frank Radway's Boston Album*, edited by Stephen Halpert and Brenda Halpert, reprinted by permission of Houghton Mifflin Company.

I wish to thank the University of Utah for the Gardner Fellowship which enabled me to complete work on this manuscript.

Kenneth E. Eble

University of Utah

Chronology

1861–1865   Consul in Venice. Marries Elinor at Christmas time, 1861. Daughter Winifred born, 1863. Brother John dies, 1864.

1865   Returns to New York. Works briefly for the *Nation*.

1866   *Venetian Life*. Becomes assistant editor of the *Atlantic*. Moves to Boston. Begins friendship with Henry James.

1867   *Italian Journeys*.

1868   Son John born. Mother dies.

1869   Meets Mark Twain following review of his *Innocents Abroad*.

1871   Becomes editor in chief of the *Atlantic*. *Suburban Sketches*.

1872   First novel, *Their Wedding Journey*. Daughter Mildred born.

1873   *A Chance Acquaintance. Poems.*

1875   *A Foregone Conclusion.*

1876   *The Parlor Car*, a farce.

1879   *The Lady of the Aroostook.*

1880   *The Undiscovered Country.*

1881   Resigns from the *Atlantic*. November, serious illness.

1882–1883   Abroad in England, Switzerland, Italy. *A Modern Instance.*

1884   Acquires house on Beacon Street, Boston.

1885   *The Rise of Silas Lapham.* Enters into publishing arrangement with Harper and Brothers.

1886   Begins "Editor's Study" in *Harper's Monthly*. *Indian Summer*.

1887   Defends Haymarket "anarchists."

1888   *Annie Kilburn.*

1889   Death of daughter Winifred. Moves to New York.

1890   *A Hazard of New Fortunes.*

1891   *Criticism and Fiction.*

1892   Brief editorship of *Cosmopolitan.*

1894   *A Traveler from Altruria.* Brief trip to Paris. Father dies.

1895   *My Literary Passions.* Begins "Life and Letters" feature for *Harper's Weekly.*

1897   *The Landlord at Lion's Head.* Trip through Germany.

1899   Lecture tour as far west as Kansas. *Their Silver Wedding Journey.*

1900   *Literary Friends and Acquaintance.* Begins "Editor's Easy Chair" for *Harper's Monthly.*

1904   *The Son of Royal Langbrith.* Receives honorary Oxford degree. Returns to Italy.

1907   *Through the Eye of the Needle.*

1908   Elected first president of American Academy of Arts and Letters.

1910   Mark Twain and Elinor Howells die. *My Mark Twain.*

1911   Visits Spain. Uniform library edition begun but stopped at six volumes.

1913   *New Leaf Mills. Familiar Spanish Travels.*

1916   *The Leatherwood God. Years of My Youth.* Henry James dies.

1917   In Carolina and the South, declines attending eightieth birthday celebration.

1919   *The Rise of Silas Lapham,* dramatic version by Lillian Sabine.

1920   Howells dies on May 11 in New York City.

Chapter One

Years of My Youth

As the foremost realist in American letters, William Dean Howells's voluminous works attest to the realist creed. Over half of his writings are nonfiction accounts, various modes of writing —essays, travel books, memoirs, letters, sketches—which capture life as he saw it and lived through it in the nineteenth and early twentieth centuries. Together with the thirty-five novels, some poems, and a large number of short stories and plays, his work constitutes an immense resource for understanding what life was like back then. Writing to his brother Joseph in 1906 he said, "I am often amazed at the quality as well as the quantity of my stuff, and feel as if it must have been done by a trust named after me" (*LIL*, 2:231).[1]

It is easy to explain the volume and nature of Howells's works, if not so easy to point out their strengths and weaknesses. Harder still to understand precisely how Howells loomed so large as an author for most of his lifetime and how little he is read or even remembered today. He began early as a writer, never deviated from writing as his occupation, and seldom took a holiday from it until his death. If he went to Heaven—and there is some doubt he would rest easy in an orthodox one—he is still writing. And as his fiction is a projection of his own experiences and of those many people he encountered in a long life, 1837–1920, we can move back and forth easily from his fiction to his nonfiction with a sense of reality created at either hand. Nor is either the fiction or nonfiction a mere record of people and events. For Howells was as interested as his friend Henry James in why people acted as they did, and as interested as his friend Samuel Clemens in capturing the emotional impact of the described past. And like both, he was a moralist, raising in his own life and in those of his created characters questions of right conduct and action.

Parentage and Ancestry

It must alter, even to a slight extent, our ideas of the American frontier, to realize how much Howells was a child of the frontier and yet how literary he was. We may forget in thinking about the frontier in this country that it was an extension of European civilization, that Shakespeare, for example, had been revered for three centuries before Howells noted that "Printers in the old-time offices were always spouting Shakespeare more or less" (*MLP*, 56). The nineteenth century, as we look back on it, appears to be an extraordinarily *wordy* age, in the length of its books, the ubiquity of the printing press, even in the length of sentences and paragraphs which made up written prose. The immigrants into the Ohio Valley, as with those into New England and the coastal colonies, brought a literary heritage with them and found themselves, even on the frontier, in a world where the written word was as much sought after as rails for fencing. In Jefferson, Ohio (population about 600), as he remembers it in the 1850s, there was a public library, "small but very well selected," in which "people met there oftener than they do in most country places, and rubbed their wits together" (*MLP*, 55–56).

Howells, to be sure, possessed traits of intelligence and imagination and makeup which inclined him toward his future career. But one cannot emphasize too greatly the part that the frontier print shop and his father's long career as a country printer played in Howells's becoming an author. It was the same school that fostered Mark Twain; Howells's retrospective essay "The Country Printer" observes: "My earliest memories, or those which I can make sure are not the sort of early hearsay that we mistake for remembrance later in life, concern a country newspaper, or, rather, a country printing-office" (*I&E*, 3). The literary entered into what he called his plain and decent, religious-minded ancestry, if at all, through the English girl his great-grandfather married. She was, so Howells wrote, "at least, a reader of the fiction of the day" (*YOMY*, 5). His grandfather, Joseph Howells, was a manufacturer of Welsh flannels, as his father had successfully been before him. In the further past, Howells's paternal ancestors were clockmakers; his father told him that as far as he could tell the family line went back to a blacksmith.

In 1883, Howells responded to an inquiry about his past by writing that his grandfather "did not go to America to 'better his condition,' for he was very well to do at home, but from a love for Democracy" (*Letters*, 3:73). Joseph Howells did give up an established family woolen business in Hay, Wales, to come to America in 1808, when Howells's father, William Cooper Howells, was but a year old. Of his grandfather's early years in America, Howells wrote: "He seems to have come to America with money enough to lose a good deal in his removals from Boston to Poughkeepsie, from Poughkeepsie to New York City, from New York to Virginia, and from Virginia to eastern Ohio, where he ended in such adversity on his farm that he was glad to accept the charge of a woolen-mill in Steubenville" (*YOMY*, 8). The wandering life, the pattern of grand hopes and scant fulfillment, and above all, the attraction of the land itself, are probably not untypical in the experiences of the many American emigrants moving west where land was cheap. Despite Joseph Howells's experience and skills in the wool trade, "the idea of living in the country," William Cooper writes, "and trying to farm, stuck by father with the tenacity of an affection for a good-for-nothing child."[2] Farming, like printing, was something that one could drift into or take up purposively without either great experience or capital. The prevailing pattern—the farms of Howells's grandfather's time and the printing establishments of Howells's own youth—was of small enterprises that failed as often as they succeeded. Even when they succeeded they provided a kind of subsistence existence as a family enterprise.

Joseph Howells's failure to improve upon his prospects in America can stand for many other examples of the contrary side of the opportunity the new world afforded for its many immigrants. So, too, he represents the many who were caught up in the religious fervor which so manifested itself early in the century in the Western lands. To note only one such manifestation, Joseph Smith's revelations at Palmyra, his forced removal to Ohio for six years and on to Illinois during the years 1820–39, roughly parallel Joseph Howells's seizure by Methodist "enthusiasm." Joseph Dylks, whose story Howells tells in *The Leatherwood God* (1916), was drawn from a real Dylks who, claiming to be God, appeared in eastern Ohio in 1828.

In Howells's own father, many of the impulses animating Joseph seem to be present, but in a somewhat tempered form. His attempts to provide a living for his family were as full of ups and downs, as transient, as Joseph's had been. In religion, he was to take up the Swedenborgian faith with somewhat the same intensity, if not to the neglect of other interests, in his middle life. Howells observed that his father was "a poet in his view of life." "I had a great taste for rural life," William Cooper Howells wrote, "because it was free, romantic and poetic."[3]

In a preface to William Cooper Howells's *Recollections of Life in Ohio, 1813–1840*, Howells writes: "He was not a very good draughtsman, not a very good poet, not a very good farmer, not a very good printer, not a very good editor, according to the several standards of our more settled times; but he was the very best *man* I have ever known."[4] The facts of his marriage to Howells's mother, Mary Dean, give us one measure of the kind of man Howells's father was. Eldest son in a family of seven with but a few months of formal education, experienced chiefly in miscellaneous labors of a farm, William Cooper nevertheless was willing to hazard marriage on the slender prospects of becoming a country printer. It is true that the death of his grandfather in Wales in 1824 gave the poor and struggling Howells family a chance for some financial stability. The actual legacy, however, turned out to be much less than expected, about $500, enough to

buy a farm near Steubenville and to provide the rural setting for
the last years of William's adolescent life. In the three years to
his maturity, the farm failed, his father moved to Wheeling to
take up work as a wool grader, and William was faced with the
choice of how to make his own living. There were, he wrote later,
"but few printing offices in the country, and they employed but
few hands."[5] He managed to get taken on by a new paper, *The
Virginia Statesman*, long enough—about two months—to learn
the rudiments of the printing trade. From that shaky basis, he
found himself casting about for other low-paying and short-
lived positions.

For a year he set himself up as a publisher and editor of *The
Gleaner*, a literary miscellany of which there seemed to be an
abundance on the frontier. Credit was easy to come by, subscrip-
tions in advance could get such ventures off the ground, but the
continuing interest to sustain them was seldom at hand. *The
Gleaner* foundered, to be replaced by *The Eclectic Observer and
Workingman's Advocate*, this time a weekly and taking on some
characteristics of a newspaper. It did no better, and was succeeded
by the appearance of William Mathers, who talked Howells
into publishing his book, *The Rise, Progress and Downfall of
Aristocracy*, which was to make both of them rich. Neither the
book's sales nor Mathers's promises of financial support proved to
have any substance, and at twenty-four, William Cooper Howells
was out of a job, with little but experience to show for his first
attempts to find a tough way to earn a small living.

His uncertain prospects, however, did not prevent him from
entering into marriage with Mary Dean a few months after they
met. The fact that Mary was from a more substantial family than
was Howells may have provided the measure of security that enabled them to risk marriage. It was Mary's father who suggested
the move to Martin's Ferry, where William Dean Howells was
born, at one of a number of low points in the young couple's fortunes. And it is the Dean aunts and uncles, profitably and ex-
citingly engaged as riverboat pilots, who helped make the years
in Martin's Ferry, according to Howells, so happy a time despite

the uncertainties. Looking back from 1910 at the years 1850–51, when his father tried to establish a Utopian enterprise at Eureka Mills, he wrote, "I should like to know what mother felt and said about the situation. . . . She had a hard part in life, but she played it greatly. She had a deep nature, and a rich mind" (*Letters*, vol. 5, to Aurelia and Annie, April 10, 1910). In *Years of My Youth*, he wrote more fully: "She was always working for us, and yet, as I so tardily perceived, living for my father anxiously, fearfully, bravely, with absolute trust in his goodness and righteousness. . . . She was not only the centre of home to me; she was home itself, and in the years before I made a home of my own, absence from her was the homesickness, or the fear of it, which was always haunting me" (20).

One can make too much, I think, of Howells's dependence on his mother; such dependence was attached to the family and home fully as much as to a single person. His relationship with his father was just as close, and it is his father's career that in many tangible and intangible ways brought Howells into his own profession. The printing trade (his father insisted on thinking of it as a "profession") was precarious but it was literary; it was dependent on the material world of business and affairs, but necessarily concerned with political and social and religious ideas which underlay the social fabric. It often attracted eccentrics and eccentric literary interests. One of William's early jobs involved printing an epic poem called the "Napoleon" after the style of Virgil and Milton, apparently to satisfy the vanity of a lawyer of some means in St. Clairsville, Ohio, a hamlet of less than 500 inhabitants.

What characterized all his father's early employment were low wages, short tenure, and an ever-present impetus for him to become an independent printer-publisher. William Cooper's career can be arbitrarily divided into the years of scant success, 1828–53, in southern Ohio, and the years in northern Ohio, 1853 to the end of his printing career, when its success had brought the Howells family a measure of financial security and political recognition. It could be argued that William Cooper Howells found such tough going as a printer in southern Ohio because his anti-slavery, generally radical views were not supported by proslavery, prosouthern conservatives. It is true that the move to Ashtabula and thence to Jefferson in 1853 was to a northern Ohio region much more sympathetic with his views. After the Civil War, Howells's father was elected state senator in Ohio, was a candidate for lieutenant governor in 1867, and was appointed U.S. consul to Quebec in 1874 and then to Toronto before his death. Howells's mother died in 1868; the widowed Howells bought a farm in Virginia in 1883 upon his retirement from the consulship, but left it to return for his last years to Jefferson.

Before leaving the subject of Howells's ancestral past, it is useful to place what seems to be his father's and grandfather's continual hazarding of fortunes against the actualities of life in frontier Ohio. Boom and bust loosely characterize much of history of American development in the middle states, but the overall pattern for Ohio during the pre–Civil War years was one of steady and spectacular growth. In 1800, there were roughly 45,000 inhabitants of the territory. Becoming the seventeenth state in 1803, Ohio had a population of 230,760 in 1810, to be doubled by 1820. At the outbreak of the Civil War, the state's population was about two-and-a-half million, exceeded only by New York and Pennsylvania among the then thirty-four states. Industry and commerce were as much a part of its fortunes as clearing land and farming. Joseph Howells's move to Ohio was clearly to the independence and opportunities it offered, and his settling in and near Wheeling, Virginia, was a taking advantage of the civilization that developed first along the Ohio River and then spread out along the river to Cincinnati in the West. Cheap land, easy credit, small farms and communities, religious zealotry, and politics were features of life among the incessant spitting Americans,[6] as Frances Trollope described Cincinnatians in the 1820s. Whatever adversities many individuals suffered along the way, the course was probably upward for the most of them. "Except for the slavery issue, Ohio in these years just before the Civil War was happier and more prosperous than it had ever been."[7]

Growing up in Ohio

One can fairly say that William Dean Howells's own career
proceeds from this Ohio of the pre–Civil War years on a course
not so different from that of his father, if one takes into consideration the greater opportunities that these later times afforded. As he enjoyed better schooling than did his father—and
yet much of it by chance and from his own efforts—so did he
have a wider scope for literary expression through his father's
printing ventures, and more direct support from many sources for
his literary bent. His father's propensity to risk and to fail probably made Howells more cautious in his own risking; he hedged
his bets much more than did his father, but his career, tame as
it may appear in retrospect, reveals a succession of risks that must
have loomed very large for a man raised amid the mixed securi-
ties and insecurities of Howells's youth.

Of these early years and the impact they had upon him, Howells
is still the best witness. Though he never accomplished a full
autobiography, detailed accounts of his early life are to be found in
A Boy's Town (1890), *My Year in a Log Cabin* (1893), *My
Literary Passions* (1895), and *Years of My Youth* (1916).
Howells deserves more recognition than he has had as a superb
writer of nonfiction: autobiography, biography, travel and other
sketches, memoirs, essays, in addition to literary criticism and reviews. His accounts of his own life and of the people around him
are often more affecting than what we encounter in his fiction.
Not facing the necessities of creating character and plot and dialogue, Howells can give all his powers of observation and language to the subject at hand. Thus, this side of his work alone
recreates life as it was for a recognizable and representative American through almost a century.

According to Howells's later account, the three years in eastern
Ohio left only two distinct impressions, one of a peach tree in
bloom, and the other of "seeing from the steamboat which was
carrying our family to Cincinnati, a man drowning in the river"

(*YOMY*, 10). A prosperous member of the Dean family had offered the elder Howells a trip with him across Ohio, and in Hamilton, about thirty miles by canal south of Dayton, he was able to buy into a Whig paper. In the spring of 1840, the family arrived in Hamilton, twenty miles or so from the big river port of Cincinnati. For a few years, until William Cooper Howells's attention was diverted by the compulsion to run a Swedenborgian religious paper, *The Retina*, his work with the *Hamilton Intelligencer* prospered. *The Retina* venture lasted for about a year, and in May 1845, he returned as owner of the *Intelligencer* until 1848, when the paper was sold, chiefly because of Howells's opposition to the Mexican War and Zachary Taylor's nomination for president. These shifting fortunes appeared to affect the young William Dean Howells but little, for he recalled the "ten or eleven years passed in Hamilton as the gladdest of all my years" (*YOMY*, 14). Here, the rest of the family, except for Henry, were born.

With the collapse of the paper at Hamilton, hard times were on the Howells family again. Their next move was to Dayton, where Howells had bought into another paper, which lasted until its failure in August, 1850. That fall, William Cooper Howells interested his brothers in buying a grist and sawmill with the intention of converting it into a paper mill to provide the economic base for a self-sustaining cooperative community. His brothers had established themselves in the vicinity before the W. C. Howells family had arrived; one was a physician, another the proprietor of the drug store in Hamilton which their father had established. The log cabin experience at Eureka Mills was the basis for William Dean Howells's later fictional account, *New Leaf Mills* (1913), but at the time it did little to aid the family's fortunes. By the second winter, the Utopian attempt was abandoned. When the opportunity came to have someone fill in at a printing office in Xenia, William Dean was sent. He was thirteen, homesick to the point of wanting to return home at once, and saved by the job's only lasting a week. Another attempt was made for him to take up paid work in Dayton, but this, too, was brief. At the end of

December, 1851, the family made a permanent move, this time to
Columbus, where Howells's father had a job through the winter in
reporting the proceedings of the Ohio State legislature.

For all the family insecurities of these years, Howells remembered life in rural Ohio as being like this description in *Years of
My Youth*:

I recall in like manner the starry summer nights, and there is one of
these nights that remains single and peerless in my memory. My
brother and I had been sent on an errand to some neighbor's . . . and
we had been somehow belated, so that it was well after twilight when
we started home, and the round moon was high when we stopped to
rest in a piece of the lovely open woodland of that region, where the
trees stood in a park-like freedom from underbrush, and the grass
grew dense and rich among them. We took the pole, on which we
had slung the bag, from our shoulders, and sat down on an old long-
fallen log, and listened to the densely interwoven monotonies of the
innumerable katydids, in which the air seemed clothed as with a mesh
of sound. The shadows fell back from the trees upon the smooth
sward, but every other place was full of the tender light in which all
forms were rounded and softened; the moon hung tranced in the sky.
We scarcely spoke in the shining solitude, the solitude which for once
had no terrors for the childish fancy, but was only beautiful. This
perfect beauty seemed not only to liberate me from the fear which is
the prevailing mood of childhood, but to lift my soul nearer and
nearer to the soul of all things in an exquisite sympathy. (*YOMY*, 51).

Howells was both romantic and realistic toward the years of
his youth; like Mark Twain and Thoreau, he could look back upon
growing up in rural and small-town America as near ecstasy. On
the other hand, long before he grew old, he wrote his brother
Joseph, April 16, 1869: "It is odd to me that we got little or no
harm out of that Hamilton life which was moral death to so many
of our mates. It is more surprising still that we were not drowned,
crushed, shot or gored to death every summer of our lives."[8]

Perhaps freedom is the key condition they all prized: space to
roam in, time not sharply apportioned, relationships to form

rather than be formed by. Howells is a representative boy in this respect. For what made Hamilton precious to him was not his parents' security or success—they had little of either—or the advantages of a somewhat settled existence, or some exceptional endowment of person or family. It was, rather, the commonplaces of the American past: children of big families so there were many companions to play with; unplotted land that included rivers and canals and woods and swamps and habitations with space between; accessibility to most of one's surroundings, including the people who figured importantly in it; a mingling of work and play in family and community enterprises; an absence of social lines and implied restrictions, and perhaps a lesser and less-pressing range of expectations placed upon the child. Thus, if such communities seem to be somewhat barren, devoid of opportunities and a sense of the variety and complexity of the world, they lift some burden of expectation and desiring from the child growing up in them.

In the world of his youth, printing, schooling, and playing were, according to his own testimony, his chief loves. One should add literature, a good deal of hard work, and an expanding and loving family. He writes, in *Years of My Youth*, that he does not in the least know "how the notion of authorship" (18) first crept into his mind, but he says later in that book, that at thirteen or fourteen, "My life, then, as always, was full of literature to bursting, the literature I read and the literature I wrote" (*YOMY*, 69).

Howells describes his printing experiences in detail in these autobiographical books, as well as in "The Country Printer," part memoir and part historical record. "I know when I could not read, for I recall supplying the text from my imagination for the pictures I found in books, but I do not know when I could not set type" (*YOMY*, 15). Howells was not quite three when his father became editor and proprietor of the *Hamilton Intelligencer*. From that time on, he was never far from the print shop. By the time he was ten, he had regular duties in the shop, and when the family moved to Dayton he was fully capable of doing everything required of a journeyman printer, editor, and writer. His first attempts at literature were not written but set into type. In his early childhood, his father indulged his interests; the printing office was inseparable from the home. Later, he took his place with Joseph, the oldest brother, as an indispensable part of the enterprise.

For Howells, the path from family journeyman printer to author was almost as inevitable as that of the farm boy who takes over the father's farm. Joseph did, in fact, take over the printing enterprise, and he carried it on almost until his death. For William Dean, the distinctive literary bent that distinguished his father from other printers had a strong impact. Poetry as such had never been the chief substance of journalism. The poet in William Cooper Howells can be found as clearly in the son, and as submerged in the reality of what supports a country printer as well as an author. The uncertainties that attended the elder Howells's printing career could not have been lost on Howells; if he always seemed to need a paying situation, if he drove hard bargains at the height of his fame which kept a half-dozen writing and journalistic enterprises afloat at the same time, it may have been the effects of the adverse aspects of being a country printer.

Two other matters deserve mention. William Cooper Howells was not a passive printer. The settled life in Hamilton came to an end because of his political views in the election of 1848. His vigorous advocacy of free soil was not tolerated as events moved closer to the breach between North and South. He would and did address himself to the causes of his time, and underneath them all are beliefs that the son was to carry on: the rights of working men, social equality, the carrying out of the best aspects of the democratic promise. Thus early in his life, William Dean Howells was not merely learning the mechanical arts of printing nor indulging himself in his passion for belles lettres, but recognizing the responsibilities, opportunities and dangers of confronting the realities of social and political life in print.

Schooling and Self-Study

Despite his long hours in the print shop and the family necessity to have him so engaged, schooling occupied a large part of

Howells's early life. It was, for him as for others, a means of escape from hard work, his being more enjoyable than that of many others, less separated from schooling, and more in harmony with his own passions. Nevertheless, his resistance to schooling and the fears it aroused are strongly set forth in his reminiscences. In both *A Boy's Town* and *The Flight of Pony Baker*, the story is told of his packing up his books and making a show of quitting school over being put back a form because of failing to respond sufficiently well in oral reading. His parents sent him back, not without some welcomed criticism of the teacher's actions. Schooling was still haphazard in the Hamilton of Howells's youth and discontinuous both while there and after moving to Dayton, Eureka Mills, and Jefferson. Early lessons were usually at the hands of lay teachers in a private house; later he went on to other private and public schools where teachers came and went with great frequency. The prevailing student mode was to resist instruction; the conventional teacher's response was a variety of pedagogical sadisms. Howells under different circumstances would have been one of those pupils teachers teach for. As it was, no one teacher remains in his memory except for "old Manson," a new teacher whose enlightened decision to get rid of the birch rod had no effect upon students, who, by silent accord, had decided to persecute him anyway.

Then, as now, schooling was predominantly verbal, and the omnipresence of the tangible word in the print shop may have helped Howells come to terms with book learning. He does remark on the discovery of prosody in the back of a book on grammar and of attempting a tragedy in the measures of "The Lady of the Lake." But for the most part formal schooling was only an accompaniment to the self-learning both forced upon him and of his own choosing. On balance, his experience in the print shop, the generally benign and literary tutelage of his father, and the acquaintances he made among printers employed by his father were as good a schooling as he might have obtained by a more systematic and required education.

Two other facts of Howells's schooling need to be mentioned: one, his extraordinary powers of learning what he wanted to learn, and two, his not extending his formal education much beyond what we would regard as grammar and intermediate schools. His mastery of languages is the best example of his talent for self-study. The best account of the beginnings of his language studies in the log cabin at Eureka Mills is offered in *A Boy's Town.* Among the barrel of books the family had transported from Hamilton, Howells discovered the poems of "a certain Henry W. Longfellow" (*YOMY*, 46). "The Spanish Student" turned his thoughts to the Spain he had already encountered in Irving's *Conquest of Granada* and *Don Quixote.* It led him "to attack fitfully the old Spanish grammar which had been knocking about our house ever since my father bought it from a soldier of the Mexican War" (*YOMY*, 46). From that time on, Howells's youthful studies were seldom without an attempt to master a language. He seemed to recognize without outside prompting that languages were a main route to literature. Spanish, German, and some attention to Latin, Greek, and French comprised his earliest studies. Though he aimed at being able to read in the languages, his sustained interest and travels made him fluent in both German and Italian, with mastery of French and Spanish sufficient to get along.

The second and closely related point is that Howells, despite all his obvious academic aptitudes, did not go on to college. The explanation does not lie in the lack of importance attached to further schooling nor even to the opportunities the times afforded. His daughter's sketch of his life observes "The whole village was proud of his studies, and a neighboring Scotch farmer offered to be one of three or four persons to send him to Harvard" (*LIL*, 1:9). But, though he was given a brief try at reading law, a schooling which might be expected to bring a much quicker financial return, he was not to be spared for four years of college. His later regret was tempered by the success he had enjoyed despite a lack of formal schooling. And though we may regard that regret as genuine, as he expresses it in detail in *Years of My Youth*, it also comes with the story of his spurning offers to become a professor, first at Union College, later at Washington University, Yale, Johns Hopkins, and Harvard itself. "It still seems to me lamentable that I should have had to grope my way and so imperfectly find it where a little light from another's lamp would have instantly shown it. I still remain in depths of incredible ignorance as to some very common things" (*YOMY*, 95). He instances mathematics beyond long division, and grammar, curious instances in that he had little need for the former and mastered to some degree the grammar of four languages outside his own before he was of college age.

Family Influences

One glance at Howells's early life reveals a boy somewhat morbid in temper, dutiful and dependent, bookish, old beyond his years, characteristics which may have fastened "the Old Man" upon him as a nickname. Another glance, however, reveals a conventional boy who has no more connection with these adult characterizations of the young or with the world of occupations and ideas and books than does a milkweed or cornstalk. In one of his many wise observations about the nature of children, he writes: "it seems to me even more true that a child is a savage. Like the savage, he dwells on an earth round which the whole solar system revolves, and he is himself the centre of all life on the earth" (*BT*, 6). It is this boy Howells has in mind when he writes, "I learned many things in my irregular schooling, and at home I was always reading when I was not playing. I will not pretend that I did not love playing best; life was an experiment which had to be tried in every way that presented itself" (*YOMY*, 17).

The Flight of Pony Baker (1902), written as a children's book, puts into fictional form many of Howells's boyhood experiences. The central story of Pony's unsuccessful attempt to join the circus grows out of an observation in *A Boy's Town* which begins the chapter on "Circuses and Shows": "What every boy expected to do, some time or other, was to run off. He expected to do this because the scheme offered an unlimited field to the imagination, and because its fulfillment would give him the highest distinction among the other fellows. To run off was held to be the only way for a boy to right himself against the wrongs and hardships of a boy's life" (*BT*, 93). *Pony Baker* reinforces the picture of Howells that the autobiographical works provide: something of a mama's boy, far more properly brought up and fussed over than Jim Leonard, a Huck Finn kind of character whose adventures occupy much of the story. Pony could never get his mother "to like Jim Leonard, or to believe that Jim was not leading him into mischief wherever they were off together" (166).

Despite chores to be done and parents who, out of family necessity and principle, saw that they were carried out, neither inhibited Howells greatly in his exploration, through play, of the world Hamilton offered. In *A Boy's Town*, the social historian in Howells gives a detailed account of the games they played and the pastimes enjoyed. The circus seized upon Howells as much as it has millions of children, and at one point traveling actors gave Howells a very early introduction to the stage. Religion, that bane of play for many children of the nineteenth century, did not act as a curb in the Howells family. The influence of Swedenborg on Howells's father was almost entirely benign; though stone throwing and fighting and some of the usual childhood cruelties figure into Howells's recreations, little took place that violated the tolerant moral and religious sympathies of the family.

It may be that what is most unusual about Howells's early Ohio years is the marked lack of separation between work, play, schooling, family obligations and enjoyments. It was a large family and not without frictions, even against the parental edict against fighting. Joseph, the oldest, was born in 1832; William Dean not quite five years later, and Victoria (1838) a scant year after that. As might be expected the three enjoyed the closest relationships, though harmony and understanding between Joseph and Will only came in Howells's late teens and following a period of great friction. By the time Howells was fifteen, the last of his seven brothers and sisters was born, Henry Israel, who suffered an undiagnosed brain injury in a childhood accident and spent the rest of his life as a mental defective.[9] Before that tragic last child were Samuel Dean, 1840, Aurelia, 1842, Annie, 1844, and John, 1846, the only child not to reach adulthood, dying of diphtheria at eighteen. "The house was pretty full of children, big and little," is Howells's dry comment forty years later (*BT*, 14).

It was within the family, even more than from schooling or outside influences, that Howells attachment to literature grew. Even so, Howells reflected, there was in him a separate inwardness, one special part of his being, that maintained a private world created and fed by reading. Thus, "while he was joyfully sharing the wild sports and conforming to the savage uses of the boy's world about him," Howells writes, "he was dwelling in a wholly different world within him, whose wonders no one else knew" (*BT*, 171). There is nothing very remarkable in his early reading, except that it was substantial, favored prose more than poetry, and set off a factual content with myth and story. Goldsmith, Cervantes, and Irving were his earliest literary passions. Goldsmith's two histories of Greece and Rome, a small book on Greek and Roman mythology, and a collection of tales he only later found to be the "Gesta Romanorum" were books he read over and over again. "What I wanted with my Greeks and Romans after I got at them was to be like them, or at least to turn them into account in verse... (*MLP*, 12). Though he read the histories earlier, he dates his love for Goldsmith from the age of fourteen, when a volume of his essays set Howells to writing sketches in the Goldsmith manner.

Don Quixote was another of the earliest of his passions. He remembers (*MLP*, 17–22) coming upon it through his father in Hamilton; he knew it well when he was ten and read it all through his boyhood. Irving's *Conquest of Granada* came after *Don Quixote*; it provided the central character, Hamet el Zegri, of the "first and last historical romance I ever wrote" (24). Even earlier he had tried imitating stories of Poe as he found them in *Tales of the Grotesque and Arabesque*. His first attempt at a novel, *Geoffrey Winter*, written in Columbus in 1860–61, has hints of Poe as well as Hawthorne all through it. The geographies, travel narratives, and poetry referred to him by his father made less im-

childish terror of hydrophobia and of years later being bitten by a dog, leaving the wound untreated, and then suffering a severe psychic rather than physical ill triggered by the village doctor's remark about hydrophobia: " 'Works round in your system,' he said, 'for seven years or more, and then it breaks out and kills you' " (*YOMY*, 79). His further description is worth quoting at some length:

I had no release from my obsession, except in the dreamless sleep which I fell into exhausted at night, or that little instant of waking in the morning, when I had not yet had time to gather my terrors about me. . . . Instinct taught me that some sort of bodily fatigue was my safety; I spent the horrible days in the woods with a gun, or in the fields gathering wild berries, and walked to and from the distant places that I might tire myself the more. My father reasoned to the same effect for me, and helped me as best he could. . . . But no doubt a more real help was his recurrence, as often as I chose, to his own youthful suffering from hypochondria, and his constantly repeated assurance that I not only would not and could not have hydrophobia from that out-dated dog-bite, but that I must also soon cease to have hypochondria. . . . My fear when it once lifted never quite overwhelmed me again, but it was years before I could endure the sight of the word which embodied it. (*YOMY*, 80–81).

Cady gives a cluster of points from which Howells's "profound psychic turbulence" might have proceeded. One is from the estrangement of Howells's family from the community; another Howells's own estrangements from his fellows by virtue of his personal intellectualism; a third, son-mother-father conflicts familiar to psychoanalysis.[11] I think the matter both more complex as regards children, male or female, coming into their own identity, and less special as an experience unique to Howells. What Howells himself later realized and what the experiences with his own children and those near to him helped teach him was that "a boy's town" is only some parts sunshine and light. Terror is never far away, as bizarre as his own believing he was dying of hydrophobia or as Thoreau's agony of lockjaw at secondhand and as common as all those unreported traumas overcome in one way or another by an organism's powerful movement toward health. Howells's hypochondria was to stay with him into his years in Venice. It illustrates the fact that growing up is often a time of profound psychic disturbances and that it can take a very long time.

I will end this chapter at this point, with Howells's youth not yet done. The move from southern Ohio to Jefferson, about seventy miles east and slightly north of Cleveland, was as consequential for William Dean as for the family. It was a time when an acknowledged search for a vocation was as strong upon him as the inward struggle for identity. It was a time when his beginning literary efforts began to see publication. It was a time when duty to family which kept him in Ohio had to give away to the need to establish his own directions. It was a time of doubts, of rapid changes, and of the first intimations that a literary career might lie open before him.

Chapter Two

Leaving Youth Behind

"My elder brother and I had several ideals in common," Howells wrote in *Years of My Youth*, "quite apart from my own literary ideals" (*YOMY*, 70). Chief among these was a desire to live in a village, as contrasted with either the country or a city, and to renounce the printing business forever. Howells's first taste of city life in Dayton offered few satisfactions; the winter in Columbus in 1851–52 had been more satisfactory. He had been able to move out of the shop of the *Ohio State Journal*, where he had earned four dollars a week as a compositor, into the book room; he had met John J. Piatt, who was to be his collaborator in *Poems of Two Friends* eight years later; and he had begun to keep a diary in which "there is evident striving, not to say straining, for a literary style" (*YOMY*, 63).

Neither he nor his brother was to escape the printing business, though Joe had gone to Cincinnati briefly in 1851 to try to become a river pilot. When their father arranged to work himself into ownership of still another paper in 1853, both brothers returned to the family print shop in Ashtabula, Ohio, on the lake some sixty miles southeast of Cleveland. Six months later the *Sentinel* moved to Jefferson, ten miles inland, and the Howells brothers were able to realize the ideal of returning to a village. The years in Jefferson were hard working years for the family, years of increased reading and study and writing for William Dean. The paper prospered generally, even achieved temporary financial success with the pub-

22

lication of a popular songbook during the Civil War, and Joseph continued the enterprise until he gained a consulate in the British West Indies in 1905.

Developing As A Journalist and Author

Howells had been attempting to write before the family moved north; he had printed pieces in his father's papers well before 1852, when his father, without his knowledge, sent one of his poems to the *Ohio State Journal,* which printed it on March 23, just after he became fifteen. At about that time, too, he was contemplating writing a life of Cervantes, and that first winter in Columbus, so he remembers, "was largely given to producing and polishing the plaster-of-paris masterpiece," a cold pastoral modeled on Pope. Various studies, sketches, and poems found their way into the *Sentinel* in the 1850s. In Ashtabula, he read *Uncle Tom's Cabin* but mainly remembered it as a means of keeping at bay the ghost of a former inmate of the house who had hanged himself there. In the summer of 1856, when he was nineteen, fears of hydrophobia incapacitated him for much of the year. The "old hippo," as he called his hypochondria, troubled him for years. In Columbus four years later he wrote his family, "As the summer approaches, I begin to feel touches of hypochondria, but I hope not to go crazy" (*Letters,* 1:55). Jim Williams comes into the pages of his diary as an acquaintance in Jefferson who greatly aided him in the education he was acquiring for himself in a study beneath the stairs. Williams is probably the J.W. of *Years of My Youth,* described there as a combination of vagabond printer, storyteller, singer, and village eccentric.

Most of the latter years of this period in Jefferson were spent with some eye to finding a vocation. The month he spent (May 1855) reading law in the Columbus offices of "Old Ben Wade," senator from Ohio, were enough to convince him that his pathway did not lie there. Family circumstances ruled out college attendance. William Cooper's careful nurturing of his son through his disabling hypochondria of the summer of 1856 was followed by his taking Will with him to Columbus when he began his second session as official clerk of the state legislature. As a natural extension of his appointment, he conceived of a legislative newsletter for outlying areas and sold the idea to the *Cincinnati Gazette*. From the start, young Will did most of the writing, and with a zest and skill that seemed to dispel the anxieties of the previous summer. In March, the *Gazette* offered him the city editorship at one thousand dollars a year, twice as much as he had been paid for the newsletter. (On their first move to Columbus, the entire Howells family was being paid at the rate of $884 a year, if the work had been steady, which it was not.) Thus, the Cincinnati offer was not only a personal opportunity for Howells but a chance to improve the family's position in its long struggle to arrive at the security of owning a home and a business.

Much has been made of Howells's brief tenure in this job, and of his shrinking from the raw facts of life as he recounts the experience in *Years of My Youth*. His reminiscences are the main source of information, though we have a letter to his brother Joseph at the time in which he seems excited, even happy, about the initial prospects. I think it reasonable to connect his giving up the Cincinnati job in little more than a month with the serious anxiety of the previous summer and with psychic disturbances which continued on the next year or two. In writing about the concealed disappointment of his father at his giving up the Cincinnati job, Howells implies that his return to Jefferson was followed by a period that summer of recovering his balance amid continuing conflicts. By late autumn, he asked for the newsletter assignment for the *Gazette* and the *Cleveland Herald* as well, and "returned to the capital with no pretence that I was not now writing the letters solely and entirely myself. But almost before my labors began, my health quite broke under the strain of earlier over-study and later over-work" (*YOMY*, 124). William Cooper Howells took over the assignment until the following spring, and at the next legislative session gave it up to Whitelaw Reid, the

first step in Reid's distinguished career. *Years of My Youth* recounts the next event:

> I was at home in the autumn, as I had been all summer, eating my
> heart out, (as I would have said in those days), when the call to a
> place on the *Journal*'s editorial staff incredibly, impossibly came, and
> I forgot my ills, and eagerly responded. I hardly know how to justify
> my inconsistency when I explain that this place was the same which
> I had rejected at twice the salary on the Cincinnati *Gazette*. (*YOMY*,
> 125).

Howells, in writing of this experience long after it happened,
may be overlooking some of its actualities at the time. With his
income from the newsletter, which could only be carried on from
Columbus, his total earnings were about the same as they would
have been in Cincinnati. Moreover, the two jobs were not the
same. His introduction to journalism in Cincinnati emphasized the
full range of reporting activities, the confrontation with the seamy
and trivial and personal that is the reporter's lot. Almost immediately in the *Journal* position, he was doing editorial work, specifically in charge of looking through the exchange newspapers,
including French and Spanish and German, for which he was
uniquely suited. Howells, his full career seems to show, was an
astute and reflective observer, but he did not have the temperament
of a newspaper reporter. His literary ambitions were probably as
much at odds with the Cincinnati position as were his personal
scruples. The position he found most congenial to his talents was
the editor's study, not the city desk. The style he pursued was that
of the "new journalism, the kind of writing which we practiced—
light, sarcastic, a little cruel, with a preference for the foibles of
our political enemies as themes" (*YOMY*, 137).

These more commonplace observations are worth placing against
interpretations which look back to Howells's neuroticism and forward to his excessive gentility. The events do seem to connect with
Howells's breaking away from home, from working through his

dependence on father and mother, and of gaining his own self-identity. They take place in a sequence that makes it possible to say he was able to succeed in Columbus as he was not in Cincinnati because he was, among other things, a year older, and in Howells's own words, "I could no longer endure the disappointment and inaction of my life" (*YOMY*, 125).

The account Howells gives in *Years of My Youth* may be more revealing of Howells in 1915, already adjudged by many of that time as out of date in his sentiments and values, than of Howells as he was in 1857–58. The ravings of a drunken woman in a police station were too much for him, he wrote, and added a sentence much used to condemn his excessive gentility: "My longing was for the cleanly respectabilities" (123). It should be pointed out that in January, 1882, Howells contributed an unblinking sketch of an ungenteel world, "Police Report," to the *Atlantic*; Mark Twain called the piece "faultless & delicious."

Howells's temper during these years is best conveyed in letters to his sister, Victoria, who was his closest confidante. On October 27, 1857, he wrote: "I'm in such a state of mind, not to say sin and misery, as hardly to be able to write. In the morning I get up in a stew, and boil and simmer all day, and go to bed sodden, and ferociously misanthropical." Having returned to Jefferson from Cincinnati, he is content with neither place, his ambitions and doubts tormenting and immobilizing him: "I am proud, vain, and poor. I want to make money, and be rich and grand.... I want to succeed, yet I am of too indolent a nature to begin.—I want to be admired and looked up to, when I might be loved.— I know myself, and I speak by the card, when I pronounce myself *a mistake*." Underneath the romantic agony is a plainer reality: "The present question with me, for instance, is, how am I to make a living?" (*Letters*, 1:13–14).

That question and many of his anxieties were temporarily resolved during the period from fall 1858 to spring 1860, the year and a half he spent on the *Ohio State Journal*. He found congenial friends at a boardinghouse in Columbus, saw his work published in national periodicals including a poem in the *Atlantic* (Septem-

ber, 1860), and collaborated with his friend Piatt on a volume
of verse, *Poems of Two Friends*, published by a Columbus firm
at the end of 1859.

Poems of Two Friends

The publication of *Poems of Two Friends* at Christmas, 1859,
is a fit ending to Howells's strivings and his coming of age in the
1850s. The words capitalized in the brief preface do much to indicate the nature of the poetry: "Tenderness," "Heart," "Oblivion,"
"Doubt," "Gracious Reader," and "Affection." The volume begins
with Howells's narrative poem, "The Pilot's Story," which was
soon to see separate publication in the *Atlantic*.

Though exact comparisons between poems written in different
languages are hard to make, reading Heine's lyrics and Howells's
side by side is revealing. His long poem, "Pleasure-Pain" and
Heine's "Homeward Bound," in Emma Lazarus's translation,[1] afford an example. Setting aside the fact that Heine's poem is a
collection of ninety lyrics and Howells's but seven, we can look
at a comparable section, in which a few quatrains take a similar
scene and incident and build on emotions created by the passage of
time, love lost and remembered, and death. Here are the first two
quatrains:

Heine

> I tread the dear familiar path,
>   The old road I have taken;
> I stand before my darling's house,
>   Now empty and forsaken.

Howells

> Through the silent streets of the city,
>   In the night's unbusy noon,
> Up and down in the pallor
>   Of the languid summer moon. . . .

One observation seems fair here. Heine is doing what Howells, later in his development, wanted to do: to capture the emotion of ordinary experiences within ordinary settings in an ordinary but not unaffecting language. Heine's poetry is more direct, less deliberately poetic than Howells's. Howells's lyric, with its "night's unbusy noon" and "languid summer moon," is "poetic" as was much American poetry of his time. Howells's poetry would not, as did Heine's elsewhere in these lyrics, include "a bony fiddler," "retching and cursing," or gods "snoring," nor would Howells have had Hetty and Julia and Kunigunda kissing the poet on successive days. In fairness, there are sighing maidens, unknown deeps, and somber woods in both, but Heine's lyrics temper the sentimentally romantic in both substance and diction with real experience finding apt words, and without sacrificing the imagination's power or fancy.

The short section of Heine's poem sampled here ends:

> Here to her vows I listened,
>   I tread the empty halls,
> And where her tear-drops glistened,
>   The poisoned serpent crawls.

as compared with Howells's:

> The summer moon is shining
>   So wan and large and still,
> And the weary dead are sleeping
>   In the graveyard under the hill. (*Poems*, 21)

Howells did not need so much to "sweat the Heine out of you as men do mercury," in Lowell's phrase (*Letters*, 1:197), as to assay Heine's lyrics to separate out ore from dross. Had he been able to do so, he might have arrived at a poetic manner and voice that more sharply separated itself from conventional poetry.

Biography of Lincoln

Poems of Two Friends sold very few copies, and though the few favorable comments it received, especially those of Henry Clapp, editor of the *Saturday Press*, and of Lowell, encouraged

Howells as a writer, they did not launch him into the poetic career he preferred at the time. Perhaps the most important consequence of this publication was the connection it gave Howells with the publishers Follett and Foster of Columbus. When his regular position at the *Journal* ended in March, he was able to get a job as reader for them. Thus, when the publishers decided to do a biography of Lincoln for quick sales during the campaign, Howells was a logical choice for the job. How little he regarded it, and how much it reinforced his disinclination to do reportorial journalism is evidenced by his sending a friend, John Howard, to interview Lincoln in Springfield. From Howard's notes and other material, he put together an admittedly "hurried" book. How hurried is indicated by the bare month between Howard's return to Columbus, June 7, and publication of the book, July 5. Howells's facility gave the book a jump on competing biographies, including one by Howard himself.

The development of his skill as a marshaller of fact is evident in the biography. Lincoln took the book out of the Library of Congress in 1863 and 1865, and annotated it lightly;[2] he must have noted, for example, Howells's summing up of personal characteristics such as "Lincoln was the favorite of the circle; admired for his gift of story-telling, and highly esteemed for his excellent qualities of head and heart, his intellectual shrewdness, his reliability, his good-nature, and generosity" (47). At the same time, Howells was capable of a more labored and affected style, even in setting forth simple facts; for example, "His grandfather, (anterior to whom is incertitude, and absolute darkness of names and dates,) was born in Rockingham County, Virginia, whither part of the family had emigrated from Pennsylvania; and had four brothers patriarchially and apostolically named Isaac, Jacob, John, and Thomas; himself heading the list as Abraham Lincoln" (18). Given such excesses, Howells may have benefited from his attention to Lincoln's style: "admirable simplicity of diction which dashes straight at the heart of a subject" (62); "excellences of Lincoln's later style—boldness, trenchant logic, and dry humor" (60).

Beginning of a New Decade

As the decade of the 1850s closed with a book, or half a one, to prove that Howells was a poet at last, so the decade of the sixties began with a number of events that importantly fore-shadowed his future. The first was the publication of the Lincoln biography in the spring, its significance enlarging with Lincoln's election and becoming an important factor in Howells's appoint-ment as consul to Venice in 1861. The second was Howells's meet-ing with his future wife, Elinor Mead, in the winter of 1860. Elinor was one of nine children of Squire Larkin G. Mead and Mary Noyes of Brattleboro, Vermont. The squire was a leading figure in the town; his wife was the sister of the founder of the Utopian com-munity of Oneida. Howells's fictional New England locales and characterizations draw more upon his wife's family than upon his own later New England experiences. It was through Elinor that he was to become closely acquainted with Rutherford B. Hayes, for her visit to Ohio was to stay with the Hayes family in Cin-cinnati. Hayes was Elinor's mother's cousin on her mother's side of the family, and in 1860 was a Republican lawyer in Cincinnati, eighteen years later to become president. The cousin she visited in Columbus was Laura Platt, daughter of Hayes's sister and one of the circle of young people Howells knew.

Elinor's wit and responsiveness to his literary interests attracted Howells. In describing her to his father, in July 1862, he wrote: "She's not violently intellectual, by any means. She has artistic genius, and a great deal of taste, and she admires my poetry im-mensely. *I* think she's good looking, and rather suppose she was picked out for me from the beginning of the world" (*Letters*, 1:119–20). She was probably the first girl outside Ohio he had ever met—and from New England and a good family, at that. Howells's wit and intelligence probably attracted her to him. The pictures we have of him during this period give off a suit-ably romantic flavor: dark hair, a mustache, eyes that could ap-pear both dreamy and penetrating. The factual description he wrote in requesting a passport gives his age as twenty-four years;

"stature, five feet and five inches; forehead, medium height; eyes gray; nose nearly straight; mouth medium size; chin somewhat short, hair brown; face oval; complexion rather dark" (*Letters*, 1:86). As Howells could not help but be attracted to a New England girl on her visit West, so she may have been led on by finding such a literary young man as Howells in the provinces. " 'Why, have you got the Atlantic Monthly *out here?*' " Howells reports her saying. And he, in reply: " 'There are several *contributors* to the Atlantic in Columbus!' There were in fact two: my roommate, who wrote Browning for it, while I wrote Heine and Longfellow" (*LF&A*, 8). Within a short time, they had reached a firm enough agreement to bridge the separations of the two years before they were to be married, in Paris, in 1862.

The third event of 1860 is Howells's first trip East. In a letter to his family in April, he notes that "as Columbus grows old to me, it seems to contract, and I begin to feel here the gnawing discontent that I felt in Jefferson" (*Letters*, 1:54). His visits to the great New England authors are remarkably set forth in *Literary Friends and Acquaintance* (1900), which begins with an evocative account of his preceding years in Columbus and reveals the naivete of his expectations: "I expected somehow to meet them all, and I imagined them all easily accessible in the office of the Atlantic Monthly" (15). Remarkably, he did meet most of them, and a dinner with Fields and Holmes and Lowell in the Parker House in Boston was as good as the imagined gathering in the *Atlantic* office. It was at dinner he has Holmes saying to Lowell: "Well, James, this is something like the apostolic succession; this is the laying on of hands" (36). Through Lowell Howells visited Hawthorne, whom he "entirely liked" (51). Thoreau he *had* to visit, not so much as the writer of *Walden*, which he had read in 1858, but for his fierce advocacy of John Brown. Thoreau, then in his declining years, disappointed Howells: "it was not merely a defeat of my hopes, it was a rout" (55). His description of Thoreau, however, is as superbly done as are the other portraits in the book:

He came into the room a quaint, stump figure of a man, whose effect of long trunk and short limbs was heightened by his fashionless trousers being let down too low. He had a noble face, with tossed hair, a distraught eye, and a fine aquilinity of profile, which made me think at once of Don Quixote and of Cervantes.... He tried to place me geographically after he had given me a chair not quite so far off as Ohio, though still across the whole room, for he sat against one wall, and I against the other; but apparently he failed to pull himself out of his revery by the effort, for he remained in a dreamy muse, which all my attempts to say something fit about John Brown and Walden Pond seemed only to deepen upon him. (*LF&A*, 54)

The visit gave him little courage to visit Emerson, and the exchanges between them were hardly more satisfactory. The mention of Poe caused Emerson to say, "Oh, *you mean the jingle-man!*" (58). He had read none of Howells's contributions to the *Atlantic*, but he pulled down bound volumes from his shelf to glance at them. He delivered a final shock by saying of Howells's interest in poetry, "one might very well give a pleasant hour to it now and then" (58).

At the end of his first round of visits, Howells proposed himself to Fields as an assistant editor of the *Atlantic*. The position has just been filled, else, Fields said, he would have been glad to hire him. Such encouragement gave Howells courage four years later to approach him again and thus begin his *Atlantic* career. In this final talk, Howells revealed his need to find economic security against a life "full of changes and chances already." Apparently an earnestness in his tone provoked Fields to ask how old he was, and to say, when Howells replied "Twenty-three," "Well, you begin young, out there!" (60).

From Boston, Howells went to New York, where he was introduced to New York Bohemian life, Pfaff's restaurant, and Walt Whitman. Whitman, so Howells recalled, "reached out his great hand to me, as if he were going to give it me for good and all" (67). Very little else passed between them; Howells was to meet him years later, was never to understand his poetry, though he acknowledged him as "a very 'imperial anarch' in literature" (68). He reviewed *Leaves of Grass* that same year; his conclusions are as judicious as one might expect from any young literary type in 1860: "He has been both overrated and underrated. It will not do to condemn him altogether, nor to commend him altogether. You cannot apply to him the taste by which you are accustomed to discriminate in poetry."[3]

When Howells returned to Columbus, it was possible for him to go back to work with the *Ohio Journal* as literary editor. His visit had apparently established an acquaintance with Oliver Wendell Holmes, Jr., four years younger than he, which led to an interesting though brief correspondence in 1860–61. "I don't quote Heine on any subject anymore if I can help it," he wrote in his first letter. "I have wearied a little of his brilliance and subtlety—both partly false" (*Letters*, 1:62). In a second letter, he turns from the literary to announce: "I have fallen in love with a white-faced being in a blue dress," and then acknowledges that he stops short of pursuing her, fearing "I should see some fault in her beauty if I did" (*Letters*, 1:64). His letters to Victoria continued the self-criticism of earlier years. A letter of March 24, 1861, avows his wanting "to do something better than achieve reputation, and be admired of young ladies who read the 'Atlantic' " (*Letters*, 1:76).

It was with Holmes, too, that Howells revealed some of his feelings about military service and the Civil War. He was curious to learn all the details of Holmes's enlisting, and he informed him, as he did his mother, of being tempted to join a company being formed by his young friends. The mood, as Howells indicated it might, passed, and he, along with the two other major prose writers of his time, Henry James and Mark Twain, played no active part in the war. His brother Sam, whose general inability to cope vexed and worried Howells all his life, went into the army in 1863. Cady concludes that "military service was psychologically out of the question" for Howells.[4] The same has been said of James. Clemens made an abortive try at being a soldier and then shipped West. Howells observed the excitement going on all round him, but neither his letters of the time nor his reminiscences seem to attach great significance to his personal engagement or lack of engagement. It is possible that he regarded the consular service he vigorously sought as a substitute. Perhaps the felt responsibilities of military service and his putting himself forward in his own interests strengthened the play of conscience often rising to guilt that is so much a part of his fiction.

The decision of Henry Cooke, owner of the *Journal*, to sell the paper and go to Washington in May, 1861, left Howells once again without a job. Other free-lance writing assignments were not forthcoming, and he began actively pursuing a consulship, not an unlikely pursuit in view of his successful biography, strong Republican affiliations, and the patronage practices of the time. Through Cooke he was able to make an appeal to Salmon P. Chase, governor of Ohio, 1855–59, and now secretary of the treasury.

Piatt was already employed in the Treasury department, and could keep him apprised of developments. An offer of Rome was extended, but the position was an unsalaried one and therefore unacceptable. It was a personal trip to New York and then to Washington that landed him the consulate at Venice, largely through Lincoln's western secretary, Nicolay. The position paid $1,500 a year. Before Howells left the country, in November, 1861, he visited Fields, Holmes, and Lowell again in Boston, made a business trip to Washington, and a personal one to the Meads in Brattleboro, Vermont.

In Italy

In the four years Howells spent in Italy, December 7, 1861, to July 3, 1865, he acquired a command of Italian language and literature which did much to establish himself in Boston when he returned. It also loosened his ties to his Ohio family, established his own family with his marriage to Elinor Mead and birth of Winifred, and moved him from being an earnest but conventional writer of poetry to becoming a sure and effective writer of prose.

All three of these developments were going on at the same time, for above all the position afforded him leisure and independent security. Though the $1,500 annual salary was not great, it was sufficient to live reasonably well, despite Howells's complaint early in his stay that he was spending one dollar a day on living costs in Venice as against living well on $3.50 a week in Columbus. Though part of his intent was to save some money toward launching a career at home, it is doubtful that he saved much. More important than income was the leisure that went with the job. Howells, as far as records tell, performed his duties conscientiously, but in Venice during these years there were not many to perform. James Woodress, the authority on Howells in Italy, says only four American ships stopped in Venice during the first year and only one took on cargo.[5] Visitors were few, American investments there negligible, and no daily time-consuming chores were expected of the consul.

Given these circumstances and Howells's fluency in languages, it is not surprising that by the first year he had gained fluency in both reading and speaking Italian. During the remaining three years he was to use that command of language in making Italian friends, gaining a firsthand as well as historical understanding of such locales as Venice, Florence, and Rome, and in becoming an authority on Italian literature. Much of this went directly into his writing while there and carried over into fiction and essays completed years after his return.

Though his Italian years were important to his gaining acceptance in Boston when he returned, they marked a definite separation from his Ohio past.[6] It was his first long and distant separation from friends and family. Though the first months were apparently lonely ones, his acquiring a language seemed to proceed at about the same pace as acquiring friends. His position as consul helped him here. Richard Hildreth, author of an antislavery novel and consul at Trieste, invited him to a sight-seeing trip, and in the summer he visited Milan and Lake Como (the account later published in the *Atlantic*, September, 1867). J. L. Motley, Charles Hale, editor of the *Boston Advertiser*, Samuel Bowles, editor of the *Springfield Republican*, and James Lorimer Graham were other visitors. Motley, the historian, was one of the Boston Brahmins, Hale's *Advertiser* became the publisher of Howells's travel sketches, and Graham was helpful in introducing Howells to the London publisher, Trübner. He made lasting Italian friends, who, in various ways, provided material for articles and later fiction.

Most important of all for his personal fortunes, he completed his courtship of Elinor Mead by correspondence, and they were married in Paris the day before Christmas, 1861. Elinor, accompanied by her brother Larkin (some five years later he married an Italian woman he met through Howells), came to England for the wedding, but a waiting period required by English law pushed them on to France. The ceremony in the American legation was the beginning of forty-eight years of married life and established the factual counterparts of Basil and Isabel March, who were to appear in Howells's fiction for almost as many years. It gave Howells companionship and personal security, two necessities of his existence, and it not only fulfilled his romantic dreams but confirmed a rise in social status already implicit in becoming a consul. Their daughter, Winifred, was born the following December. These first years of marriage in Venice remained happy memories for both Howellses the rest of their lives.

Time in establishing residence, his work on the language, and his marriage consumed much of Howells's first year. None of them distracted him from indulging his somewhat abstract poetic aspirations as well as pursuing concrete literary ventures. How artistically inclined Howells was in these years, and how hard it is to perceive that persona in light of the middle-class image of stolidity created later in his life. Elinor, herself, was a fashioner of creditable sketches; the one she did of Howells at this time, like extant photographs, is the sketch of an artist, pen in hand, cape, mustache, beard. The priority Howells gave to poetry, and the schooling he and Elinor put themselves through in exploring the art history of Venice and Florence, as well as the topics he chose for poems written in Italy, are overtly "arty." "Recent Italian Comedy," accepted by the *North American Review* in 1864, exemplified his allegiance to art. Gaining a reputation "amongst the Italian literati," as he wrote his father (*LIL*, 1:94), is a far distance from the realities of commonplace American life in any age.

From Romantic Poetry to Prose

The state of art in America of the 1850s may account in part for the general failure to recognize how much the romantic posture of the artist was part of Howells's makeup. His poetry is commonly passed over as betraying little but the conventions of nineteenth-century verse or the influence of Heine and Longfellow.[7] But an examination of the poems both before and during his stay in Italy more clearly reveals a Howells overwhelmed with artistic posturing. In the earlier poems, where little in the American locale provided descriptive or historic artistic touches, poetic art as conceived of in America of that time placed stress upon the transitoriness of human affection, the loss of love, the melancholy of remembrance.

Howells's late adolescent years, when he was shaping his destinies toward poetry, were years in which Longfellow's popularity was at a peak. *Hiawatha* appeared in 1855; *The Courtship of Miles Standish* in 1858. Longfellow's mastery of language, use of commonplace American legends, his fondness for stories, even his rise from Portland, Maine, to becoming a professor at Harvard, had obvious meaning for Howells. Howells's essay "The White Mr. Longfellow" in *Literary Friends and Acquaintance* is suffused with the warmth of the personal acquaintance with him which began in 1866 and lasted until, poignantly, Howells went out to see him in 1882 and was told, " 'Oh, the poor gentleman has just departed!' " (*LF&A*, 177). In considering the shaping forces in Howells's early and middle life, one must consider how powerfully and long the venerated New England writers ruled over him and others of his generation. When Howells, barely twenty-three, first met these men, Emerson, Hawthorne, Whittier, Longfellow, and Holmes were all past fifty. Lowell, closest to Howells in personal association, was forty-one, and was to address him as "My dear boy" the rest of his life. With the exception of Thoreau and Hawthorne, who died within five years of Howells's meeting them, all lived on until Howells himself was forty-five; Holmes died when Howells was fifty-seven.

Howells's poems written in Italy are "artistic" in the extreme. "It is not Heine, now," he wrote Moncure Conway in 1863, "but Dante, and perhaps Art more than either" (*Letters*, 1:145). "Pordenone" (*Poems*, 201–22) is a tale of jealousy between the young artist, Pordenone, and the mature Titian. Its underlying subject is the nature of art; its characters require footnoted explanations for readers not immediately conversant with sixteenth-century Italian art. The poem was done, as were most of his long poems of these days, in Longfellow's hexameters, and its cadences are as evident (if not as regular) as Longfellow's:

Hard by the Church of Saint Stephen, in sole and beautiful Venice. . . .
Otherwise Violante, and while his pupils about him
Wrought and chattered, in silence ran the thought of the painter. . . .

"No Love Lost," written in Venice but not published until 1867, compounds the artistic pretensions of "Pordenone." So, too, with "The Faithful of the Gonzaga," which differs only in adopting the ballad stanza and then is off on another romantic tale taken from "a most romantic incident of the history of Mantua." It was not only Heine that Howells must rid himself of but an entire romantic afflatus that fell upon him somewhere in his self-acquired education as what an Ohio boy striving for Art must embrace.

Howells remembers (LF&A, 80) that he sent verse to "magazines in every part of the English-speaking world, but they came unerringly back." "Louis Lebeau's Conversion," modeled on Longfellow's narrative poems, was accepted and published by the *Atlantic* in November, 1862. Prior to that time, he had published seven poems in 1860 and 1861. "Saint Christopher," "The Faithful of the Gonzaga," "Disillusion" (published as "No Love Lost"), and "Pordenone," are all products of the Italian years, though the last was not published until 1882.

For the *Harper's Bazar* series "The Turning Point of My Life" (March, 1910), Howells picked out Lowell's praise of his essay on recent Italian comedy in 1864 as decisive in turning him from poetry to prose. His difficulties in getting poetry accepted must have played as large a part. Equally important, Howells had continued to be a literary journalist all the while he was indulging his poetic ambitions. Travel letters appeared in the *Ashtabula Sentinel* in 1862 and regularly in the *Boston Advertiser* beginning in March, 1863. Later in the year, the *Advertiser* took seventeen of his Venetian sketches, which had been turned down by the *Atlantic*.

Venetian Life and Other Reflections of Italy

These articles became the basis for *Venetian Life* (1866), a highly successful fusion of Howells's literary and journalistic talents. The book did not easily burst into print, nor did it make Howells an immediate fortune. It did, however, establish him as a writer of more than common abilities, and it went into revisions and reprintings well into Howells's late years. It was turned down initially by the London publisher Trübner unless Howells could find an American publisher to share the risk. A chance meeting with M. M. Hurd aboard ship on Howells's return to America and a subsequent meeting in New York secured an American printing by Hurd and Houghton. The first edition appeared in June, 1866.

Venetian Life, though not one of the books that is often referred to now, deserves brief mention here for both its substance and its style. Mark Twain quoted extensively from it when he appraised Howells's work in 1906. He had read it forty years before, and rereading Howells's descriptive prose, he wrote: "The spirit of Venice is there."[8] The book states its intent at the outset through the metaphor of the stage. Venice, as customarily described, has all "the sham and cheapness" (*VL*, 10) of the popular theater, and Howells's intent is to describe it as it is, stripped of "the sentimental errors" (12) other writers have passed on. The first chapter most obviously carries out that realistic intent, dwelling on Venice's poverty, its commercial decay, and its subjection to Austrian rule—causes, according to Howells, for the end of "the old merrymaking life of the city" (16). In leaving Venice, he describes her as "a phantom of the past, haunting our modern world,—serene, inexpressibly beautiful, yet inscrutably and unspeakably sad" (413). In between these melancholy reflections, both realistic and romantic, is a historical and contemporary account of the city, made personal by the quietly dramatized incidents that befall a young American couple living there.

A second travel book, *Italian Journeys*, was written as a series of sketches of places Howells visited before he left Italy, though it was not published until 1867, after various individual sketches had appeared in the *Advertiser*, the *Nation*, and the *Atlantic*. In sum, the Italian years were very profitable ones in providing marketable materials and in shifting Howells's energies to development of a prose style that could move readily into the writing of fiction. A complete accounting of the literary use Howells made of these first Italian years is given in James Woodress's *Howells and Italy*. Here, I will just mention the major works which directly emerged: the novels *A Foregone Conclusion* (1875), *A Fearful Responsibility* (1881), and to some degree *The Lady of the Aroostook* (1879); articles, "Italian Brigandage," "Ducal Mantua," and "Modern Italian Poets," all in the *North American Review*; and stories and sketches, "Minor Italian Travels," "Tonelli's Marriage," and "A Year in a Venetian Palace," in the *Atlantic*. He returned to Italy for an extensive visit in 1882–83 and again in 1904. These visits like others later in life furnished him with material for numerous articles and travel pieces; the 1882–83 trip gave him basic impulse and setting for the novel *Indian Summer*.

Though Howells seems so preeminently an "American" writer, as does Longfellow, neither should be forgotten as forging essential ties with European thought and letters. The interest in Italian writers from Goldoni to Verga, which Howells stimulated in others, also played a part in his development as a realistic novelist. By the time of his return, Howells was an immensely more sophisticated person than when he left Ohio in 1861. Marriage and a child were part of it, as was his establishing his independence by holding a responsible position in a distant country. The self-study he had pursued with no immediate ends in Ohio had given way to learning and experience which he had already drawn on extensively. He was ready, in every way, to establish himself in his own country.

Chapter Three

Journalist and Author: 1865-79

Homecoming for Howells in 1865 must have aroused some memories of more poignant returns home from briefer departures in his boyhood. Only nine months earlier he had written to his mother: "Home! How my heart leaps at the thought! O mother, you mustn't think that this separation has not been as hard for me as for you. Many a time I've been so homesick I hardly knew what to do—almost as homesick as in the old childish days when it almost broke my heart to be five or ten miles away from you" (*LIL*, 1:91).

Nevertheless he had, somehow, borne up, and his note to his father from off Halifax reminds him of the new obligations he has taken on: "We're all perfectly well, and tremendously delighted to think of being so near home. Will go to Brattleboro from Boston. . . . We shall be only detained a short time in Vermont, and shall come to you as quickly as possible" (*LIL*, 1:95). Like Bartley Hubbard in *A Modern Instance*, Howells's first need was to find a "basis," a steady job to support wife and family and still permit pursuit of his literary aspirations. Though he had taken a four-month leave from the consulship, by the time he resigned he had fulfilled his four-year obligation.

Editor of the *Atlantic*

Offers of positions were not immediately forthcoming. The main prospect in Boston, the *Atlantic*, may have seemed less a possibility in light of the rejections of both poetry and prose Howells had sent from Italy. James T. Fields was apparently out of the city when he arrived; neither had picked up the talk they had once had about Howells's coming on as an assistant. Lowell was as cordial as before and much more inclined to treat Howells as an author already in stride. But his advice was for Howells to seek opportunities in the West. When he did visit Ohio, within ten days of his arrival, a round of inquiries in Columbus, Cincinnati, and Cleveland turned up nothing. One option he did not seem to seriously entertain: returning to the family enterprise—though he did accept his brother's offer to meet Trübner's condition by publishing an American edition of *Venetian Life.*

The visit to Ohio was short and largely concerned with his search for a job. He may have been relieved that nothing in the West was available, for it forced his next move to New York, to reacquaintance with friends there, and a job offer almost the moment he arrived. It also resulted in a chance meeting with M. M. Hurd, who agreed on the spot to publish *Venetian Life*, thus making it unnecessary for Howells to fall back upon the family. The job offer came from Edwin Lawrence Godkin, publisher of the *Nation*. Howells wrote Elinor, October 27, 1885, of his showing Godkin a play review he had done. "Mr. Godkin said, 'How would you like to write exclusively for the *Nation*, and what will you take to do it?" (*Letters*, 1:234). Howells said fifty dollars a week, and the matter was left with Godkin to think over. By this time, Howells was confident enough to write: "I should prefer this sort of connection with the paper, but I don't care a great deal, for I foresee that if these journals live they will take my articles at my own prices" (*Letters*, 1:234). A month later, Godkin secured Howells's services for forty dollars a week but left him free to write for other papers and to be paid extra for articles on Italian subjects and poems. Of his contributions to the *Nation*, a column, "Minor

Topics," on New York City life, was the most significant. Though its manner was urbane, its substance included a fair amount of attention to the underside of New York life. Howells saw the column as an opportunity to do "some sketches of New York life, just in the spirit I should write of Italian life" (*Letters*, 1:239).

His stay on the *Nation* was brief, only until his twenty-ninth birthday, March 1, 1866. It ended when Fields made him a similar offer on the *Atlantic*, which Howells accepted after ascertaining that Godkin would not object and that the terms constituted a step forward. He was to receive $2,500 a year and was to sift manuscripts, correspond with contributors, oversee proofreading, verify facts, and write regular book reviews.

If these specified duties included most of the routine chores of editing a magazine, they were chores that Howells could do well. Moreover, aside from the attraction that Boston had always held for him, there were other reasons for taking the job. Boston was closer to Elinor's family; it was the home of more and more important literary acquaintances; and it somehow was a return to another village, a vastly more cultured one than Jefferson and Columbus, and one in the process of drastic change, but a village all the same.

The *Atlantic*, moreover, was still a provincial New England literary magazine, its purpose, as avowed by Francis Underwood, one of its founders, that "of concentrating the efforts of the best writers upon literature and politics, under the light of the highest morals."[1] It had begun in 1857, and had its growth in that period after the Civil War when there was "a mania of magazine-starting."[2] Frank Luther Mott estimates that there were 700 periodicals in 1865, which increased to 3,300 by 1885.[3] When Howells became editor, the magazine had established itself as the literary periodical that might be expected to emerge from Boston. Its national and commercial status was much more modest. When its first owners sold it to Ticknor and Fields in 1859, no bids other than Ticknor's for $10,000 were received.[4] Its circulation was never large, about 30,000 in 1860, and about 50,000 in 1870. Nevertheless, both the *Nation* and the *Atlantic* can be put with small-circulation periodicals which then and since "exerted a strong influence on thinking people."[5]

Howells's personal life in Boston, Cambridge, and Belmont parallels his professional life. Indeed, they were carefully intertwined, and probably more often than not in conflict. Howells's early writing came after hours, and the arrival of a second child, John, in 1868 added to the demands on both parents. They kept in close touch with both families. Howells thanks his mother for sending them an obstreperous live peacock and adds, "If you have any thoughts of giving us Charles, the horse, please consider our unprepared state" (*Letters*, 1:280). Though they stayed at their first house in Sacramento Street for almost five years, they moved to a boardinghouse in Boston for three months to spare Elinor housekeeping, then permanently to Berkeley Street in Cambridge, and in 1873 built a house around the corner at Concord Avenue. Mildred, their last child, had been born the previous year. The young family, the moving, Howells's increasing responsibilities, and the beginnings of an ambitious fiction writer's career, which included social obligations most often of a literary kind, must have taken a good deal from both of them.

Elinor maintained her artistic interests by becoming greatly involved in the planning and decoration of the houses they occupied, particularly the ones they had built. Her brother, William Rutherford Mead, was the architect for their country house in Belmont, to which they moved in 1878. Very early in this period, however, about the time of John's birth in 1868, Elinor began to suffer from a chronic delicacy of health which may have been the age's reaction to the position many women found themselves in. Denied opportunities for her own development, and faced with the acceptance of a secondary position in relation to a professional man's career, a woman's unconscious defense might include the neurasthenic ills which constituted both a withdrawal and a demand for attention.[6] The relationship between Basil and Isabel March in Howells's fiction is surely revelatory of William Dean's and Elinor's relations. Basil for the most part is detached, polite but tolerant, engrossed in other matters than those which occupy Isabel, and Isabel is often condescended to, appreciated at some little distance, and though possessed of a sharp tongue, not distinguished either as a thinker or a person of much emotional depth.

"I am a mill that runs day and night," Howells wrote his mother in 1867 in a conscience-stricken explanation of why the demands of his career had reduced his connection with his parental family.[7] Summers in Cambridge were often as hot as the winters were cold. On one of the hottest of July days in 1868, he wrote his mother: "The summer puts me in mind of that awful year of drouth which to me is now shrouded in what I must almost call the blackness of insanity. Now, however, I have not a shadow of hypochondria upon me. But I must always be a different man from that I could have been but for that dreadful year" (*Letters*, 1:296). That same summer he put off returning to Ohio during the onset of his mother's final illness, and arrived there only after her death. That loss on his side was followed by the death of Elinor's father, the dominant parent in her life, during the summer of 1869. The tempo of Howells's work, both the editorial routines in which he was involved and his own disciplined writing, may have made it easier for him to weather his mother's death than for Elinor to recover from the death of her father. But despite the losses, they both may have felt freed, to some extent, from the generation past.

Throughout his life, Howells moved between the need for stability and security and an inner compulsion toward freedom and change. The classic and romantic existed side by side. The poetic impulse that clouds almost every poem with romantic melancholy was part of what he was leaving behind as he pursued an upward path from beginning as assistant editor of the *Atlantic* to becoming full editor when Fields turned those duties over to him in the summer of 1871.

But Howells's steady rise in fortune and reputation was not without conflict. The picture of a methodical, hard-working, and steadily more successful editor, author, and family man exists beside one of an often frustrated writer and wage-earning husband with hostages to fortune. On the positive side, his financial situation improved greatly; as early as 1868 his *Atlantic* salary had been raised to $3,500 a year. Sales of his early books and continuing success with articles and other literary work added to his income. In 1867, Harvard awarded him an honorary degree of master of arts. The first offers of academic positions came during the 1870s, and he received and accepted an invitation from Harvard to lecture from 1869 to 1871. He gave the Lowell Lectures in Boston in 1870, the result of which was eventually the book *Modern Italian Poets* (1887). His acceptance into the Dante Circle was followed by his joining the Saturday Club and Tavern Club. From late summer 1867, when he was able to spend a month at Elinor's parents' house in Brattleboro, he moved within a decade not only to a succession of better houses in the Boston area but to the pattern of spending summers in the country at one site or another.

On the debit side, Elinor's ill health became an increasingly disturbing fact, and the promise that lay in new and grander houses had to be put against the realities of how an ailing wife could maintain such establishments. The financial panic of 1873 came upon Howells with great force. The problems Howells was personally experiencing in the 1870s are part of the substance of "The Man of Letters as a Man of Business," published in *Scribner's,* October, 1893, in which Howells looked back on his own career. "I do not think any man ought to live by an art," he wrote. "I am tempted to begin by saying that Business is the opprobrium of Literature" (*L&L,* 1–2). Though he acknowledged that after the Civil War, chiefly because of the growth of magazines, many authors could be supported by their work, he also pointed out that two thirds of magazines were made up of material which "however excellent, is without literary quality" (*L&L,* 11). Through most of the 1870s the *Atlantic's* circulation, never large, was in decline. As to his success as a writer of books, "in the United States," Howells wrote, "the fate of a book is in the hands of the women" (*L&L,* 21).

Howells's Fiction and Nonfiction: 1866–79

"I'm thinking now about commencing a romance—" Howells

wrote to his sister Victoria, in June, 1866, "the scene of it to be laid in Italy, or Venice, rather—but I have ever so much work begun which I must finish first" (*LIL*, 1:113). The idea was still with him the next fall, when he wrote M. M. Hurd, September 8, 1867, "I've now got all other work off my hands, and am pleasing myself with the idea of a romance ... everybody writes a novel, sooner or later, and I expect it is also my destiny" (*LIL*, 1:121). We do not know how much of these intentions moved into manuscript form soon after. In June, 1869, he told Henry James that he was nearly finished with "A Pedestrian Tour," "which is nothing but an impudent attempt to interest people in a stroll I take from Sacramento Street up through the Brickyards and the Irish village of Dublin near by, and so down through North Avenue. If the public will stand this, I shall consider my fortune made" (*LIL*, 1:144).

Though James was writing fiction at the time and talk about fiction must have occupied many of their hours, Howells's movement to becoming a fiction writer was gradual and along a natural path. Seeing if what he had done with Venice could be done with suburban Boston was one step. That step coincided with the *Atlantic*'s need for material and Howells's need to make his observing and writing pay his *Atlantic* wage and advance his own writing career. As a recognition of his worth to the magazine, he had been relieved of some routine duties and asked to make regular creative contributions to the magazine. "Mrs. Johnson," the piece with which his next published book, *Suburban Sketches* (1871), begins, initially appeared in the *Atlantic* (January, 1868) as a part of his regular duties.

Suburban Sketches is important in one way in showing Howells that he could fashion magazine pieces out of commonplace American fare. It gave him additional practice in the creation of character and the handling of narrative, and it reveals, read closely now, a disturbing condescension toward the "lower classes":

I say, our last Irish girl went with the last snow, and on one of those midsummer-like days that sometimes fall in early April to our yet bleak and desolate zone, our hearts sang of Africa and golden joys. A Libyan longing took us, and we would have chosen, if we could, to bear a strand of grotesque beads, or a handful of brazen gauds, and traffic them for some sable maid with crisped locks. . . . if we desired colored help, we must seek it at the intelligence office, which is in one of those streets chiefly inhabited by the orphaned children and grandchildren of slavery. To tell the truth these orphans do not seem to grieve much for their bereavement, but lead a life of joyous and rather indolent oblivion in their quarter of the city. . . . How gayly are the young ladies of this race attired, as they trip up and down the sidewalks, and in and out through the pendant garments at the shop doors! They are the black pansies and marigolds and dark-blooded dahlias among womankind. . . . More rarely yet than the gentleman described, one may see a white girl among the dark neighbors, whose frowzy head is uncovered, and whose sleeves are rolled up to her elbows, and who, though no doubt quite at home, looks as strange there as that pale anomaly which may sometimes be seen among a crew of blackbirds.

An air not so much of decay as of unthrift, and yet hardly of unthrift, seems to prevail in the neighborhood, which has none of the aggressive and impudent squalor of an Irish quarter. . . . a ragged gayety, which comes of summer in the blood, and not in the pocket or the conscience, and which affects the countenance and the whole demeanor, setting the feet to some inward music, and at times bursting into a line of song or a child-like and irresponsible laugh—gives tone to the visible life. (*SS*, 18–20)

A modern liberal must blink hard in the reading of this. It mirrors that Cambridge world which so impressed Howells when he first arrived. It fully accepts the distance proper and wealthy Bostonians maintained between themselves and the colored help or the Irish or almost anyone else not born to their position. *Suburban Sketches* has some importance as a measure of how far Howells had to go to reach the perceptions of American society he entertained in the 1890s.

Suburban Sketches may have freed Howells for the writing of fiction, just as it freed him from the great dependence upon his Italian materials revealed in his publications of these early years.

poem that had apparently not found acceptance elsewhere, and the chapter ends with the Marches' plans to return down the St. Lawrence via Montreal and Quebec. Kitty is brought in again in the next chapter, and Montreal and Quebec furnish opportunities for the kind of mingling of physical description and past history so successful in Howells's previous travel books.

A bit of dialect humor gets into the Quebec chapter with the appearance of a troupe of "black haired British blondes of Jewish race," who say things like "W'at a guy she'll look!" and "Nonsense! Bella's too 'eavy for Wenus!" The Ellisons, Kitty's guardians, come prominently into the dialogue, through another farcical scene involving a mix-up in hotel rooms in which the London Hebrews apparently have received the favor of the hotel clerk, "the Benjamin of his wicked tribe." The resolution is a long paragraph in which Basil reflects that "our commonplace time and hemisphere" has so furnished the "commonness and cheapness of the *mise en scène*, for that . . . helped to give it an air of fact and make it like an episode of fiction" (*TWJ*, 172). The comedy here plays upon racial stereotypes, providing for superior Bostonians mild amusement and discrete irritation from the vulgar talk and antics of the Hebrews or the Irish. A last short chapter sees the Marches safely home with a bit of fuss about customs, the kind of comic confrontation that also found its way into Howells's farces later.

Their Wedding Journey is more important as Howells's first big step into fiction than in its own merits as a new form of fiction. It gave him, as his travel writing already had, a kind of writing which he could do easily and which came to constitute a large part of his total fiction. It may have had the adverse effect of not demanding the exercise of great imaginative power and a compelling language. Its direct contributions to his later fiction were the establishment of the central characters, Basil and Isabel March, who became familiar figures in other novels, and the introduction of one of the most familiar character types in his fiction: the innocent young girl. Inevitably that character had to be provided with various kinds of young men. The young men in Howells's fiction, as in James's, often came in pairs, the one inclining to vices that males incline to, the other holding a more steady course.

Basil and Isabel March incorporated some novelty into fiction and matched reading tastes of a populace in which marriage and family so prevailed. They offered a useful counterpoint to the young couples whose courting behavior was given so much attention by Howells and other nineteenth-century authors. They also helped establish an engaging authorial tone and voice, the Howellsian blend of tempered cynicism, satire, bemusement, acceptance, and comedy, in which the human fallibility of the author is as exposed as that of the characters.

The innocent young woman and her not quite so young men became staples not only of Howells's fiction but of Henry James's as well. Daisy Miller and Lydia Blood are closely related, as are Miles Arbuton and Roderick Hudson. It could hardly be otherwise for either writer, dependent as each was on writing a marketable fiction and on using the social milieu with which he was familiar. A limitation in the fiction of both, I think is that they had matured into comfortable upper-class American lives which they valued even as it limited the material at their command. It is something of an oddity that Howells waited so long to draw upon his Ohio past, a world he knew emotionally and in its particulars far more keenly than he knew Italy and Cambridge. But perhaps the answer is simply that, in the years he began to write fiction, it appeared to be a more distant, less usable past. Still, his feelings for his youth come through in the many outlanders, women and men, who populate his fiction.

Nothing of what I am discussing here went unnoticed by Howells. He moved to fiction cautiously, and though he did a great deal of talking about it with Henry James and others of a kind that could be called theoretical, his impulses were mostly practical. As James said of him to Charles Eliot Norton: "His talent grows constantly in fineness, but hardly, I think, in range of application. . . . the trouble is he never will read Sainte-Beuve, nor care to. He has little intellectual curiosity, so here he stands with his admirable organ of style, like a poor man holding a diamond and wondering how he can use it."[9] In commenting on James's remark much later in life, Howells was still uncertain about being an artist, but he was assuredly an editor and writer, with a multitude of possibilities for exercising his talent. His feelings about *A Chance Acquaintance* show some of his uncertainties. Writing to James in September, 1873, he confesses having experienced "triumphal feelings" when he finished it in July, but "Now I regard it with cold abhorrence, and work it over, shuddering" (*LIL*, 1:171).

A Chance Acquaintance (1873) takes up Kitty Ellison, the character introduced in *Their Wedding Journey*, and involves her in a tentative romance with Miles Arbuton, a superior young man. James and Howells were agreed in Howells's success in creating Kitty Ellison. "I like her," Howells wrote, "because she seems to me a character; the man, I own is a simulacrum" (*LIL*, 1:174). Kitty is an orphan; her father was killed in a border feud and her mother died soon after. Her uncle Jack, a strong antislavery country doctor, has been responsible for her upbringing and education. Like Howells, Kitty is largely self-educated, with the help of a "library pretty well stocked with the elderly English authors, poets and essayists and novelists" (*CA*, 37). Her education gave her "a great liveliness of mind and several decided opinions." She could rattle on "in a free, wild, racy talk, with an edge of satire for whoever came near, a fantastic excess in its drollery, and just a touch of native melancholy tingeing it" (39). Kitty meets both the Marches and Miles Arbuton on her first trip away from home. Miles is the kind of young gentleman who likes to be mistaken for an Englishman. Kitty, in a letter home that takes up one chapter, tells her friends that "he has been a good deal abroad, and he is Europeanized enough not to think much of America, though I can't find that he quite approves of Europe..." (80–81).

The progression of the story is of innocence coming into awareness. Kitty's initial attraction to Miles gives way to a rejection of him, not because he's conceited and patronizing and refined to excess, but because "he seems to have nothing natural to fall back upon" (90). The conflict between them is clearly one between the American West and East. It is informed throughout not only by Howells's current ambivalent feelings about Boston, but by his memories of life in Ohio and his observations of Americans in Europe. The new Boston associated with Mr. Arbuton is described as a place of "mysterious prejudices and lofty reservations ... of high and difficult tastes ... a critical, fastidious, and reluctant Boston, dissatisfied with the rest of the hemisphere, and gelidly self-satisfied ..." (91). That, of course, is not the Boston that Kitty (or Howells) idealized from afar. But it was fast becoming the Boston of Howells's mature perceptions.

Like *Their Wedding Journey, A Chance Acquaintance* is interesting in some relation to what a reader knows about Howells. Kitty and even Miles are satisfactory enough characters, but they become more interesting as one realizes how much they are made up of different sides of Howells's own character. More than with any writer of my acquaintance, Howells needs to be known in order to heighten interest in his work.

This novel also reveals Howells's uncertainties when the story requires climactic action. In one such moment, Miles leaps forward to save Kitty by taking the full onslaught of a savage dog on his manly breast; Howells has his vicarious revenge on all those snarling and hydrophobic dogs of his youth when a shopkeeper applies a red-hot cooper's iron to the dog's muzzle, forcing it to slack its grip and slink away. The last scene is of another kind, requiring no melodramatic postures to make its effect. In the midst of his protestations of love for Kitty, two Boston ladies of a previous acquaintance engage Miles's attention. Kitty realizes he is ashamed to introduce her to them; she summarily dismisses him and brings the story to its realistic conclusion.

From the American scene and from romance still intertwined with travel narrative, Howells moved back to an incident from his Italian years for his next fictional work. Cady makes much of the fact that Howells wrote on the flyleaf of *A Foregone Conclusion* (1875), "my first novel," and goes on to discuss the distinction being made at the time between the novel and the romance.[10] Howells accepted the general distinction that made Hawthorne's *The House of the Seven Gables* a romance and *Great Expectations* a novel, but he was not inclined to place Hawthorne in an inferior category as a romancer. He accepted the common-sense distinction between fictional works invested with more of the remote and imagined as contrasted with those using the near-at-hand and factual; between an elevated, lofty, and literary language and conception and a language and conception tied more closely to actual events; between a story aimed primarily at entertainment and one having serious intents. Romance in most common parlance is what goes on between young men and women in the many stages of romantic love. Invest such goings on with a seriousness clumsily and constantly urged by the author and you have the sentimental novel, the form Howells most distrusted.

These distinctions, few of which strictly hold up against the reality of major works of fiction, were not shaping considerations of Howells's early fiction. *Their Wedding Journey* and *A Chance Acquaintance* had pushed a kind of departure from fact into fiction in the direction of the novel as a serious and highly regarded work, but the characteristics of the central characters in both had affinities, perhaps uncomfortable ones for Howells, with the romance. In calling *A Foregone Conclusion* a novel, Howells may have meant no more than that he was raising his sights somewhat, dealing not merely with the "romantic" situation of Don Ippolito, or spinning a tale from a far-off place, but taking up in fictional form such a question as clerical celibacy. An article on that subject attributed to him, "Marriage Among the Italian Priesthood," had appeared in the *New York Times*, October 19, 1865.

The plot for *A Foregone Conclusion* is drawn from Howells's years in Venice. The central character, Don Ippolito, is modeled after a priest who helped Howells with Dante, and the details of setting and action draw heavily on his own experiences in Venice. The other characters are Florida Vervain, the young vibrant American girl who is the object of his mistaken passion; her mother, who is something of the typical wealthy American widow abroad; and Ferris, a young artist serving as consul in Venice during the

Civil War. Such a cast of characters enables Howells to exercise his satirical bent even more than in *A Chance Acquaintance* and to point out more complex contrasts in manners and morals. Faced with the basic story of Don Ippolito's falling in love with Florida, Howells must work more with plot, making the novel more truly a work of fiction but raising questions about his skill in handling incident and character.

Ferris meets Don Ippolito and the Vervains through his duties as consul. Engaged through Ferris to be a language teacher for Florida, the priest falls in love with her and pours out his story of how his father had forced him into a priesthood for which he is temperamentally unsuited. Responding as a free uncomplicated American girl might, Florida urges him to give up the priesthood and come to America. Mistaking this as an affirmation of her love for him, he confesses his own passion, and Florida, horrified now by a response beyond her experience and imagination, flees back to America. Ferris remains in Italy to see Don Ippolito contract a fatal illness and die. He returns to America, serves two years in the war, and marries Florida. Since he is an artist and she has money, he finds himself in a somewhat dependent but tolerable position. To the whole story he provides an epilogue, a realistic and ironic commentary following a discussion between Ferris and Florida trying to reach full understanding of the plight of Don Ippolito. Has he died because of an unfulfilled love, as Florida is inclined to think, or has he died simply of fever, as Ferris assures her he has? The authorial last word suggests that the real tragedy of the story is that Ferris, the man who owes so much of his happiness to Don Ippolito, should be so blind to the priest's genuine passion.

A Foregone Conclusion was an immediate and continuing success. Howells could write his father that it had not received one bad review; James reviewed it in the *North American Review*, calling its ending the only flaw in an otherwise superb work. The novel confirmed Howells's command of the novelist's crafts, and together with the earlier novels fairly represents Howells in the first stage of his fictional career.

The number and variety of Howells's other writings of the period indicate what a literary engine he had become. In addition to books already mentioned, Howells published between 1872 and 1879 *Jubilee Days*, humorous features of the world's peace jubilee, in collaboration with Thomas Bailey Aldrich (1872); *Poems* (1873); *Sketch of the Life and Character of Rutherford B. Hayes* (1876); *The Parlor Car*, a farce (1876); *Out of the Question* and *A Counterfeit Presentment*, comedies (1877), in addition to articles, reviews, and one short story. One of his poems, "The First Cricket," was set to music by F. Boott. He had written the words for a previous song, "The Battle in the Clouds," song and choruses inscribed to the Army of the Cumberland, in 1864. Unpublished in book form but serialized in the *Atlantic* beginning November, 1875, was the novel *Private Theatricals*, not printed as a book, *Mrs. Farrell*, until 1921. Two other novels were planned and not completed. All this in addition to his regular work for the *Atlantic*.

The publication of collected poems in 1873 (he was grateful to James for an unpublished, but favorable, review) is an example of how almost everything Howells wrote found its way into print, and often in two or more contexts. Ten of the poems are from "Poems of Two Friends," but by far the greater number are those written and published after 1865. We have already discussed Howells's limitation as a poet and his turning away from poetry. Plays were a new interest of this period, and they began somewhat as his first novels emerged from his travel books. In this instance, Howells's obvious ability to write clever dialogue and his keen eye for topical subjects gave him reason to try his hand at farce. These short one-act pieces, with names like *The Elevator, The Mouse-Trap, The Parlor Car, The Register*, appeared with some regularity in the 1870s and 1880s. The mystery of their popularity does not disclose itself on the printed page; we must take the word of such a witness as Booth Tarkington who remembers the great fun of doing a Howells farce when the young folks were home at Christmas time. The two longer plays Howells wrote during this period move beyond the limitations of the one-act farce into full-length comedy. Given his interest in the Italian stage, there is

nothing unusual in his turning his hand to the form itself. Some
mention of Howells's efforts as a dramatist will be made in later
chapters.

Associated with the stage by its title and its central character
Belle Farrell, an actress, *Private Theatricals* is a curious work that
deserves attention beyond its associations with drama. It is unusual
in Howells's early work for its darkness of tone; not until *The
Landlord at Lion's Head* (1897) was Howells to describe a New
England landscape as stark as this. Indeed, its failure to be published as a book came about because of the threat of a suit following its serialization in the *Atlantic*. Reading it even today, one can
understand how boardinghouse keepers dependent for a livelihood
on attracting summer boarders might feel maligned by the severity
of Howells's descriptions of both setting and characters. Fanny
Kemble, the American actress whom Howells had induced to write
her memoirs for the *Atlantic*, apparently felt no such outrage.
"Your Mrs. Farrell is terrific—" she wrote, "do for pity's sake give
her the Small Pox—she deserves it" (*LIL*, 1:205).

Private Theatricals is also unusual in Howells's fiction for its
choice of a somewhat "bad" woman as the heroine. Her badness
is relative, however, for she has probably been viewed by later
readers not as a mere trifler with young men's affections but as a
charming woman who chooses to display her charms rather than
slip into pious widowhood or a second vacant marriage. All the
sneering at Howells's sexual timidity sets aside his obvious concern
all through the 1870s and 1880s for the place of women in
society. Mrs. Farrell's sexuality is a part of the problem she presents for herself, for the young men in the novel, and for society.
We forget how great a denial there was of woman's sexual nature
in the society Howells occupied. Mildred Howells looked back
upon that world from 1929 and wrote: "One notes with surprise
after the feminine activity of the present, the general resignation
of even faintly middle-aged ladies to headaches and invalidism,
and the walks taken through woods and meadows in trailing
draperies."[11]

The novel is rich with suggestions about Howells's inner life.

While not a repudiation of his rural past or an indictment of the present, its beginning is an almost misanthropic piece about a wandering preacher, Nehemiah Woodward, "a dreadfully dull man," who is saved from utter failure by his father's leaving him a farmstead in West Pekin, the setting of the novel. Mrs. Woodward settled for Nehemiah only after the death of her true love. It is largely her bitter energy which converts the failing farm into a summer boardinghouse. As the novel introduces the Woodwards' daughter, Rachel, talented enough perhaps to be an artist, one cannot help but be reminded of Howells's own provincial past.

The plot moves somewhat away from this dark beginning to concentrate on the summer visitors at the Woodwards' place. Mrs. Gilbert is the social center of the group, but Belle Farrell is the center of most of the talk. She is the object of pursuit by two young men, deliberately set forth to be contrasting types—Wayne Easton, an intense young artist, and William Gilbert, the nephew of Mrs. Gilbert and inclined to more worldliness than Easton. Easton as might be expected falls under Mrs. Farrell's spell. She leads him on, though she is really more disposed toward Gilbert. To further complicate matters, Rachel is also in love with Easton. The two friends quarrel, are reconciled, learn something of Mrs. Farrell's flighty affections, and fade out, leaving some small possibility that Gilbert may come back to Belle after all. Rachel's goodness throughout the book raises a question of whether Howells is portraying New England rectitude sympathetically or satirically. At the end, she reconciles herself to the loss of Easton, whose fastidious artistic intensity makes one wonder again whether this is an attempt at individualizing a character or at caricature. Mrs. Farrell seems untouched by it all, and is last seen appearing as Juliet, and provoking the comment that her talent is really for "private theatricals," after all.

Almost everything of interest in the novel is below the surface—Howells's attitudes, for example, toward art, sex, morality, rural virtue. Sexuality is as much the underlying theme as any, revealing itself, at one point, in a scene between Easton and Mrs. Farrell in which her hat has become entangled in her hair:

She turned the wonder of her neck toward him and bent down her head. "Is it caught, anywhere?"

"It's caught," he answered, gravely, "on a hairpin."

"Oh dear!" sighed Mrs. Farrell.

"May I?" asked Easton, after a pause.

"Why—yes—please," she answered, faintly.

He knelt down on the rock beside her and with trembling hands touched the warm, fragrant, silken mass, and lightly disengaged the string. (70)

Critics have observed that Howells awakened interest in Turgenev, which came in the early 1870s, may account for some of the gloom and the intensity of novels like this one and *A Foregone Conclusion.* Acknowledging such an influence, one still considers the tensions in Howells's own life, beneath the surface of the placid New England society which he uneasily occupied, as having helped create these novels. Like his caustic observations of rural life, his depictions of the excesses to which artistic idealism, Puritanism, and false heroism can bring young people, his exposure of the shams that pass for diversions with Mrs. Gilbert and her group, and the sexual tensions bespeak a Howells who thought and felt more widely and intensely than he wrote.

The final novel of the seventies is *The Lady of the Aroostook* (1879), which James called, "the most brilliant thing you have done."[12] What James was affirming was Howells's bringing to perfection what he had begun in *Their Wedding Journey* and had quickly advanced in *A Chance Acquaintance.* Clearly it has more substance than the earlier works, comes together in all respects in ways that *A Foregone Conclusion* does not, and has far more consistency of tone than *Private Theatricals.* Howells's perceptions of provincial Americans and superior Bostonians and Europeans are the sharper for his having experienced them all. The novel breaks no new ground, but it sums up a side of his work so well as to afford a division in his early work from that which was to follow. From this point on, though there were to be reversions to this earlier manner, Howells's novels took on a wide range of problem subjects, escaped the restrictions that stories of courting entailed, and were consistently darker in tone.

The plot of *The Lady of the Aroostook* is as simple as that of *A Chance Acquaintance*, even acknowledging that the heroine covers more territory in going from South Bradfield, Massachusetts, to Venice and back. Lydia Blood is a proper, provincial, New England girl raised by her aunt and grandfather in a New England town north of Boston. Her aunt, Mrs. Erwin, invites her to Venice, and she finds herself on board the *Aroostook*, not, as it was planned, a lone child passenger in the care of the captain, but a young unchaperoned woman among three male passengers, two of them young enough to be suitors. The moral dilemma this represents, the contrasts brought out between Lydia's natural innocence and acquired Puritan morality, and the pretensions and behaviors of the American and Europeans in Venice, occupy much of the book. The rest is taken up with the growing love between James Staniford and Lydia, which must overcome various moral scruples on both sides before it can receive the blessings of marriage. Staniford's jealousy of his friend Dunham and various misunderstandings have to be resolved before the story ends. The couple returns to America, not to New England nor even to Ohio but to some long entertained fancy of Howells, life on a sheep ranch in California.

I do not think that very much of this novel or romance—neither term fits well—is to be taken seriously. Its triumph is the mock-heroic tone which Howells maintains throughout, with only an occasional lapse in the characterization of Lydia and in such melodramatic embellishments as the drunken Hicks, for example. Its most successful characterization is not Lydia Blood, though she is an interesting variant of Kitty Ellison; it is James Staniford, Howells's most engaging fictionalizing of himself. Talent, art, literature, criticism are looked at with a comic subtlety worthy of Cervantes. Staniford represents preeminently the rational man, not bereft of a sense of beauty or romance, who can maintain an idealism which only occasionally gets in the way of living in the world. He is not a model of manly virtue or aesthetic or moral sensibilities. Seriousness need not be solemnity, sensibility need not be sentimentality, satisfaction need not be complacency, he seems to say. He is beyond the ordinary man, if at all, in the full development of his conscience and in a heightened ability to see the comic side of what may well be a tragic life. He is a younger version of Basil March, more engaging here because he has not yet been drawn into marriage. He escapes, therefore, somewhat as Basil does not, the impression that he sits too smugly at the center of things, looking neither out too far nor in too deep.

It is this portraiture which makes *The Lady of the Aroostook* the most successful result of Howells's first years' practice of fiction. For him as a writer, it represents a hard-won and not consistently maintained equanimity amid a busy and conflicting life. With but three exceptions, the short novel *A Fearful Responsibility* (1881), *Indian Summer* (1886), and *April Hopes* (1888), all of his novels of the next decade are novels which concern themselves with social problems and which extend his canvas beyond the two or three characters his early fiction examines so well.

Chapter Four

Growth as a Novelist:
A Modern Instance

Toward Literary Independence

In a long letter to James Russell Lowell, June 22, 1879, Howells reviewed his own situation as well as that of literary America. In light of the apparent approval granted by Lowell, he happily acknowledged that he was somehow deserting Lowell by leaving Cambridge and moving to Belmont. From some reminiscing about Cambridge life and remarking about how his two children are now enjoying the country, he moved to discussing how "Harry James waked up all the women with his Daisy Miller." He then went on to say he had "come to understand fully what Hawthorne meant when he said to me that he would like to see some part of America on which the shadow of Europe had not fallen. But it's no deeper than a shadow." Howells was to develop these ideas in his review of James's *Hawthorne*, which appeared in the *Atlantic* the next February. "In the meantime," he went on to Lowell, "it seems to me that we are in a fair way to have a pretty school of really native American fiction. There are three or four younger fellows than myself writing, and there are several extremely clever, but not too clever, young women" (*LIL*, 1:271–72).

As quiet as the passage is, it is Howells's declaration of literary independence, not from the shadow of Europe, but from the shadow of Lowell himself and the literary New England which had hung over him from his first pilgrimage in 1860. The actual break from Boston was not to take place until 1888 when he moved to New York, but clearly at this time he was preparing the way.

Howells's feeling about literary New England are best conveyed in his reminiscent volume, *Literary Friends and Acquaintance* (1900). "Literature in Boston, indeed, was so respectable," he writes of the years he first spent there, "and often of so high a lineage, that to be a poet was not only to be good society, but almost to be good family" (*LF&A*, 125). The Boston patricians he named were Prescott, Motley, Parkman, Lowell, Norton, Higginson, Dana, Emerson, and Channing, men who gave Boston "her supremacy in literature during that Unitarian harvest-time of the old Puritanic seed-time which was her Augustan age" (*LF&A*, 125). As for Cambridge as he remembered it, he wrote:

People held themselves high . . . their civilization was still Puritan though their belief had long ceased to be so. . . . Family counted in Cambridge, without doubt, as it counts in New England everywhere, but family alone did not mean position. . . . Money still less than family commanded. . . . I look back at my own life there with wonder at my good fortune. . . . I was young and unknown and was making my way. . . . At times, when I had experienced from those elect spirits with whom I was associated, some act of friendship, as signal as it was delicate, I used to ask myself, how I could ever do anything unhandsome or ungenerous toward any one again, and I had a bad conscience the next time I did it. (*LF&A*, 240–41)

The impression that these figures made on a talented, literary, but plebeian young man cannot be underestimated. As he grew in stature as both editor and author, however, he tempered his reverence for the Brahmin culture. Contemporary acquaintances became more important to his development. These included Thomas Sergeant Perry, who opened to his view the great Russian authors (Russian was a language Howells did *not* master); John Hay, whose *Castilian Days* appeared in the *Atlantic* and aroused Howells's warm praise: "I've loved Cervantes ever since I was ten years old, but vastly more I'm sure I owe to your beautiful, exquisite treatment of it" (*LIL,* 1:161–62); Edmund Clarence Stedman, poet and friend from meetings in New York before Howells went to Boston; and Thomas Bailey Aldrich, author and editor of *Every Saturday.* His work on the *Atlantic* brought him into acquaintance with a great many other writers and public figures both inside and outside Boston.[1]

Henry James

None of these became as close friends or as important to his literary development as Henry James and Mark Twain. Howells was turning twenty-eight, James twenty-three, when they met soon after Howells arrived in Cambridge. The James family had moved to Cambridge in 1866, but Henry had been there since 1862, enrolled in Harvard Law School part of that time but occupying himself with serious attempts at writing. His first story in the *Atlantic,* "The Story of a Year," appeared in March, 1865, just as Howells was concluding his tour in Venice. It was Howells the next year who urged Fields to accept "Poor Richard" and "to take all the stories you can get" from him.

At the outset, Howells was the more experienced writer and in a position to further some of James's ambitions as well as to afford him the literary stimulation that relieved some of the personal tensions in James's life. When James went abroad, first in 1869–70, then in 1872–74, they continued to correspond. In a letter of 1873, Howells wrote: "I thank you for not telling me too much about Rome. Such things are hard to bear. I hate the American in Europe,—because I am not he. At times the longing is almost intolerable with me, and if I could see any way of keeping the bird in the hand while I clutched at those in the bush, I should go" (*LIL,* 1:176–77). In December of the same year he thanked James for an unprinted but favorable review of his poems and acknowledged the rightness of his strictures on *A Chance Acquaintance.* "By the way," he writes, "I hope you won't send any of your stories to *Scribner's.* We have of course no claim upon you, but we have hitherto been able to print all the stories you have sent, and so it shall be hereafter" (*LIL*, 1:181).

How much each writer influenced the other with respect to "realism" is still conjectural, despite all that has been written on the subject, most of it from the vantage point of their later criticism and observation. Few of James's early tales are very "realistic" in the sense we now associate with the term, and as he acquired his peculiar strengths he moved far away from the kind of realistic novels Howells was writing in his later years. James's first two novels, *Watch and Ward* and *Roderick Hudson*, were serialized in the *Atlantic*, in 1871 and 1875, and have most of the faults of conventional fiction of the time—sentimentality, melodramatic posturing, and a subject matter congenial to the tastes of a feminine audience. What must have attracted Howells's attention were similarities to his own fictional approaches and a familiarity with both the New England and European cultural contrasts James was weaving into his fiction. The character study in which plot turned on nuances of moral and social behavior was the kind of work Howells was also doing. *Daisy Miller*, which appeared in the English magazine *Cornhill* before its publication in the *Atlantic* in 1879, was anticipated in *A Chance Acquaintance* by five years, and that particular kind of young lady was a triumph of Howells in *The Lady of the Aroostook* the year after.

James departed from his first long stay in Europe in 1875, and thereafter his relationship with Howells was maintained by infrequent visits and more frequent correspondence. In 1904, Howells carefully advised those who were arranging for James's American tour, and that summer, on one unusually hot day, Howells and James spent the day at Howells's summer home at Kittery Point, Maine, talking in their old way. In 1911, he joined with Edith Wharton and others in some quiet but unsuccessful maneuvering to get James the Nobel Prize. Throughout the last years of James's life, when James, in both England and America, had still not securely established his literary reputation, Howells continued to give him encouragement and support. During the last weeks of Howells's life, he was working on two essays about Henry James.

Mark Twain

Howells's friendship with Mark Twain is too rich and long-lasting to be described in short space.[2] The bare facts are that they met in 1869 in the offices of the *Atlantic* to which Mark Twain had gone to thank the anonymous reviewer of his first book, *Innocents Abroad.* The reviewer was Howells, and from that time on until Mark Twain's death in 1910, they enjoyed a warm and professionally stimulating friendship. Mark Twain's settling in Hartford in 1872 made it possible for the two men to see each other fairly often, some times on visits between the two families.

Similarities in their family situations as well as in their past experiences and in their ambitions as writers helped establish and maintain their close relationship. Both were Westerners, short on formal schooling, money, and family status; apprentice printers and fledgling journalists; ambitious authors, inclined both to the romantic and realistic; anxious fathers, and husbands of women who seemed never for long to be physically well. Both realized their literary way was not to be that of the New England Brahmins who dominated respectable literature nor that of the sentimental storytellers and poets who pleased the popular audience.

Howells's championing of Mark Twain's genius is well known.[3] He published reviews of most of Mark Twain's books, plus three long summary articles about him in 1882 and 1901. He was instrumental in getting Mark Twain's first contribution, "A True Story," into the *Atlantic* in 1874, though he rejected the "Fable" which Mark Twain had submitted at the same time. It was Howells's continuing encouragement that led to the serializing of "Old Times on the Mississippi" (*Atlantic*, January–June and August, 1875), and that, in turn, to *Tom Sawyer* and *Huckleberry Finn.* Howells read *Tom Sawyer* in manuscript, making "some corrections and suggestions in faltering pencil", (*MT–HL*, I, 111) mostly in the first third, and the generosity of his offering to read the proofs of *Huckleberry Finn* took Clemens's breath away (*MT–HL*, 2:482). In letters or conversation or in print, Howells responded to most of Mark Twain's work.

Less well known is that Mark Twain was a sensitive and admiring reader of Howells's work.[4] He read virtually everything Howells wrote, and though we have no such abundance of systematic criticism as Howells made of Twain's works, we do have a continuing stream of specific praise in the letters. Reading *The Lady of the Aroostook* in Munich, January 21, 1879, he wrote:

If your literature has not struck perfection now we are not able to see what is lacking.—It is all such truth—truth to the life; everywhere your pen falls it leaves a photograph. I *did* imagine that everything had been said about life at sea that could be said,—but no matter, it was all a failure & lies, nothing but lies with a thin varnish of fact,—only *you* have stated it as it absolutely *is*. And only you see people & their ways & their insides & outsides as they *are*, & make them talk as they *do* talk. I think you are the very greatest artist in these tremendous mysteries that ever lived. . . . You ain't a weed, but an oak; you ain't a summer-house, but a cathedral. In that day *I* shall still be in the Cyclopedias, too,—thus: "Mark Twain; history & occupation unknown—but he was personally acquainted with Howells." There—I could sing your praises all day, & feel & believe every bit of it. (*MT-HL*, 1:245–46)

As to the importance of their relationship in helping each find his own independent way, the Whittier birthday dinner of December, 1877, is particularly revealing. The occasion was both Whittier's seventieth birthday and the *Atlantic Monthly*'s twentieth, and at Howells's invitation, Mark Twain made an after-dinner speech that seemingly revealed the fool he was to the whole New England patriarchy. In actuality, he delivered a funny and typical bit of Western humor, a tale of how he had been visited in a California mining camp by three rogues passing themselves off as Longfellow, Emerson, and Holmes. His caricature of the three, who were all in the audience (Holmes, at sixty-eight, was the youngest), was at the heart of the jest: Emerson a "seedy little bit of a chap—red-headed," Holmes "fat as a balloon," Longfellow "built like a prizefighter." The tale ended with a snapper: the miner who has been telling the story to Mark Twain, who has presented himself as an author, is told by Mark Twain that these poetry spouting vagabonds were imposters, to which he replies: "Ah—imposters, were they? Are *you?*"

In *My Mark Twain* (1910), Howells recalled the speech as "the amazing mistake, the bewildering blunder, the cruel catastrophe," and probably magnified both the audience's "appalled" response and Twain's feelings of utter humiliation. The speech may, as Lynn argues, have betrayed Twain's animosity to New England and specifically to "all Westerners who played the man-of-letters game in New England as small-time frauds who had sold out to a larger fraudulency."[5] The number included both Howells and himself. Henry Nash Smith comments: "However the actual audience may have responded to Mark Twain's speech, his career as a writer did represent new perspectives and new energies which threatened the New England literary tradition."[6] When Howells advised Clemens to write letters of apology to each of the supposedly offended authors, his concluding comment fits with other indications that Howells himself was coming out from the shadow of New England: "They would take it in the right spirit, I'm sure. If they didn't the right would be yours" (*MT–HL,* 1:213). His quiet reminder to Lowell that there are young men and women in New England who can write now is just such another indication. More important, the work he was to do prior to his actual departure from Boston left much of the New England attachment to polite letters behind and used aspects of contemporary life at some odds with the image of New England gentility.

Four Minor Novels

Before discussing *A Modern Instance,* the novel which most clearly marks Howells's growth as a novelist, I wish to mention four other novels: *A Fearful Responsibility, Dr. Breen's Practice, A Woman's Reason,* and *The Undiscovered Country.* None of these is a novel that must be restored to public attention. *A Fearful Responsibility* can be set aside quickly both for its brevity (it occupied but two issues in *Scribner's Monthly*, June–July, 1881) and for its use of the courting theme and Venetian background more successfully set forth in other works. It has some added interest in relation to Howells's life in the person of Professor Elmore, who is in Venice during the Civil War writing a history of that city. He debates, as Howells must have debated, the ethics of going to Venice while the war is going on. The other characters are Lily Mayhew, the familiar Howells ingenue, and Clay Hoskins, a young sculptor-consul, who is one of four men attracted to Lily. Professor Elmore and his wife dissuade Lily from marrying any one of them and then worry about their meddling after she has returned to America unmarried. Both are relieved when they hear, some years later and after she has passed the awful age of thirty, that she has married a clergyman from Omaha.

Dr. Breen's Practice (1881) is worth mentioning, if only because it is in connection with this novel that the "palpitating divans" remark comes into print. "John is at this moment curled up on the lounge reading *Doctor Breen's Practice*," Howells wrote to John Hay in 1882. "For this reason, if for no other, I could not have palpitating divans in my stories; my children are my censors" (*LIL*, 1:311). They do not, however, censor his reading, for he admits to reading everything by Zola he can lay his hands on, even though he has to hide such books from the children.

No strong case can be made for Howells's not showing an extraordinary delicacy in sexual matters in his voluminous writings. Still, he was not quite as oblivious of or hostile to sexuality in fiction as some critics claim. He wrote to J. W. DeForest, December 9, 1886: "it was your bold grappling with the fact of the robust love-making among three-fourths of our nation that gave me courage to deal with it in Lemuel, and A Modern Instance. It's odd that no one touched it before you" (*Letters*, 3:170). By now, the sexual revolution and its effect on literature may give us a useful perspective toward Howells and his capitulating to the reticences of his time. The situation has reversed itself; modern writers are as much constrained to write explicitly about sex as

Howells was constrained not to. As Lowell, for example, explicitly cautioned Howells about not writing anything that a young girl could not read (it was Lowell, too, who removed a supposedly irreverent mention of a pine tree from a Thoreau essay), so modern editors, publishers, and audiences have encouraged the inclusion and elaboration of explicit sexual scenes in popular fiction. Without arguing whether the understanding of human beings and their actions is furthered more by one set of tendencies than the other, one must by now acknowledge that our time is as peculiar, with regard to sex in literature, as was Howells's.

Neither Howells's nor the Victorian attitude toward sexual relations in fiction should obscure the fact that women in Howells's time were restricted in many ways. The suffrage movement served to point out how women were denied opportunities for education, faced great difficulties in finding suitable occupations or careers, and contended in many ways with the effects of the limited roles society forced upon them. These latter questions were much a part of Howells's fiction of this period. In making a young and pretty single woman *doctor* the protagonist of *Dr. Breen's Practice*, Howells was challenging, however politely, the conservative opinion of his time.

One cannot argue that Howells debates the place of women in the professions in an energetic way. But perhaps that is because such a debate is only a part of what is on his mind. Some are old concerns—the differences between East and West, for example, brought out in this novel by introducing a Westerner from Cheyenne into the central action. Others are topical, the conflict between homeopathic and allopathic medicine, which was a matter of controversy at the time. Another is a general topic which was to preoccupy Howells for the next three decades: the efficacy of social reforms. Dr. Breen is examined in the course of the novel chiefly in her own inner conflicts between fulfilling herself in marriage or in a life of service and in examining how much of her behavior comes out of honesty with herself about her desires and satisfactions. "At the end of the ends," Howells concludes the book, "she was a Puritan; belated, misdated if the reader will, and cast upon good works for the consolation which the Puritans formerly found in a creed" (270).

A Woman's Reason, not published until 1884, but which Howells was working on as early as 1878, further pursues the position of a woman forced to survive under straitened circumstances in the Boston of that time. Even more, it is a study of New England as it might have been and as it was now becoming, a contrast not unlike that which Willa Cather creates for mid-America in *A Lost Lady*. Like that novel, the social changes are mirrored in the central woman character. One can see in the novel the New England of the India trade, full of men of courage, daring, and unshakable honesty, being replaced by a commercial New England at worst populated by outright villains (one is a suitor for Helen Harkness's hand) and at best by young men like Robert Fenton (who eventually marries Helen), who are nice enough chaps but hardly looking for more in life than a comfortable existence. *A Woman's Reason* is too full of melodrama to be convincing, but it is also packed with observations about contemporary society that were to be put to more focused use in later novels. In one respect it is startling among Howells's novels, for a part of the machinery of the plot requires that Robert be shipwrecked on a desert island, thus making Howells create a scene, very effectively executed, almost completely out of his imagination.

One other novel precedes the publication of *A Modern Instance*. This is *The Undiscovered Country*, a novel that has been urged by Kermit Vanderbilt as among Howells's best works.[7] My own reservations about the novel are almost as strong as toward *A Woman's Reason*. Still, the stronger connections of this novel with the tormenting personal concerns of Howells do give it considerable power despite an often unintended murkiness. Even that may not be just to Howells's intent, for his "notion," as he wrote to W. H. Bishop, "was not to explain anything in my story" (*LIL* 1:282).

The main sources of emotional power in *The Undiscovered Country* are the familial relationships which also give *A Modern*

Instance its stature, for, as in *A Modern Instance*, a father's tyranny over a daughter is a powerful theme here. Exploring the nature and consequences of Dr. Boynton's tyranny over Egeria is central to the novel, but *The Undiscovered Country* also draws upon characterizations found in earlier novels and creates many of its specifications out of current social phenomena. From the earlier novels, a pair of male protagonists are developed, both gaining strength from Howells's ponderings about his own divided nature. From a wave of spiritualism now infesting New England and from a long held interest in religion itself and specifically in the place of the Shakers within a changing society he creates a backdrop for the entire story. In this respect and in its main theme, the story very much resembles James's *The Bostonians*, which was to appear in 1886.

The novel opens on a back street in Boston which has become the haunt of spiritualists. The two young men, Mr. Ford, "tall and spare," and Mr. Phillips, "much shorter and stouter," are witnessing a seance most importantly involving Dr. Boynton, who is convinced of the spiritualistic powers of his daughter, Egeria, sometimes called the Pythoness because of her powers.

Howells gives more attention to the characterizations of the young men than he had done in earlier novels, in part because the central conflict is both a love conflict between a modern rationalist not altogether skeptical of religion and a spiritualist whose beliefs approach lunacy. Ford is a moody chap, not fond of bric-a-brac, polite society, or ladies. He is not a Bostonian by birth, but arrived there as a young man from the provinces. He writes a "caustic style," knows something of science, and is poor as befits one who has not yet settled on a vocation. Most of the women at his lodgings are afraid of him, but Mrs. Perham, who is not, says: "He is as natural as the noble savage, and twice as handsome. I like those men who *show* their contempt of you.... Mr. Ford's insolence has a sort of cold thrill about it that's delicious" (47). Phillips is a deliberately contrasting male character, something of a caricatured Howellsian or Jamesian young man whose interest in arts is dilettantish, feminine, and in tune with polite society's general regard. "Such men as Phillips consorted with," Howells writes, "were of the feminine temperament, like artists and musicians (he had a pretty taste in music); or else they were of the intensely masculine sort, like Ford, to whom he had attached himself" (37).

The rising action of the story is Ford's unsparing desire to expose Boynton as a fool and charlatan. Egeria is caught in the middle, feeling some of the delicious cold thrill in Ford's presence that other ladies feel, but also perceiving in him a savagery that threatens both herself and her father. Events conspire to avoid an early confrontation between Ford and Dr. Boynton over a proposed test of Boynton's faith in Egeria as a medium. Instead father and daughter leave Boston and make a journey to a Shaker community, doubtless modeled on the one Howells had visited in Shirley, Massachusetts. This hapless trek of the Boyntons makes Massachusetts seem as vast as the Russian steppes; never did Howells depict a pair of human souls less capable of fending for themselves and subject to more mischance. One place of temporary refuge is a tavern, the landlord of which is described as "a short, stout man, with a shock of iron-gray hair and a face of dusky red, coarse and harsh; his blood-shot eyes wandered curiously over Egeria's figure" (149). Egeria at this point, sinking into illness, is hardly a figure to be noticed except by a truly depraved and drunken male, but only the intervention of a spiritual experience—or so it is interpreted by Dr. Boynton—gets her out of the tavern owner's clutches.

In the Shaker village, Egeria takes to her sick bed. As she recovers her physical health in the spring, her father becomes more unhinged, and some loony talk which purports to explain the equally loony conviction that Egeria has spiritual powers leads to his proposing to the Shakers another test. The reader now sees the ugly side of Boynton's spirituality; it is the means by which he maintains power over Egeria, and even she begins to divine this aspect of their relationship. As might be expected, Ford and Phillips arrive by chance in the vicinity; they have taken to the country to escape the summer malaise in Boston. The test destroys all the props of Boynton's shabby spiritualism, though Howells keeps Ford discreetly off stage during the old man's unmasking. What follows are some Lear-like roamings and ravings of Dr. Boynton who, coming upon Ford, seizes upon his presence as being responsible for his defeat. Boynton then falls into an illness from which he does not recover and which provides space for some reconciliation between Ford and the old man before the novel ends.

The rest of the story pursues the welling up of love between Ford and Egeria. A pastoral scene, not unlike that between Mrs. Farrell and Easton, hints at Ford's sexual aggressiveness, which, apparently, must be tempered in order to make marriage possible. Ford is gathering maple leaves for Egeria:

> He caught it about the slender stem well up towards the limbs, and, bending it over, began to break them away and fling them on the ground.
> "Oh, no!" cried Egeria from where she stood. "Don't!"
> "Don't what?" asked Ford, turning half round, without releasing the tree.
> "You seemed to tear it so. You have enough. . . ." (295)

Eventually they are married. Mrs. Perham, who has well characterized Ford at the beginning, says of Egeria: "I've an idea that the Pythoness is insipid; but if Mr. Ford likes insipidity, I want him to have it" (383). Insipidity, if it be so, seems quite compatible with comfort, and the Fords settle down to a comfortable life in the suburbs of Boston, not unlike that of Mr. and Mrs. W. D. Howells. Phillips no longer visits them because they have "neutralized each other into the vulgarest commonplace."

In such a placid ending, one in which both the author's acceptance and irony are present, the tensions sustained in three fourths of the novel are all but forgotten. The basic question of belief has dissipated in Boynton's disavowing spiritualism before his death and professing a hope that perhaps science will solve the mysteries of "the undiscovered country"—the line is from *Hamlet*—"from whose bourne no traveler returns." Ford does not share his wife's Episcopal leanings, and his dabbling in science has turned, at her suggestion, something called the Ford Fire Kindler into a respectable income. His earlier inclinations toward becoming a writer have been set aside, leaving, however, such direct ties with Howells as this (Ford is speaking): "and after I got here I sent a letter to a newspaper about it. You might think that would end it; but you don't know the economies of a hack-writer. I've taken my letter for a text, and I'm working it over into an article for a magazine. If I were a real literary man I should turn it into a lecture afterwards, and then expand it into a little book" (321).

Far from creating an impression that confinement to the commonplace gave Howells too little to write about, *The Undiscovered Country* makes an impression that too many matters both on the surface and beneath were pushing for Howells's attention, diverting him from a sustained and intense work of fiction. A verifiable movement in Howells's handling of fiction is his moving away from the Turgenev-like study restricted to a central character with a supporting cast of two or three to the more populated social novel which accommodates a number and variety of characters, themes, and actions. The weakness in *The Undiscovered Country*, however, is not so much in the handling of Dr. Boynton and Egeria and the spiritualists and the Shakers as well as Ford and Phillips and their Boston acquaintances; these matters are handled well and made to fit with some excusable contrivance and disjunctions. The weakness is the more serious one of backing away from the pursuit of a dominant and powerful theme. Dr. Boynton is a tamed and excused Lear, even before he is given a peaceful death. Egeria is, indeed, insipid, when she need not be. Ford is surly and savage and sexual, but to little point, as it turns out. For the most part, *The Undiscovered Country* remains tied to Howells's and his readers' topical interest in spiritualism. When it manifests its real power it draws upon the inner tensions between parent and child, the ambiguities of love and passion, which Howells had long and deeply felt.

A Modern Instance

The shortcomings just given attention are less apparent in *A Modern Instance* (1882). There is a relentlessness and a single-ness of purpose in the pursuit of Bartley Hubbard which is absent from *The Undiscovered Country*. So intense does it become in the latter part of the novel, indeed, that the reader thinks back upon the beginning and may be provoked to a sympathy with Hubbard that Howells did not intend. Or, he may decide that the premises upon which the entire novel is built become suspect in the weight Bartley Hubbard's wickedness is made to carry.

Lynn attributes Howells's nervous collapse in the fall of 1881 to his reaching the crucial point in the novel where Bartley deserts his wife and child: "It is clear that Bartley's flight set in motion an anxiety that completely overran the castle of Howells's defenses."[8] Cady, who freely speculates on the sources of Howells's breakdown in 1856, restrains himself here. "No one now can really tell anything except that it was a long and critical sickness. . . ."[9] Howells, himself, attributed it to "long worry and sleeplessness from over-work" (*LIL*, 1:303). I cannot help but be sympathetic to Lynn's view, for there is a disjunction in the novel at about the point Howells was forced to set it aside. The completion of the novel, rather than showing the backing away and ameliorating I have called attention to in *The Undiscovered Country*, which might be an expected result of exhaustion and recovery, shows a relentless-ness toward Hubbard which can be interpreted as a means of dis-sipating a guilt which was strongly at work in Howells's psyche.

What the illness does confirm is the presence of tensions in Howells's life quite at odds with the image of steadily increasing success that appears as its surface reality.[10] An indication of the tensions Howells was under, close in time to the writing of *A Modern Instance*, is in a letter to Horace Scudder, February, 1881: "But I have grown terribly, miserably tired of editing. I think my nerves have given way under the fifteen years' fret and substantial unsuccess. At any rate, the MSS., the proofs, the books, the letters have become insupportable" (*LIL*, 1:294). Howells resigned the *Atlantic* editorship shortly before this letter was written, in part as a way of resolving a quarrel between Houghton and Osgood which had dissolved their partnership. Though Howells entered into a contract with Osgood for a book a year at a guaranteed annual salary of about $8,000, plus royalties for sales beyond 10,000 copies, the arrangement left him only relatively free. He continued to take on many money-making literary chores and to operate under the pressure of books he was now obliged to write.

Another great source of worry, a new worry since the summer of 1880, was the mysterious illness suffered by his sixteen-year-old daughter, Winny. The story as it played itself out until her death in 1889 is tragic in details as in outcome. The attempts to diagnose her condition, ostensibly of psychic origins, the methods of treating it, and the remissions and recurrences could not help but be agonizing to Howells. Appearing as it did the summer before his own illness and bringing with it memories of his own earlier breakdown, Winny's decline must have been a strong contributing cause of his own malaise.

The idea for *A Modern Instance* came to Howells as early as the summer of 1876 when he saw a performance of *Medea* in Boston.[11] Thereafter, the novel became "a new Medea," and, under that title, engaged Howells in some preliminary writing in 1878. The *Medea* Howells saw, however, was not the original but an English translation of a melodramatic version by the Austrian playwright Franz Grillparzer (1791–1872). Grillparzer, like Howells, domesticated the classical tragedy; both played down the violence and universality of the Euripides play. But both focused on the discord that arises between husband and wife and which Howells used for his study of an American divorce.

In April, 1881, he went to Xenia, Ohio, to see the old Eureka mills where he had lived for a year and on to Crawfordsville, Indiana, to witness a western divorce case, which was to play an important part in the novel. It was to begin serialization in the *Century* in December, and, as he wrote to Mark Twain, he planned to finish it by that time and cut for Europe. He had finished 1,466 manuscript pages before his illness, much of that to be revised and 300 or 400 pages yet to be written while the first parts were being serialized. Howells's professionalism is remarkable in his being able to bring the novel to as satisfactory a conclusion as he did.

It was the theme of *Medea*, translation or version aside, which must have attracted Howells. Like other works of Euripides, *Medea* places a reader's sympathies with a woman wronged and has passion operating as the tragic force. Medea is the wife Jason brings back from the East at the conclusion of his trip to find the golden fleece. A faithful wife, and a passionate one, she kills Creon, Creon's daughter, and their own children in revenge for Jason's leaving her for Creon's daughter. No proper story for the Victorian, obviously, and yet it was both translated and played before Victorian audiences.

Medea dominates any version of the play. Her temper and jealousy and the awful power of her passions are central to her character. Jason is a less commanding figure; his easy assumption of masculine prerogatives and his failure to comprehend the strength of Medea's feelings are in both Euripides' and Grillparzer's characterizations, and in Howells's delineation of Bartley Hubbard. The attention Howells was giving to women's role in American society made *Medea* a play to which he could strongly respond, perhaps specifically to such a passage as this in the Euripides play as translated by E. P. Coleridge:

Of all things that have life and sense we women are the most hapless creatures; first must we buy a husband at a great price, and o'er ourselves a tyrant set which is an evil worse than the first; and herein lies the most important issue, whether our choice be good or bad. For divorce is not honourable to women, nor can we disown our lords. Next must the wife, coming as she does to ways and customs new, since she hath not learnt the lesson in her home, have a diviner's eye to see how best to treat the partner of her life. If haply we perform these tasks with thoroughness and tact, and the husband live with us, without resenting the yoke, our life is a happy one; if not, 'twere best to die. But when a man is vexed with what he finds indoors, he goeth forth and rids his soul of its disgust, betaking him to some friend or comrade of like age; whilst we must needs regard his single self.[12]

What Howells adds which is not in the original play is the prominence given to Medea's father—Squire Gaylord in the novel— a projection, perhaps of attachments to and conflicts between Howells and his parents and Elinor Mead and her father. In Euripides' *Medea*, little attention is given to Medea's father and none to their relationship aside from the fact that she betrayed her father and killed her brother in order to follow Jason. But in Howells's novel, a triangle of conflict involving Bartley and Marcia and Marcia's father was not lost on the Victorian audience, how- ever its sexual basis might be denied. It may have aroused some readers to find the story "unwholesome,"[13] and such readers were not likely to be appeased by Bartley's getting what he deserved, shot down well before the novel ends by a man of violence in Whited Sepulchre, Arizona, who has been outraged by Bartley's pen. What may have stayed with readers and what they would not have chosen to mention is the picture of the squire and Marcia, as queer as her mother, living out their equally queer lives in Equity, Maine.

Most of the novel, almost all of the part Howells finished be- fore his breakdown, concentrates on the three central characters, with Equity, Maine, at one pole, Boston at the other. Were it not for the tension one feels at the outset, the novel could have become a politely amusing one about mating and marriage. Equity is not a bad place, pastorally beautiful in summer and full of skating and hot mince pies, even in winter. The squire, of course, is uncom- monly grim, but Marcia loves him, and her liveliness arises above her family's barren condition. Bartley, an orphaned country boy, would be an engaging figure anywhere. He is clever, articulate, and pointed toward worldly success. He goes away to school where he excels. He thinks of taking up law, and amazes Squire Gaylord by the rapidity with which he absorbs Blackstone. He edits the village newspaper in what he regards as a "hick" town, and he is fond of dress, his horse and cutter, and flirting with girls. Certainly, there is nothing in him to suggest the burden of evil that the novel is going to force upon him.

The characterization of Marcia, on the other hand, is serious from the start, if one gets past the surface playing that attends her relations with Bartley. She is not orphaned, as is Bartley, and left free; rather she is delivered over to a father's love and passion out of a failed and sinister marriage, sinister in the pallid figure the mother cuts, in the vacancy that exists between husband and wife, and in the turning to Marcia that gives Squire Gaylord what vitality he possesses. The passionate nature of Marcia and her father's power over her are revealed in the reaction to her father's question after Bartley has given her a good-night kiss:

The blood flashed up from her heart into her face like fire, and then, as suddenly fell back again and left her white. She let her head droop and turn till her eyes were wholly averted from him, and she did not speak. He closed the door behind him and she went upstairs to her own room; in her shame she seemed to herself to crawl thither, with her father's glance burning upon her. (15)

One can see this as the stuff of melodrama, particularly when it is followed by the scene which describes Bartley's reaction. Back at his hotel, he kicks off his boots, warms a mince pie over the coals, and reflects that he had had "a grand good time; but it had left him hungry." But that, I think, is not quite fair to Howells's intent nor even to his execution. He is working his way into his material along familiar lines, albeit the idea for a modern tragedy is still operating as a compelling impulse. The focus properly falls on Marcia and her wrenching herself away from Equity, her insufficient even pathetic attempt to adapt not only to Boston but to Bartley. Given her nature and the situation she finds herself in, we relinquish the notion that this woman might be fitted into a domestic comedy, a farce by Howells for example. We accept the truly pathetic, if not tragic, position she finds herself in, caught between her love for a husband who she must believe has done her wrong and her love for a father who she cannot believe has wronged her but most certainly has. It is harder to give up our notion of Bartley as a not-so-bad fellow who has an eye on the main chance, a fondness for Tivoli beer, an inclination to stoutness, and a somewhat wandering eye, and make him into a Jason, a figure suitable to tragedy.

The involvement of secondary characters in the novel, which most critics have acknowledged as a weakness, is not just padding nor even floundering while Howells was recovering his health. Ricker and Kinney, whose involvement is almost entirely with Bartley, are efforts to give him some dimensions beyond those provided by the domestic scenes. Both characters are effectively drawn and provide more support for taking seriously Bartley's moral defects, the worst being a rationalized dishonesty that dims his perceptions of himself as well as of those around him.

The Halleck family and Clara Kingsbury are less necessary, the latter probably not necessary at all expect as, once again, Howells turns to a satirical type which will be put to better use in a later novel, *Annie Kilburn* (1889). There is little in the portraiture of Clara Kingsbury and Mr. Atherton that helps set off the serious plight of the Hubbards or to emphasize serious aspects of the story not already conveyed through the main characters and their actions. Atherton's pronouncements on separation and divorce are, as Kenneth Lynn has called them, "hysterically pompous." Perhaps Howells was not unaware of the temptations (not yet opportunities probably) divorce offered. We have no direct evidence that Howells ever felt this way, though the chances of such questions not arising in almost fifty years of marriage are very slim. But there is abundant indirect evidence that Marcia borrowed some of her most irritating characteristics from Elinor Howells, and evidence aplenty in the depictions of Basil and Isabel March that Howells sometimes found his wife a pain.

The Hallecks occupy a more interesting, if hardly more justifiable, place in the novel. Ben Halleck, who has the most excuse for being, is probably the most insufferable characterization of goodness that Howells allowed himself to create. If it were clear that Howells recognized this and eventually allowed Marcia to marry him, it might atone for the death of poor departed Bartley. But his recognition of Ben as being as crippled emotionally and morally as he is physically is fitful at best; too much of the time we are expected to both pity and admire him. This error in characterization may extend to the entire Halleck family. One side of Howells brings them forward as exemplars of the old New England faith, admirably if old-fashionedly alive in present-day Boston. Another side might have had them exercising a crippling effect upon Ben fully as powerful and inexcusable as Squire Gaylord's over Marcia. Questionable as I think their presence is in this novel, they are nonetheless an important part of the fabric of New England society, with old values struggling to stay alive amid great change.

A Modern Instance both reached more readers and aroused more criticism than any of Howells's previous novels. His reputation in England, never as large as in this country, was enhanced by Edmund Gosse's calling the novel "altogether the greatest work of fiction that America has given us since the death of Hawthorne" (*Letters*, 3:27). His notoriety, if not reputation, increased by a testy letter from Robert Louis Stevenson, whose wife had divorced her previous husband to marry him, saying he desired "to know no one who considers himself holier than my wife" (*LIL*, 1:333). Almost all the reviews by American literary people Howells respected were favorable, an indication of the quality of the book and of the coming to age of younger critics with opinions less ruled over by attitudes of the past.

In the early 1880s, Howells was becoming aware of both good and bad effects of his increasing fame. His friendship with Edmund Gosse, the English critic, speaks of his wide acceptance among English readers. In 1882, the Howellses were not only entertained by Americans then in London—Lowell, who was the American ambassador, John Hay, Clarence King, Harte, Aldrich, and Warner—but were welcomed by British social and literary figures. In November, the publication of his essay "Henry James, Jr." in the *Century* (Thomas Sergeant Perry had done one on Howells for the March issue) exposed Howells to another side of fame. His

remark that the artistry of James made that of Scott, Dickens, and
Thackeray crude by comparison brought harsh attacks from British
quarterlies.

Outside the high literary circles, Howells was receiving attention
of various kinds. To an inquirer in March, 1882, he wrote that
he never used tobacco, and "when I take wine, I think it weakens
my work and my working force the next morning" (*Letters*,
3:10).[14] To an inquiring biographer in 1883, he replied that
"Heine, Thackeray, & Tourguènief are the writers who have helped
me most" (*Letters*, 3:73). To another writer inquiring about his
work habits he wrote in June, 1884: "I am lazy, and always force
myself more or less to work, keeping from it as long as I can invent
any excuse. I often work when dull or heavy from a bad night,
and find that the indisposition wears off. I rarely miss a day from
any cause.... For a lazy man I am extremely industrious" (*Letters*,
3:102).

More flattering even than these evidences of interest in him as
an author was an offer of a professorship at Johns Hopkins from
President Daniel Coit Gilman. In a long reply, December 3, 1882,
Howells set forth at length a reasoned analysis of his strengths
and weaknesses as a professor of literature and a careful account
of how he would teach if he were to accept the position. In the
end, as his letter clearly indicated, he put his writing of novels
first and hinted at conditions and salary which Hopkins would not
be able to meet. He sought Lowell's advice, and made his formal
refusal of the offer the afternoon after he received Lowell's reply.[15]
A letter to his father from Florence at the end of January, 1883,
sums up Howells's feelings about his growing fame: "Of course it's
a pleasure to have people wanting to see me, but it's a vain and
empty one—the very most insubstantial of all pleasures, I think;
and this is what I so long longed for!" (*Letters*, 3:51).

Chapter Five

Indian Summer
and April Hopes

To Europe and Back: 1882–83

Howells did not quite cut for Europe, as he told Mark Twain he would, as soon as he had finished *A Modern Instance*. His illness slowed down his completion of the novel, and his own and his family's illnesses made it necessary to give up the Belmont house permanently before their departure in July, 1882. The year the Howellses and their three children spent in Europe included stops in London both before and after revisiting Italy. Henry James found charming lodgings and introduced Howells to the London literary circle. Later in Florence for the winter, James was living close by, and he and Howells talked literature "perpetually, as we used to do in our walks ten years ago." As always, Howells used his time well, working on *A Woman's Reason*, polishing his spoken French, compiling the material for *Tuscan Cities* (1888), completing notes for another travel book, *A Little Swiss Sojourn* (serialized in *Harper's Monthly*, February, 1888), and renewing old memories of Venice, much of which found its way into *Indian Summer* (1886), written not long after his return.

The European trip acted as a restorative for Howells following his years of hard work and the severe illness of the year before. Even Winny, he wrote from Venice, "Down for nearly two years with nervous prostration, is now quite herself again." His return, however, brought him back to the realities, both good and bad, of his upward progress. Financially the Howellses were well enough off to move out of the rented house in Louisburg Square to which they returned and occupy the house Howells had built on Beacon Street, the place for a successful man to live in the Boston of the 1880s. Professionally, having severed his ties with the *Atlantic* in 1881, he was free for a period of about two years from meeting a regular journalistic deadline. Nevertheless, he was busy: working with Mark Twain on the play *Colonel Sellers as a Scientist*, writing the libretto for an opera, *A Sea Change, or Love's Stowaway*, music by Georg Henschel, putting three articles into book form, *Three Villages* (1884), collaborating with Mildred by writing a text for her drawings, *A Little Girl Among the Old Masters* (1884), doing two or three farces, and still managing to complete two ambitious novels. Once again he saw himself as a hard-driven literary engine. "The expenses!" he wrote to the biographer James Parton from Beacon Street, March 27, 1885. "I am on the fire, and I *must boil*" (*Letters*, 3:119).

Both Elinor's and Winny's health continued to fail, despite periods of comparative well-being. In June of 1883, his father retired from the consulate and moved to a Virginia farm. Sam, his indigent brother, continued to borrow and depend on the family for support. In 1886, Howells bought a small-town paper, the *Madison* (Indiana) *Index*, for him, thinking, incorrectly, that it might provide for him a permanent situation. That same year, his brother Joseph, now fifty-four, traveled to England for his health, and Victoria, the sister closest to him in age, died of malaria in Jefferson. An end of the year letter to Henry James faced the fact that he would be fifty on his next birthday: "I've heard people say that they are not conscious of growing old; but *I* am. . . . I feel my half century fully. Lord, how it's slipped away!" (*LIL*, 1:389).

Indian Summer

It is out of a combination of nostalgia aroused in revisiting Italy and the reflections that accompanied his return to his professional and personal responsibilities at midlife that Howells wrote *Indian Summer*. The book was probably essentially completed by July, 1884, when he began to write *The Rise of Silas Lapham*, though *Lapham* began serializing in November, 1885, and *Indian Summer* did not begin in *Harper's Monthly* until the following July.

Indian Summer is a difficult novel for critics to confront, both underpraised and overpraised and seldom read with a willingness to grant that this relating of a May–December romance deserves a place with the serious social novels that both preceded and followed it. Clearly it is the best of Howells's novels of "mating and marrying," and the best, too, at displaying Howells's mastery of comic irony.

Howells had suggested as a name for the story, "September and May," for it is, like Chaucer's *Merchant's Tale*, the story of an older man's attraction to a very young woman. Its mood is that of Howells writing to James Russell Lowell just after Christmas in 1882: "We are here in Italy again, in the old soft air, under the same mild old sky, out of which all snap and sharpness have gone as out of the mood of a man too much experienced to be eager about anything. I don't know whether the old charm is here or not: it is by brief surprises, and all sorts of indirection, I suppose" (*LIL*, 1:335). From Venice, in April, he wrote Mark Twain: "Winny, who had been drooping in Florence, and getting so that she could not sleep, has recovered in her native air as if by magic; she takes the deadly romantic view of Venice, and doesn't hesitate to tell me that I did the place a great injustice in my books. It is quite amusing. She thinks it is *all* beauty and gayety..." (*LIL*, 1:340).

It is in Florence that the central figure of the novel, Theodore Colville, meets a friend and confidante of his past, Mrs. Bowen, and her companion, Imogene Graham. Colville is patently Howells, or what Howells might have been had his course kept him in Ohio. At forty-one, Colville has sold his successful paper, the Des Vaches, Indiana, *Democrat-Republican* and has come to revisit the Italian scenes he had first encountered as a twenty-one-year-old idealist hoping for a career as an architect-author. Like the broken engage-

ment which kept the Marches apart after their first meeting in
Italy, Colville had been rejected by a beautiful young girl on his
first Italian trip. His years as a bachelor since make him the more
susceptible to Imogene, who, barely twenty, is both the past repeating itself and a present opportunity altogether too tempting to be
set aside. Most of the novel is taken up with the love affair between
Colville and Imogene, in the serious yet comic tone that seems to
best fit stories of this kind.

What is somewhat surprising about the novel is that Howells
would attempt the subject at all. If it were not to offend the audience of his time, it must be handled delicately. And Howells could
well be accused of having experiences in real life at odds with
his image of trusted respectability. That he was able to carry it
off so well is attributable to his comic sense. In the novel, he was
able to sustain the tone which made him such a popular writer of
farces, and over a longer span and with genuinely and fully created
characters. Though one can find conventional and stereotyped responses in both Imogene and Colville, for the most part both are
individual and authentic. Imogene had been rehearsed often in
previous versions of the ingenue of which Howells was so fond.
Howells loved his ingenues, and creating a situation wherein that
love might almost be vicariously consummated must have given
him great satisfaction. At the same time, the novel has other
sources for its superior vitality. Winny's presence and the fresh-
ness of her response to Italy was one source. She was twenty; the
companionship she gave to her father, the counterpoint she provided to the Howellses' earlier experiences provided both incidents
and emotion Howells could draw on directly. Elinor furnished much
that is in the character of Mrs. Bowen, particularly that New
England rectitude that inclines toward both self-sacrifice and ideal-
ization of self.

It may be a fault in the novel that Colville and Imogene do
not convince the reader that they will really become lovers. But
"lovers" is our word, and however well Howells might handle his
characters, he worked within conventions that said couples must
marry first and love after. Nevertheless, he creates convincingly the

subdued yearning, the flattery, the self-delusion through which Colville moves from a kind of avuncular fondness to a genuine love affair. Imogene is drawn along by her own romantic fancies and by the genuine attraction an older man often possesses for a young woman. Mrs. Bowen is created with the right amount of charm in her own person to make it believable that with the engagement broken between Colville and Imogene, he will turn to Mrs. Bowen and conduct a courtship which will lead to marriage.

In many ways, this is Howells's most successful dramatization of the romantic-sentimental as against the realistic point of view, the one associated with youth, the other with maturity. As should be expected, maturity has the last word. And yet, maturity has by no means said it all. While Colville is caught up in his romantic fancies, an older, wiser gentleman, the Reverend Mr. Waters, is observing and commenting on the action. After Colville has broken with Imogene, Waters comments:

Oh, I don't know that I blame people for things. There are times when it seems as if we were all puppets, pulled this way or that, without control of our own movements. . . . Most of us, in fact, go sounding on without any special application of breath or fingers, repeating the tunes that were played originally upon other men. It appears to me that you suffered yourself to do something of the kind in this affair. We are a long time learning to act with common-sense, or even a common sanity, in what are called matters of the affections. (269)

There is in *Indian Summer* a glow about the love affair of Colville and Imogene that testifies to its "fidelity to experience and probability of motive" which Howells regarded as the essential condition of great imaginative literature. With no disservice to Howells and his wife and his children, a reader can imagine that he might have felt past forty, in Florence, in the spring, the attractions of the sweet soft life and even entertained fancies that such might be possible. One feels in the novel the mood lying behind Howells's advice to a young friend which Henry James appropriates for *The Ambassadors*, "Live all you can; it's a mistake not to."[1]

Indian Summer, then, does not need to be put with or against any other novels. It was a moment of free imagining arising out of the details of actuality that Howells fashioned into literature. It was not the first nor the last of his essentially romantic reflections about the curse of old age, the glories of the past, the wistfulness of remembered pleasures, the sober contemplation of roads not taken, which are a creditable part of both his fiction and his nonfiction.

April Hopes

April Hopes (1888) may be conveniently linked with *Indian Summer*, for it is almost an unintended parody of Howells's novels of mating and marriage which he could not easily forswear.[2] *Indian Summer* is, in my opinion, the vastly better novel, but the two novels both represent the fiction of the 1880s which lies largely outside of Howells's novels of social concern. Cady calls *April Hopes* "a neglected little masterpiece," a position that can best be maintained by reading a great deal into Howells's intentions and by discounting the importance of Howells's execution.

On the surface, the novel appears to be a quite conventional love story, set in motion by its opening scene during Class Day at Harvard. Howells's later view is right, I think, in finding "little but a contrast of temperaments" in the story, though an interviewer also has him remembering some ten years later that it was "the first he wrote with the distinct consciousness that he was writing as a realist."[3] What this realism appears to consist of is chiefly the author's intention of unsparingly exposing the follies of romantic selfishness and sentimentalizing as the way to a successful marriage. In Howells's own words, the "social intent" of the book is "the teaching that *love is not enough in love affairs*, but that there must be parity of ideals, training and disposition, in order to insure happiness. . . . an engagement made from mere passion had better be broken" (*LIL*, 1:410).

To readers of Howells's earlier fiction, then or now, there is little new in the message, and neither the characters Howells creates nor the situations he places them in hold one's interest. Both of the male protagonists, Dan Mavering and his newspaperman friend Boardman, have appeared before and more engagingly in other Howells novels. Alice Pasmer is such a vacancy of a girl as to defy a reader's entertaining serious reflections about her displays of female temperament. The one convincingly drawn character, Mrs. Pasmer, ultimately becomes tiresome in the obviously contrapuntal realism of her views. As if that were not enough, Howells bends the novel to a happy ending despite the repeated broken engagements that mark the young couple's courting. In so doing, Howells can have his realism both ways. The sardonically inclined can reason that such shallow types as Mavering and Pasmer will, indeed, marry in spite of all the self-created vicissitudes of their courting, and can relish Howells's parting shot delivered by the narrator at the end: "If he had been different she would not have asked him to be frank and open; if she had been different, he might have been frank and open. This was the beginning of their married life" (*AH*, 354). The conventional reader can find that once again love has won out and that whatever future may lie ahead for the Maverings, Howells's depiction of the ups and downs of romantic love has been both entertaining and true to life.

In fairness to Howells's competence as a novelist, *April Hopes* does not entirely depend on the central couple nor on Howells's success in deflating romantic passion. The delineation of upper-class and wealthy Bostonians and how they got that way occupies many of its pages. The Harvard scenes are convincingly drawn (Howells's son John was accepted into Harvard with only one condition the spring of 1887), and Howells's treatment of class and social structure throughout the novel adds to the evidence which shows him drawing away from the Bostonian culture which he had once sought. The novel's merits, however, do not much alter my feeling that, however ironic Howells is in the treatment of a familiar subject, the novel is still a turning back to his earlier stock in trade.

Although *Indian Summer* and *April Hopes* can be related to important events in Howells's life, to his other fiction, and to his avowal of literary realism, they are somewhat apart from his major fiction of the 1880s. Most of his novels as well as much of his periodical writing show an ever-deepening concern for the problems arising from a competitive, economic-chance society. *The Rise of Silas Lapham*, to be discussed next, is the first among a number of novels that explore the nature of a competitive business society and the one closest to examining Howells's own rise up the ladder of materialistic success.

Chapter Six

Silas Lapham and the Economic Novel

The Rise of Silas Lapham

As a still developing novelist, Howells occupied himself through-out the 1880s with serious concerns about the American social and economic system which fostered so much inequality within a supposedly democratic society. Howells's own rise to affluence and social position seemed to be accompanied by a corresponding rise in his social conscience. Though *A Modern Instance* was a kind of social problem novel, as, to a lesser degree, were *The Undiscovered Country* and *A Woman's Reason*, none of his earlier works came to grips with the broader manifestations of the American social and economic system. Howells's celebrated move from Boston to New York at the end of the 1880s would be not so much a shift in physical residence or even in alliances with mag-azines and publishing houses, but a widening of horizons in an at-tempt to take in the truths of the powerful commercial society that America was becoming.

In July, 1882, while Howells was readying his departure for Europe, Osgood, acting as his agent, informed him of an offer of $6,000 from Henry Mills Alden of *Harper's Monthly* for a story, provided it " 'shall be a story of American life & character with sufficient humor to meet popular requirements and having no such singularity of plot as characterized' *An Undiscovered Coun-*

try, 'i.e., no plot based on exceptional or unusual manifestations of human character' " (*RSL*, xii). Later in the year, Howells submitted, perhaps because of his revisiting Venice, his "notion" for the story as involving a young American skipper going to Venice from a New England port at about the turn of the century. Other writing and traveling intervened, but by 1884, in a letter to Gilder, Howells clearly saw the story as one of "a rude, common, unrefined nature [striking?] out against a temptation which must break many business men and accepting ruin rather than inflict it" (*RSL*, xiii). About this time, he must have written out the five-page handwritten synopsis, "The Rise of Silas Needham," which contains the essentials of the main plot.[1]

In this synopsis as in the completed novel, Howells has his central character introduced through an interview with Bartley Hubbard. That beginning effectively ties the story with *A Modern Instance*, the two novels that were Howells's favorites, and marks a practice of using characters from novel to novel which gives a Balzacian dimension to his work. Though Bartley Hubbard fades from the scene in *The Rise of Silas Lapham*, the initial course of both novels is to chart the upward strivings of two provincial young men. In *Lapham*, Silas, an up-country Vermont boy born of poor parents, makes his way into a million-dollar paint business largely because of the discovery of a mineral element for a superior paint on his father's farm. He moves to Boston, aspires to a social standing his wealth seems to entitle him to, and hopes to see his two daughters successfully married. Mrs. Lapham, like many of the older married women in Howells's fiction, occupies a distinctly secondary position, retaining more of the provincial values and attachments than does Silas. Into this story of American business success is introduced a complication rising out of Lapham's having squeezed out a partner in the early days of the business. Playing on Silas's guilt, the former partner returns and secures a loan from Lapham pledging as security certain lands in the West. When business reverses, poor investments, and, in particular, the competition of a new paint firm with a cheaper manufacturing process force Silas to near-bankruptcy, he must choose between selling lands of dubious worth or bankruptcy. Lapham wrestles with his conscience, decides not to sell, and leaves Boston for Vermont to live out his life in materially reduced but morally satisfying circumstances.

In addition to this central plot line, a romantic plot has the two Lapham sisters falling in love with Tom Corey, son of the Boston aristocrat, Bromfield Corey. The two sisters are contrasting types: Penelope, the elder, is "small, dark, and ugly" by her own admission; Irene, the younger, is beautiful and vacuous. When to everyone's surprise Tom turns out to be in love with Penelope— she is witty, oftentimes ironic, and a reader of books—and not Irene, Penelope must, before she can consider marriage, assure her overly refined conscience that she has not deliberately set out to take Tom away from Irene.

Further, the novel as a whole contrasts different aspects of two types of American families: the Laphams as a provincial family before they gained wealth; the Laphams coming into wealth and Boston society; the Bromfield Coreys as representative of Boston aristocracy, but specifically in a position of declining wealth though still possessed of social position and graces. All are treated with both respectful and satirical attention. A number of other characters play some part in the action, principally the Reverend Mr. Sewell, who will appear in other novels, and who here is the literate clergyman expounding realism. Zerrilla, the daughter of a Civil War buddy of Silas's, whose problems include a drunken mother and husband, adds another dimension of realism to the novel.

One cannot but think of Howells's great fondness for Thackeray in this social and satirical novel. I don't think that Howells's satire is as pointed as Thackeray's, and in his moving to a large array of characters there is some diffusion of effects. Nevertheless, what is in the novel is a remarkable balance and wholeness in looking at a society about which he is having much grave doubt and which he will address in more pointed terms in subsequent novels. It is not for him to say here that the *nouveaux riches* need be gross, stupid, cunning, or crooked, or that the poor folk are necessarily good, or that moneyed and unmoneyed aristocrats are of finer stuff, or the reverse, that their sophistication hides a rottenness at the core. Nor is his examination of the social and economic structure of American society as strenuous as it was to be in later novels. At this point, Howells seemed content to examine how a provincial man of conscience, somewhat like himself, would react to the moral and social strains that accompany the acquiring of wealth.

It may be a weakness of this novel that for all the contrasts of characters and families, everyone turns out to be a pretty decent sort, even though out on the edge of those whose lives Howells looks at closely—like Zerrilla in Lapham's office—*are* people who are *not* decent, are *not* successful, are *not* even touched by the minimum benefits a democratic society might be expected to provide. Howells located basic ills in the inequalities between classes supposedly tempered in a democracy, but the muted tone of *Silas Lapham* in this respect is well conveyed in Howells's authorial comment on the "uneffacable" differences between the Laphams and the Coreys: Our manners and customs go for more in life than our qualities. The price that we pay for civilization is the fine yet impassable differentiation of these. Perhaps we pay too much; but it will not be possible to persuade those who have the difference in their favor that this is so (*RSL*, 361).

The battle in *The Rise of Silas Lapham* is the battle of individual conscience against the forces of materialistic business success. It is clearly Howells's view that Lapham's choice is superior to the choices condoned and even encouraged by the ethics of a business society, and that his choice is little assisted by the force of religious and social ethics. Howells carefully creates a number of conditions and rationalizations that might have let Lapham compromise with his conscience. If he sells the western lands, he will be saving Rogers, the man he has wronged; he will be assuring a future for those he loves; he will not, in any case, be deceiving those he is directly dealing with; he can act honestly in the light of what he knows and disregard what he is only pretty certain of; and he can pursue a course which may, in the long run, actually work more good than harm. In the end, Silas must make a moral choice based on his own sense of right and wrong and policed by a not always active conscience. In former times, Howells seems to imply, the American conscience was more healthily developed, not just by an institutional church, but by the family, the social setting, the culture at large.

Religion was much a part of that past culture, and Howells's fiction of the period as well as his periodical writing gives attention to the religious conflicts of the time.[2] His most sweeping perception is that of the ethical effects of religion being overwhelmed by economic and social forces, symbolized in *Annie Kilburn* (1889) by the Reverend Mr. Peck's being crushed by a train after he has made his decision to go minister to the poor. Conscience and even acts of conscience are clearly not enough to resist the adverse effects of a success-oriented, economically driven society. Increasingly, Howells dwelt upon the effects of society and environment on individual ethics and acts. His questioning of individual morality turned to social morality, and to an increasingly severe criticism of American society.

The attention in *Silas Lapham* falls chiefly on the individual moral choice, though the social class structure is also an object of Howells's scrutiny and satire. There is a marked difference between the concentration on the individual here and the depiction of a wider social scene in *A Hazard of New Fortunes*, to come five years later. While *Silas Lapham* was appearing in the *Century*, Mark Twain praised Howells by letter for his "marvelous facility" in writing stories that made "all the motives & feelings perfectly clear without analyzing the guts out of them." "What people cannot see," Howells replied, "is that I analyze as little as possible, but go on talking about the analytical school—which I am suppose[d] to belong to" (*MT-HL*, 2:535–56). Howells's comment notwithstanding, most of the novels which preceded those of the late 1880s were to some degree limited in their examination of the social milieu and most heavily invested in studying a limited number of individual characters and character types. As Howells's social convictions grew and his identification as a literary realist strengthened, so did his ability to observe and record the harsh facts of the social and economic world in which he lived.

The Beacon Street house, which provides so much perspective for *The Rise of Silas Lapham*, provoked a reflection to his father, August 10, 1884: There are miles of empty houses all round me. And how unequally things are divided in this world. While these beautiful, airy, wholesome houses are uninhabited, thousands upon thousands of poor creatures are stifling in wretched barracks in the city here, whole families in one room. I wonder that men are so patient with society as they are (*LIL*, 1:363–64). When this mood and substance gets into the novel, it is toned down from the passage as originally written which suggested dynamiting empty mansions as a fit recourse of the poor. "If I were a poor man," Howells revised the passage, "with a sick child pining in some garret or cellar at the North End, I should break into one of them, and camp out on the grand piano" (*RSL*, 194).

Howells's Beacon Street house gives us another measure of how rapidly his attention was shifting toward forthright attack on American society. Only a few weeks after the letter to his father, he is writing to Henry James, describing his move to Beacon Street, observing this time that the sun sets over the Back Bay much as it does over Cambridge. That leads to his reflecting back on his building a house on Concord Avenue when he had barely enough money to buy the lot. He asked himself, " '*Can* blood be got out of a turnip?' " and answered, "Now I know that some divine power loves turnips, and that somehow the blood will be got out of the particular turnip which I represent. Drolly enough, I am writing a story in which the chief personage builds a house 'on the water side of Beacon,' and I shall be able to use all my experience, down to the quick. Perhaps the novel may pay for the house" (*LIL*, 1:366). As one examines other letters written at the time, one to Clemens, for example, which refers to "a mighty pretty house here on the water side of Beacon st." (*LIL*, 1:365), the questioning of his good fortune is but a passing thought amid a prevailing mood of fulfillment. Like the debate within *Silas Lapham*, Howells's own questioning in 1885 is still remarkably in check.

Two years later, however, freshly under the influence of Tolstoy, he wrote to his sister Annie: "Elinor and I both no longer care for the world's life, and would like to be settled somewhere very humbly and simply, where we could be socially identified with the principles of progress and sympathy for the struggling mass" (*LIL*, 1:404). In a letter to James, October 10, 1888, Howells wrote what I think is the most characteristic letter of this period of his life. "I should hardly like to trust pen and ink with all the audacity of my social ideas; but after fifty years of optimistic content with 'civilization' and its ability to come out all right in the end, I now abhor it, and feel that it is coming out all wrong in the end, unless it bases itself anew on a real equality. Meantime, I wear a fur-lined overcoat, and live in all the luxury my money can buy" (*LIL*, 1:417).

Howells's Economic Novels

Some of what I am documenting here can be charged to Howells's changing moods, likely to be present in many observant and sensitive persons of modest origins who have arrived at great financial success and social position. Some can be related to the profound effect of reading Tolstoy. Some can be directly related to events in Howells's immediate life, the execution of the Chicago anarchists being the most notable. But all these merely accelerated the steady movement Howells's thought was taking. The most convincing documentation of this progress is in the books he wrote, beginning with *Silas Lapham* and followed by *The Minister's Charge* (1886), *Annie Kilburn* (1889), *A Hazard of New Fortunes* (1890), *The Quality of Mercy*, *The World of Chance*, and

A Traveler from Altruria (all 1892). He did not give up his other writings, any more than he gave up his fur-lined overcoat or retired to a Tolstoy-like peasant life. But the voice that was most prominent, the one which establishes him most clearly as a novelist of substance and power, is that which takes up the cause of social injustice and the need for founding a society on better principles than those dominated by economic chance and individual greed.

Though all of these novels have the larger number of characters and the increasing complexity of relationships which mark Howells's development as a novelist, a clear line of social criticism can be seen in each. In *The Minister's Charge* it is, as he says in a letter to Henry James, "the frankness about our civilization which you have sometimes wondered I could practice with impunity. The impunity's gone, now, I assure you" (*LIL*, 1:387). *Annie Kilburn*, he tells Hamlin Garland, is "from first to last a cry for *justice*, not *alms*" (*LIL*, 1:419), and an attempt to examine the differences that divide social classes and the vain attempts being made to ameliorate them. *A Hazard of New Fortunes* depicts finance capitalism as not only dividing society but dividing families, as well. *The Quality of Mercy* examines embezzlement and its effects and the conditions of competitive capitalism which seem to bring it about. *The World of Chance*, which was rumored to be "a socialistic novel," was denied being such by Howells, "except so far as every conscientious and enlightened fiction is of some such import" (*LIL*, 2:40). In it, he chooses a young western newspaperman come to New York to sell a novel as the means of illustrating the workings of economic chance. The explicitly socialistic element is the character of David Hughes, a former resident of Brook Farm and a socialist, who debates his views with the central character, Shelley Ray. Ray "abhorred all sorts of social outlandishness; he had always wished to be conformed, without and within, to the great world of smooth respectabilities" (*WC*, 126). Against that bit of self-flagellation, Howells presents Hughes's ideas that competition is the devil in the bottle, that a monopoly by the people is the only solution, and that a world people's trust will grow as the idea roots and spreads under the blossoms over the existing system. Hughes's ideas were to be given more detail in *A Traveler from Altruria*, written the same year.

These novels make up an impressive body of work concerned with social and economic issues, and they were accompanied by much reading and reviewing and essay writing going over the same ground. In all fairness, it should be said that, clearly as they indicate Howells's mood and shifting interests, these novels, with the exception of *A Hazard of New Fortunes*, were not particularly successful. *A Hazard of New Fortunes* looms so much larger than the rest and so well represents Howells at the peak of his powers as both novelist and social critic that it will be discussed separately in the next chapter.

The Minister's Charge

Modern readers are not likely to come to a novel called *The Minister's Charge; Or, The Apprenticeship of Lemuel Barker* without some negative reactions created by the title. The novel begins as a story William Dean Howells was eminently qualified to write, a story he did write in a number of other books: that of the young provincial person of talent trying to make his way in a more sophisticated society. With some typical Howellsian ironies, the novel does take that course. Lemuel's talent seems to have been less than would fairly have brought him to Boston, but once there he learns rapidly, is able to gain Bromfield Corey's notice, and even to make it plausible (though Howells closes out the novel without its happening) that he should marry into society in the person of Lily Vane. The Reverend Mr. Sewell, who created no particular alarm in his appearance in *Silas Lapham*, figures in this novel because it is his mistaken but well meaning generosity— he has given more praise to Lem's pitiful poems than they deserve—which has aroused the young man's literary hopes and

set him on the road to Boston. Thus, Lemuel becomes "the minister's charge," and Sewell's conscience as to his responsibility for
Lemuel is scrutinized throughout the novel.

All this is not done very well, but Boston reviewers were
not reacting to something not done well; they were plainly put
off by something done well enough to have an effect. If Howells
had kept Lemuel within the mock-heroic, or if he had even sympa-
thized and gently satirized him at the same time, as with Bartley
Hubbard, he probably would have turned out an acceptable entertainment. But, from the first of this novel, which he took up very
soon after completing *Lapham*, Howells was serious about what
he was doing.

What Howells was most serious about, I think, was that the
society Lemuel found himself in was not going to give him a
fair break, and by implication, was not going to give a fair break
to a majority of its citizens. Worse than that for the genteel reader,
Howells took that question, which doubtless had been raised in
some parts of polite society, out of the drawing rooms altogether
and portrayed it through Lem's adventures in the nether-world
of Boston. As commonplace as such excursions were to become,
they were not common to Howells's fiction of the time nor to
the audience who read his books. Read today, Manda Greer and
Statira Dudley, the factory girls Lemuel meets, *are* farcical. In
being swindled on the Commons and jailed on a false charge,
Lemuel is more of a bumpkin than a victim of evil. But, to the
readers of Howells's time, it must have been unnecessary and in-
sulting to be dragged through the mud in order to get Lemuel to Bromfield Corey's house where such things might be discussed discreetly and Lemuel either brought up to a level of
refinement consonant with his remaining there or sent back to
Willoughby Pastures.

Less troubling, but still unsettling, is the growing seriousness
of Sewell, whose struggles with his own conscience in regard to
Lem move him to doctrines more disturbing than those he was
used to espousing. The chief doctrine he calls complicity, which
identifies even those who live in comfort and refinement as some-

how responsible for the degraded conditions Howells described.[3] "Complicity" is not a very strong doctrine today, and it was, as Sewell was aware, a reaffirming of the central Christian doctrines, rooted in being one's brother's keeper. It was the animating force for the social gospel which gave religion considerable vigor in the 1880s and 1890s. It borders upon the ecological awareness of our own time. It struck Howells's audience with particular force, because it questioned the charitable impulses by which good Christian rich preserved their religious principles and kept the poor at bay.

The Minister's Charge is no great novel, not even for Howells, but in retrospect it was a clear indication that while the public might expect him to continue with writings more to their taste— *April Hopes*, for example, which appeared the next year, or *The Mouse Trap, The Sleeping Car, The Albany Depot, Evening Dress*, and *"A Sea Change,* or *Love's Stowaway,* a lyricated farce"— he would not be silent about the multitudinous injustices and inequalities cheapening and debasing American life.

Annie Kilburn

Annie Kilburn is a strong economic novel, what *Hazard* might have been had Howells remained confined to New England. The setting is a New England manufacturing town, Hatboro, Massachusetts, and the satire falls chiefly upon the remnants of New England aristocracy, no longer thinking high and living plainly, but self-righteous, snobbish, and faddishly interested in helping the working class. Judge Kilburn and Squire Putney are no longer the dominant figures, and the older aristocracy is threatened by the rising middle class of merchants typified by Mr. and Mrs. Gerrish (a particularly well-chosen name). Annie Kilburn has just returned from eleven years in Italy, and sees the society into which she was born from a fresh and critical perspective.

Two main plots run through the novel. One involves Annie's ponderings over what constitutes the right kind of social involvement and action. The other is the conflict between the Reverend

Mr. Peck and Mr. Gerrish, which divides the town and leads to Peck's resignation. The two plots are intertwined, for the arguments being made within the community are the conflicting voices from her past, her family, and the community's traditions that Annie must wrestle with in deciding her personal course of action.

Other characters are Squire Putney, whose decline is symbolized by his ruining his life with drink, and Dr. Morrell, something of a conservative who takes a middle position between Peck and Gerrish, and whose acquiring of more liberal views may make it possible for him to marry Annie. The most dramatic event in the novel is the Reverend Mr. Peck's decision to leave the community and set up a cooperative home in Fall River to minister directly to the working classes. In a sense, he has lost his fight with Gerrish, who has been incensed by Peck's refusal to preach a businessman's Christianity. More significant, even this gesture comes to nothing; he is struck down by a train and dies with Annie at his side as he is about to leave town. After his death, Annie decides with Putney's and Dr. Morrell's help that she will give up such charities as the Indigent Surf Bathing Society and make some small but positive and personal steps to alleviate suffering close at hand.

Howells's position is one he has expressed before: that charity is not the answer to the worker's disadvantaged position, that lines of social cleavage dividing society, as the town of Hatboro is divided, are set down by the capitalistic competitive system, and that workers might have some chance of tempering the worst abuses of the system if they had the education and financial help that might enable them to deal with the worst of their conditions. Though he does not explicitly set it forth, Howells makes clear in this novel that the particular ills that fall upon the lower classes are the result of a social system which will not be remedied by charitable gestures from a well-meaning aristocracy or by appeals to past traditions of morality or power, or by aroused and socially responsible clergy. He does not pose solutions as such, but clearly he perceives the need for changes far more sweeping than those envisioned by most members of the middle- and upper-class society he occupies. In *The Quality of Mercy* (1893) he has his idealistic journalist, Maxwell take a "very high philosophical view" of an embezzler's illegal act, and accuse "the structure of society" (157). Maxwell's editor blue pencils this part of his essay as "rank socialism."

The Quality of Mercy

The Quality of Mercy is a character study of an embezzler, but like most of Howells's novels of the period, it is awash with other characters and actions. Though the novel does not abandon the idea of individual responsibility for one's acts, it does emphasize the workings of both chance and society upon an individual's ethical choices. Much of the first part of the novel dramatizes the doctrine of "complicity," introduced in *The Minister's Charge,* in dwelling upon the web of consequences Northwick's act leaves behind. The second part returns the focus to Northwick and attempts to probe the nature and consequences of his act upon himself.

Northwick, the central character, is described in Howells's outline of the story as "a man of great force, great apparent wealth and high social standing, who had worked himself up from simple New England beginnings, to the head of a great manufacturing interest. At the opening of the story, he is in the secret which cannot be kept any longer—that he had embezzled and muddled away the company's money to an amount that makes him a hopeless defaulter."[4] Three courses are then open to him: "to kill himself ..., to stand trial ...; to go to Canada as so many others have done." The completed novel proceeds in just this way. Northwick's background is sketched in. Early in his life he disappointed his father by his pursuit of narrow materialistic ambitions which gain him financial security. Few people know that it was through his wife, now deceased, that he founded his fortune. They see him as a man of some culture, living with his two grown daughters a quiet, reserved life in Hatboro, Massachusetts, also the setting of *Annie Kilburn.* In truth, he possesses little culture; he has lived to accumulate possessions. His carefully maintained outward refinement is a consequence of an "instinct of respectability, the wish to be honored for what he seemed" (12). The reasons for his financial manipulations are hardly more than this, though they become the subject for prolonged discussion in the novel. Human frailty yielding to the pressures of an acquisitive society seems to be closest to Howells's own judgment of Northwick's case. Within the novel, Lawyer Putney pronounces, "His environment made him rich, and his environment made him a rogue" (359).

After Northwick's flight to Canada, attention shifts from him to a cast comprising a grand assemblage of characters from Howells's other novels. Lawyer Putney, Gerrish, and Dr. Morrell are there from *Annie Kilburn*, each playing roles consistent with their earlier appearances. Putney, like Eben Hilary, chairman of the board of Northwick's firm, represents an earlier order of blunt and shrewd but honest Yankee. Dr. Morrell, now married to Annie Kilburn, is still a trimmer. From *A Modern Instance*, Pinney and Ricker, the newshawk reporter and editor, are brought in, chiefly as a means by which Northwick is found and brought back, voluntarily, from Canada. *The Rise of Silas Lapham* contributes the Boston characters, Bellingham, Bromfield Corey, and the Reverend Mr. Sewell, all of whom comment on the cause and effects and meaning of Northwick's crime. Matt Hilary, Eben's son, is created to provide a love story with Northwick's daughter Sue, and to depict a businessman's son who repudiates business and, in fact, seems strongly inclined to socialism.

The most important new character introduced is Brice Maxwell, a familiar young journalist figure but one who has artistic aspirations. The piece he writes about embezzlers can stand for much of the discussion of business ethics in the novel. Drawing upon "a rapid array of defaulting treasurers, cashiers, superintendents, and presidents," he comes to this conclusion about their conduct:

On one hand you had men educated to business methods which permitted this form of dishonesty and condemned that; their moral fibre was strained if not weakened by the struggle for money going on all around us; on the other hand you had opportunity, the fascination of chance, the uncertainty of punishment. . . . it behooved society to consider how far it was itself responsible, which it might well do without ignoring the responsibility of the criminal. (125–26)

At the time this novel was published in 1892, white-collar crime was drawing attention to the broader question of ethics in a business society. The extreme that Howells creates—defaulters shooting and hanging themselves or populating Canada—faced another extreme in the urgency of such famous speakers as Russell Conwell, whose "Acres of Diamond" speech made of business a sacred calling. ". . . . 98 out of 100 of the rich men of America are honest. That is why they are rich," he proclaimed. Bishop William Lawrence of Massachusetts went further: "Godliness is in league with riches."[5] The underlying question of Howells's economic novels, the responsibility of those who *have* to share with, do something about, those who *have not*, is one aspect of ethics; a more specific question is whether it is possible to acquire wealth without being dishonest.

From the ethical discussions which conclude part one, Howells returned in part two to the main plot, the flight and pursuit of Northwick. Afflicted with a mysterious fever which plunges him into fantasies of guilt and discovery, Northwick becomes more abject and pitiable without, however, adding much to his credibility as a central character. Pinney finds him in Canada and brings him back. At the border, Northwick seems to reach out for the atonement that may signify his full recognition of the criminality of his act. He asks Pinney to put him in handcuffs; the gesture comes too late. Northwick tumbles forward, dead, and "the loosened handcuffs fell on the floor" (355).

The staginess of the ending suggests that this novel, for all its earnest realism, does not succeed very well either in probing the nature of criminality or in going beyond what Howells has already done to see the American economic world both realistically and convincingly. The theme of social responsibility for individual acts, the ruinous workings of economic necessity, and the possibility that both of these are to be seen as the amoral and unfeeling workings of chance are set forth amid much that diffuses attention. The parading of points of view may (inadvertently on Howells's part in fiction but perhaps not in his life) excuse the reader's withdrawal from the actualities of social conflict into more commonplace and comfortable aspects of life.

I think it fair to say that this novel and a closely related one, *The Son of Royal Langbrith* (1904), fail to carry the conviction which comes through in *A Hazard of New Fortunes*. Too much going over the same ground and too much acceptance in the absence of solutions weaken them. When Howells did offer a specific solution in *A Traveler from Altruria* (1892), he moved away from realistic confrontation into a form of fantasy which permits him both to shape the world as he would like to see it and to expose American competitive capitalism as it was. The sterner realism with which Howells faced New York life in *A Hazard of New Fortunes* and the Christian-Socialism which underlay the Altrurian fantasies are the subjects of the next chapter.

Chapter Seven

Hazarding New Fortunes

Facing a Harsher World

Howells's life from the publishing of *The Rise of Silas Lapham* to *A Hazard of New Fortunes* showed an intensification of his personal and social concerns and no letup in his varied literary work. In his personal life, the death of Winny brought to a sad end a decade of hopes and despair. The family's move from Boston was brought about in part by their seeking treatment for her in various places. When they first moved to lower Manhattan, Winny had been admitted to a Philadelphia hospital under the care of S. Weir Mitchell, known both as a novelist (*Hugh Wynne: Free Quaker*, 1897) and as a foremost specialist in nervous disorders. Within six months of their move, March 3, 1889, Winny was dead. "The blow came with terrible suddenness," Howells wrote Edward Everett Hale in April, 1899, "when we were hoping so much and fearing nothing less than what happened" (*LIL*, 1:424). Elinor's ill health worsened with the death of Winny, their mutual social life was much curtailed, and she remained a semi-invalid the rest of her life.

Despite this stress and amid a series of moves—from Boston in 1887 to Rochester to Little Nahant, Massachusetts (summer 1888) to lower Manhattan back to Boston to a Cambridge suburb "not far from Winny's grave" (summer 1889) back to Boston back to New York and finally to 40 West Fifty-ninth Street (1892)—Howells wrote as much as ever. Having signed in Oc-

tober, 1885, a lucrative contract with Harper and Brothers—
$10,000 plus royalties for a novel a year and the new feature in
Harper's Monthly, "The Editor's Study"—he was back to meeting
regular salaried commitments. Chief among these was *A Hazard of
New Fortunes*, written during the year preceding September, 1889,
and serialized in *Harper's Weekly* beginning March 23, 1889.

A Hazard of New Fortunes

The framework of the novel clearly reflects Howells's own
hazarding of new fortunes in leaving a comfortable and established
existence in Boston. The title, like so many of his titles, was taken
from Shakespeare, this time *King John*, act 2, scene 1. Basil and
Isabel March are the central characters. Basil's hazarding of fortune is his leaving his insurance position in Boston to accept the
editorship of a new periodical, *Every Other Week*, in New York.
Fulkerson is the go-getter from the West who talks March into
taking the position. The magazine is financed by Dryfoos, an Indiana farmer made a millionaire by the discovery of gas on his farm.
His son, Conrad, is bookkeeper for the magazine but critical of
business and turned toward religious and social reforms. Mrs. Dryfoos is a pallid figure, uncomfortable at being uprooted from
Indiana and limited in the role she plays in the family. Dryfoos's
two daughters, Mela and Christine, are given a social chaperone,
Mrs. Mandel, to teach them the social graces which might gain
them advantageous marriages.

In addition to these central characters, Howells brings in a
circle of social and business acquaintances, among whom Lindau,
the German socialist, modeled on the Ohio printer who helped
Howells learn German in his teens, is most important in repre-
senting the causes Howells was espousing. A trio of characters,
Beaton and Wetmore and Alma Leighton, represent artists and
artistic talent, bringing out relations between art and business
and providing a romantic subplot. Beaton is an interesting figure,
betraying an ambivalence Howells felt toward art. Chiefly an
opportunist and a rationalizer of his self-serving acts, he has an

abundance of talents somewhat dissipated in a restless turning from one art to another. A similar lack of moral certitude affects his behavior with Alma, Christine, and Margaret Vance (a figure like Annie Kilburn in that novel), who is genuinely if ineffectually searching for the best way of alleviating the lot of the poor. In the end Beaton is rejected by all of them. His rejection by Christine, to whom he has come after being set aside as "loathsome" by Alma, takes place as a violent outburst in which she threatens to tear his eyes out.

Colonel Woodburn and his daughter are Southerners whose characterizations add another dimension to the novel. Woodburn's analysis of the development of an America ruled over by commerce allies him with Howells's own thought, but the solution he brings forward is a return to a planter aristocracy in which a kind of top-down responsibility of the rich and powerful to those beneath them is a way of meeting the demands of complicity. Lindau calls it feudalism. Margaret Vance and Conrad Dryfoos, whose relationship comprises another subplot, end up as victims of chance seemingly abetted by the economic system. Conrad is killed in the strike by a stray bullet; Margaret becomes a nun. That part of the novel's resolution seems to derive from Howells's feelings both of frustration with and of wan hope in a purposeful universe and a benevolent if inscrutable God. Kendricks, a somewhat superfluous writer of social verses and short stories, rounds out the cast of characters.

Overall, the novel shows the Marches drawn into the lives and experiences of these characters and reacting to the events which take place during their first year in New York. As with *Silas Lapham* the most illuminating scene is a dinner party, engineered by Fulkerson, and bringing the other characters to the Dryfoos place. The conflicts between Dryfoos, the almost stereotyped capitalist, and the others, who hold various social views, prepare the way for the street-car strike and the violent events in the last section of the novel.

Howells's satire in the dinner scene takes on seriousness in light of the violent events to follow. His depiction of the bringing in of

a white sugar oil-derrick lit by a gas flame as the caterer's tribute
to Dryfoos is as good as any single scene in *Silas Lapham*. It reminds one again of how deftly Howells appropriated fictional materials from life. In May of 1887, he had written to Mark Twain
from Findlay, Ohio:

> They are going to have a Natural Gas Jubilee in this wonderful
> place on the 8th or 9th of June, and they are going to ask you, of
> course. I think if you will come you will enjoy a No. 11 astonish-
> ment, and it will fit you comfortably. The wildest dreams of Col. Sel-
> lers are here the commonplaces of everyday experience. I wish I could
> blow off a gas-well in this note, for then you would have some notion
> of what a gas well is. But I can't, and so you had better come, and see
> what thirteen of them all going at once, are. (*MT-HL*, 2:593-94)

But satire of this sort is not the main purpose of the dinner
party. Rather, the restrained quarrels that break out within this
group mirror the uglier disparities which divide American society.
Dryfoos proudly tells how he broke a strike in his plant by secretly
hiring strikebreakers and driving the old employees out. Lindau
is incensed, and March has difficulty in keeping him from walking
out. Lindau and Colonel Woodburn join in denouncing the com-
mercialized society but arrive at completely opposing views as to
solutions. Fulkerson tries to steer the conversation out of its dangerous paths; March takes it all in and reflects upon it with
Isabel after.

The last section of the five-part novel shifts to the actualities of
a real strike. Dryfoos is infuriated by it; Lindau takes an actual
part in it; Conrad and Margaret Vance are sympathetic to the
strikers' cause; and Fulkerson tries to think of ways it might prove
profitable to the magazine. In the midst of this public violence,
the Dryoos family's private life breaks apart. Christine calls Mrs.
Mandel a meddlesome minx and flings down her jewels on her
father's plate. Dryfoos, in part goaded by his daughter's insolence
but principally infuriated by the strike and Conrad's sympathies
with it, strikes his son, and as Conrad is killed shortly after, has

to live with that memory. Conrad is killed by a stray bullet in the act of trying to protect Lindau from a policeman's club. Lindau is clubbed to the street and falls beside him. Howells has Conrad making this observation at the moment of violence: "The policeman stood there; he saw his face; it was not bad, not cruel; it was like the face of a statue, fixed, perdurable; a mere image of irresponsible and involuntary authority" (422). March arrives on the scene just as they fall, and his later reflections provide a kind of coda for the more violent actions.

Dryfoos leaves the ownership of the magazine to Fulkerson and March and departs for Paris. "There the Dryfooses met with the success denied them in New York; many American plutocrats must await their apotheosis in Europe..." (495). In March's philosophizing over the impact of the events upon Dryfoos, which precedes the final tying up of the threads of plot, he espouses what Isabel labels "fatalism." Of what has happened to Dryfoos, he says: "It was an event, like any other, and it had to happen as much as his being born. It was forecast from the beginning of time, and was as entirely an effect of his coming into the world—" (486). Earlier, with Conrad's death and Lindau's clubbing hard upon him, March makes the strongest statement of the novel:

> But what I object to is this economic chance-world in which we live, and which we men seem to have created. It ought to be law as inflexible in human affairs as the order of day and night in the physical world, that if a man will work he shall both rest and eat.... But no man can feel this as things are now; and so we go on, pushing and pulling, climbing and crawling, thrusting aside and trampling underfoot; lying, cheating, stealing; and when we get to the end, covered with blood and dirt and sin and shame, and look back over the way we've come to a palace of our own, or the poorhouse, which is about the only possession we can claim in common with our brother-men, I don't think the retrospect can be pleasing. (436–37)

The dark mood of the novel may arise in part from Howells's personal loss that accompanied its writing. Years later, he wrote to Brander Matthews about his struggles with the novel: "It cheered me to know you liked it, for I like it myself, all but the beginning, where I was staggering about, blind and breathless from the blow of my daughter's death, and trying to feel my way to the story" (*LIL*, 2:301). But the Marches' search for a house, upon which much criticism has been focused, is less important to the novel than the impact New York made upon them. Though Howells made an uneasy peace with New York (the apartment facing Central Park was a haven within the city through the 1890s), he describes it in *A Hazard of New Fortunes* as "the abode of . . . a poverty as hopeless as any in the world, transmitting itself from generation to generation, and establishing conditions of permanency to which human life adjusts itself as it does to those of some incurable disease, like leprosy" (65). A few pages later, at the climactic point of the introductory section, Isabel sees a "decent-looking man with the hard hands and broken nails of a workman," hunting for food in the gutters.[1] Basil gives the man a coin, and this dialogue follows. Isabel says:

> ". . . I shall not come to a place where such things are possible, and we may as well stop our house-hunting here at once."
> "Yes? And what part of Christendom will you live in? Such things are possible everywhere in our conditions."
> "Then we much change the conditions."
> "Oh no; we must go to the theatre and forget them." (71)

Howells's Social Thought

No more than Basil March could Howells change the conditions of the city or of the larger America shaped everywhere by the forces of competitive capitalism. But he could not easily get the images of people living in want and squalor out of his mind. In March, 1892, he wrote C. E. Norton, "I lay yesterday wondering at the great mass of human suffering, and getting a kind of objective perception of its bulk and variety. What a hideous spectacle life is from that point of view!"[2] It is typical that in 1896, not long after settling in New York, Howells bought a house in Far Rockaway, Long Island. "We have long idealized our home as on a village street" (*LIL*, 2:69), he wrote, but it satisfied the Howellses only one summer. They gave it up, perhaps recognizing it as a romantic hope similarly expressed in a letter to Clemens in 1898: "That is now our ideal—Elinor's and mine—to keep house somewhere in a little place with one girl" (*LIL*, 2:99).

Though a host of forces were at work in the 1880s shaping Howells's social attitudes, Howells himself makes much of the change that came over him with the reading of Tolstoy, which begin with *The Cossacks* in early 1886. "The whole of his testimony is against the system by which a few men win wealth and miserably waste it in idleness and luxury, and the vast mass of men are overworked and underfed... he bears perpetual witness against the life that Christendom is now living—the life that seeks the phantom of personal happiness, and ignores the fact that there is and can be no happiness but in the sacrifice of self for others."[3] His impact as Howells describes it in *My Literary Passions* was both ethical and aesthetic, but Howells closes his tribute with the lines, "I came in it to the knowledge of myself in ways I had not dreamt of before, and began at least to discern my relations to the race, without which we are each nothing. The supreme art in literature had its highest effect in making me set art forever below humanity..." (189).[4]

The importance Howells attached to Tolstoy is further reflected by the amount and kind of reading and reviewing he was doing during the years he was reading Tolstoy's works. Though such specifically relevant books as Gronlund's *The Cooperative Commonwealth*, Bellamy's *Looking Backward*, and Ely's *Social Aspects of Christianity* did not alone bring him to his kind of Christian Socialism, they played an important part in his analysis of economic conditions and in the tentative solutions he permitted himself to offer. Most of the books both helped define and were read in the light of the kind of literary realism he espoused. In *A Hazard of New Fortunes*, the two come together much as Tolstoy's aesthetic and ethical impact had come together earlier. Howells achieved in the novel an effective management of a large number of diverse characters, each carefully chosen for the perspective it could give to an examination of both self and society, and all placed against the backdrop of an American life broader and more significant than he had portrayed before. And here, too, he argued out at great length the kind of beliefs that were to be given more direct expression in his essays of the period and in the Altrurian romances.

Clara Kirk in *W. D. Howells, Traveler from Altruria*[5] has well described the directions Howells's thought was taking and the various forces which contributed to its direction. She argues convincingly that a social Christianity grounded in the life and example of Christ and reinforced by the democratic conceptions of Greece in which self-interest gives way to civic responsibility are fundamental to his thought. The doctrine of "complicity" which the Reverend Mr. Sewell sets forth in *The Minister's Charge* begins as an "evolution from the text, 'Remember them that are in bonds as bound with them' " (*MC*, 457), and is a natural step to the "altruism" with which Howells attempts to reconcile the insistent demands of self with the needs of others. *A Hazard of New Fortunes* embraces in a dramatic and more complex form what Howells was to write out in his Altrurian essays.

The Haymarket Square bombing and subsequent events, coming closely upon Howells's first reading of Tolstoy, intensified Howells's distress with American society. The bombing grew out of a strike at the McCormick Reaper plant in Chicago which resulted in police firing upon the strikers. On May 4, 1886, at a mass protest meeting, a bomb was thrown which killed one policeman, wounded six others fatally, and injured others. The rounding up of strikers and those associated with them led to the trial and conviction of eight men generally identified as "anarchists" but specifically attached to the bombing by circumstantial evidence at best. The case dragged on for more than a year when the Illinois Supreme Court in November, 1887, upheld the conviction of seven (the eighth, Louis Lingg, had committed suicide in his cell). Four were executed on November 11. The remaining three were given long prison sentences, but in 1893 were pardoned by Illinois governor Altgeld for lack of evidence of guilt.

Howells came into these events November 6, when he wrote

a public letter to the *New York Tribune* appealing for clemency for the men: "That court [the Supreme Court] simply affirmed the legality of the forms under which the Chicago court proceeded; it did not affirm the propriety of trying for murder men fairly indictable for conspiracy alone; and it by no means approved the principle of punishing them because of their frantic opinions..." (*LIL*, 1:399). That letter, which called upon others to join in his appeal, is greatly restrained compared with letters he wrote to others at the time. To his sister, Annie, he wrote: "It's all been an atrocious piece of frenzy and cruelty, for which we must stand ashamed forever before history. But it's no use. I can't write about it. Some day I hope to do justice to these irreparably wronged men" (*LIL*, 1:404).

With this real strife fresh in his mind, Howells brought an intensity to *A Hazard of New Fortunes* not often found in his work. A strike provides the central violent action of the novel. Here reality provided much material. The Reading Railroad was the target for a strike in December, 1887, the Burlington Railroad the next year, both unsuccessful. A streetcar strike in New York, in January–February, 1889, gave Howells the setting for the novel's denouement.

There were other violences of the time that remind a present-day reader that Howells's writing of this period both risked the respectable reputation he had established and gained strength and currency from the prevalence of social unrest. On the risk side was that of aligning himself too much with genuine revolutionary thought and actions. This time was not so long removed from the violence that took both Lincoln's and Garfield's lives. The Carnegie strike at Homestead, Pennsylvania, in spring 1892, led to a bloody battle between the strikers and Pinkertons hired by the company in which eleven workers and nine detectives were killed. Just after, in New York, Henry Clay Frick, president of the company, was stabbed and shot in his office. Both in the letters he wrote during the period and in his fiction, Howells disavows violence and emphasizes the necessity of bringing about reform by the ballot. Writing to his father, he calls the attempt on Frick's

life "a wicked and foolish mistake. . . . In one thing the labor side
is wrong. It has the majority of votes, and can *vote* the laws it
wants . . ." (*LIL*, 2:26).

Countering these risks was the fact that social protest was coming from many respectable quarters. Such a shrewd journalist as
John Brisben Walker, who secured Howells's services for the
Cosmopolitan, knew there was a large audience receptive to new
social thought. Though that alone does not account for the success
of his magazine, circulation of the *Cosmopolitan* under his editorship went from 20,000 in 1889 to 300,000 by 1898.[6] Howells's
Harper's editor, Henry Mills Alden, approached Howells in 1888
about carrying out a series of sketches of New York life which
they had previously discussed. The Harpers, he tells Howells, have
"the same kind of interest which first inclined your heart to the
subject—one based on the social meaning of such sketches."[7]
Howells's polite Altrurian letters of 1892 were to be succeeded
within the decade by muckraking journalism that both exposed
social ills and built the circulations of newspapers and magazines.

The decade of the nineties found the country in one of its worst
depressions since the Civil War. Despite his severe criticism of the
economic chance world, Howells, like others of the affluent class,
trusted in the economy enough to take his lumps from that trust.
In 1884, he had asked Clemens for a check for his work on the
Library of Humor. "I shouldn't have thought of turning to you
if it hadn't been for the shameful behavior of C.B. & Q., which
seized the moment of my buying a house to go down 13 points . . ."
(*MT-HL*, 2:494). In 1890, according to Cady, Howells had
$6,000 worth of Atchison and Topeka stock fall from $1.13 to
twenty-four cents a share.[8]

The Altrurian Romances

The social consciousness that produced *A Hazard of New For-
tunes* found its next outlet in a series of letters, "A Traveler from
Altruria," which began in the *Cosmopolitan* in November, 1892.
Howells's relationship with John Brisben Walker, the new editor-

owner of that magazine, might have come out of the pages of
A Hazard of New Fortunes.[9] Walker was a powerful self-made
man for whom journalism was but one of a number of successful
commercial ventures. Howells's editorship of the *Cosmopolitan*
lasted less than half a year, probably because of dissatisfactions on
both his and Walker's part. His severance from the magazine did
not end his friendship with Walker nor stop the appearance of
the Altrurian series which he had planned before he left the magazine. They were published from November, 1892, through the next
year, and after they were completed, Walker printed a second
series, "Letters of an Altrurian Traveler," from November, 1893,
to September, 1894.

Later published in book form,[10] these essays add to our knowledge of Howells's social thought. Once again, Howells turned to
that most congenial of literary forms, the travel-fiction, to amplify
his views. The central character, Aristides Homos, comes to America
from a recently located remote island civilization. His name,
Aristides, is that of the Athenian statesman and general at the
Battle of Marathon in 490 B.C., who won a lasting reputation as a
model of just behavior. Howells was probably also aware that
Aristides was ostracized from Athens by ballot, presumably because the citizens got tired of having him always held up as a
model of justice. To temper such a fate for his fictional traveler,
Howells created as his host a reasonable replica of one of his own
selves. This is Mr. Twelvemough, whose popular novels appeared
in duodecimo volumes—thus the play on words for his name. Between the two of them, they can register surprise and wonder both
ways, on Homos's part that American civilization could really be
as barbaric as it is, and on Twelvemough's part that supposedly un-
solvable social problems had been solved in Homos's country,
Altruria.

As the series progresses, other figures are introduced, Mr. Bullion,
the banker, for example, who explains that the business of this
country is business, and Mrs. Makely, who reminds Mr. Homos
that Christ himself said, "The poor ye have always with you." The
representative figures from American society come together in the

central portion of the series to illuminate for Mr. Homos the character of American society. Mr. Homos responds by telling the company how Altruria has gone beyond the competitive society that prevails in America. The key is that of providing the conditions by which egotism can shift to altruism, competition to cooperation, and inequality to true democracy. Public ownership, which came about after Altruria had experienced the same baneful economic strife now going on in the United States, was the necessary social condition. Thereafter, Altruria was able to reduce working hours to three a day, to eliminate both poverty and excess accumulation of goods, to foster the artist in every one, and to restore equality and brotherhood.

In 1907, Howells collected six of the letters of 1894 and used them as the first part of *Through the Eye of the Needle*, tying them to the earlier visit of Mr. Homos and adding a second part. Again, the central vision is of the awful contrasts between the lives of rich and poor and the inability of democratic or religious institutions to deal adequately with the injustices of a capitalistic economic system. Howells had brought the earlier "Letters" to a close by having Aristides fall in love with a New York society woman, Eveleth Strange, who is cut from the same cloth as Annie Kilburn and Margaret Vance. Aristides gives her the choice of his love and returning to Altruria or keeping her money and remaining in New York. Temporarily overcome by the romance of the moment, she agrees, but overnight she recovers her good sense and decides to keep her money and give him up. *Through the Eye of the Needle* picks up this broken romance and accomplishes the marriage of Eveleth and Aristides and their return to Altruria. The letters Eveleth writes back describing her life there comprise the second part of *Through the Eye of the Needle*. Around them, Howells creates a dreamlike aura, softening somewhat the implication of his earlier conclusion that materialism and altrurianism were irreconcilable and vaguely hinting that though Altruria was a dream it might yet be realized.

Though Howells did not in this final Altrurian book greatly depart from his basically Christian Socialist position (he supported

Debs as the socialist candidate for president in 1906), he did soften his passionate convictions of earlier years. His most powerful social statements are to be found in *A Hazard of New Fortunes*, where, for example, he has Colonel Woodburn declaim

how commercialism was the poison at the heart of our national life; how we began as a simple, agricultural people, who had fled to these shores with the instinct, divinely implanted, of building a state such as the sun never shone upon before; how we had conquered the wilderness and the savage; how we had flung off, in our struggle with the mother-country, the trammels of tradition and precedent, and had settled down, a free nation, to the practice of the arts of peace; how the spirit of commercialism had stolen insidiously upon us, and the infernal impulse of competition had embroiled us in a perpetual warfare of interests, developing the worst passions of our nature, and teaching us to trick and betray and destroy one another in the strife for money.... (337)

It can be said of *A Hazard of New Fortunes*, as of the Altrurian pieces, that in the end there is little but faint hope that can be held out for a society to build itself upon Christian-Greek principles which reconcile self and society. And yet Howells's view of man is neither superficial nor hopeless. Man is born into conflicts, both within and without. It is the ethical choices which are most important, and it is their subtlety, not their magnitude, which makes them both terrifying and difficult. The first step toward right choice is the step of the realist: to see things as they are, not clouded by sentiment, posturings, conventions, dogmas, and a haze of personal and social delusions. Second is the development of the inner voice, the conscience which adjusts self-interest to the common good. The adjustment is not abnegation; the eremite, the prophet are too far from mortal men to be very effective in answering this world's needs. They are necessary, just as Conrad Dryfoos was necessary, but their necessity is inscrutable to most mortals. Third, in the conflict of self with society, the responsibility for others is complete; man's complicity is all embracing, centered in the hand of God. But even though a man heeds all these precepts, he is not sure that he has found the truth. One doubts, and doubts must have their province. Chance may be the explanation of suffering without cause, advancement without toil, and evil despite good works, but such an explanation must not deny the possibility of a higher moral law. What appears as chance is often the conjunction of circumstances with personality, of environment with character, of what Mark Twain called "circumstances and temperament." But Howells does not accept Mark Twain's darker mutterings that man is the "poorest joke of all" in a meaningless cosmos; he retains a faith in man's ability to act for the right which may be, at heart, his only divinity.

Chapter Eight

Fiction and Fact
of the Nineties

In June, 1892, Howells and his daughter Mildred sailed for Europe to visit his son, John, studying architecture in Paris and for Howells's first vacation abroad since 1882–83. He was able to visit with Mark Twain in Paris shortly after his arrival, but his father's serious illness (he was to die in August) brought him home in July. He wrote to C. E. Norton: "It has aged me as nothing else could have done. I am now of the generation next to death" (*LIL*, 2:53). The works of this decade when Howells moved into his sixties can be divided chiefly into fiction, personal and literary reminiscences, and literary criticism, with acknowledgment of a volume of poems, one travel book, the first Altrurian material, and a flood of articles and reviews on a wide range of subjects. One of his best novels, *The Landlord at Lion's Head* (1896), comes during this decade; the beginnings of his reminiscences appear as a fresh body of materials; and his views on literature come into a substantial form in *Criticism and Fiction* (1891), *My Literary Passions* (1895), and *Heroines of Fiction* (1901).

Fiction: *The Landlord at Lion's Head*

"My story has only the personal interest, I'm afraid," Howells wrote to Sylvester Baxter in the summer of 1896. "The Harvard part is perhaps important as studying a 'jay' student. I hope you

will find Jeff justifying the pains I have taken with him, and I
have dealt with two neurotic types who are new. They will appear
in due course" (*LIL*, 2:70). Howells's uncertain praise of *The
Landlord at Lion's Head* matches a general response to it through
the years. Howells was not assured of its publication in advance,
and when it was accepted by the editor of *Harper's Weekly*, his
relief was a measure of the uncertainty he felt about it. Howells's
attitude toward the novel's central character, Jeff Durgin, was
ambiguous; he conceived him to be a mixture of good and bad,
could call him a "brute" in later letters, and confess at another
time to liking him "more than I have liked worthier men."

The appearance of the first installment of the novel on July 4,
1896, is regarded by Kenneth Lynn as "a fitting date for a new
beginning in American literature"; it celebrates Howells's breaking
"through the self-concern of the post—Civil War novelists to the
broader outlook of twentieth-century naturalism."[1] Lynn's regard
for the novel seems particularly just, both in giving it a high place
in Howells's fiction and in associating it with literary naturalism.
For part of Howells's mixed feelings about the novel must have
arisen from his having created in Jeff Durgin a "naturalistic" hero,
a twentieth-century man, powerful, amoral, and superbly adapted
by nature to win out in the competitive struggle for existence.
What must have been disturbing for Howells was that, for all
these characteristics, he had created an immensely attractive man.

The novel opens against a naturalistic background, the harsh,
much-depleted terrain of upper New Hampshire under the shadow
of Lion's Head mountain. There the Durgins, not unlike the Woodwards in *Private Theatricals*, have managed to scrape out a bare
existence. Four of Jeff's older brothers and sisters have died; his
father and the five living children are all wasted by tuberculosis.
Only Jeff and his mother retain any vitality, sufficient in his
mother to bring Jeff to manhood despite the poverty in which
they live. Like Mrs. Woodward's taking over for an equally incapable husband, Mrs. Durgin is the one who turns the family
from marginal farming to running a boardinghouse.

Into this harsh scene wanders a young and typical Howells artist.

His name is Jere Westover, an apt name in obvious and not so obvious ways. Beyond the simple connection of "west" with Westover is an intimation of "warmed-over" or "leftover," that becomes more apt as his character develops. He, too comes out of nature, living in the woods of Wisconsin until he was sixteen and then breaking away to pursue an artistic career. Westover has many of the characteristics of Howells himself, and they are treated respectfully, if often ambiguously. He has started out in New York, but, made to feel inferior there, has schooled himself in Italy and come back to Boston to pursue a career. He travels to Lion's Head to paint the mountain as it is.

Part of what Howells is doing in this novel is clarifying his views toward realism. Westover's role is not only that of providing a point of view through which we see Jeff Durgin, but of setting forth the artist's quest for reality. Lion's Head is not only a social metaphor, reminding a reader of Garland's story "Under the Lion's Paw," but an aesthetic one. Westover's attempt to capture the essence of Lion's Head mountain under the favorable conditions of his youth at the first of the novel are repeated at a later age and in the coldness of winter in the second part. His relative success and failure in both instances are, to some degree, Howells's questioning of both the artist's perception and understanding of reality and his ability to render it. That questioning parallels and strengthens the other theme of the novel, the difficulties of perceiving and understanding social reality and judging it. Beyond both, in Howells's scheme of aesthetics and social ethics, lies the question of use: to what purpose our perceiving and rendering and understanding and judging in a scheme of things which may have no scheme?

In Westover's first attempt to render Lion's Head, the boy Jeff Durgin looks over his shoulder and says, "I don't think that looks very much like it." Westover, caught up in the necessity of finding just the right tint, replies, "Perhaps you don't know." "I know what I see," Durgin says. " 'I doubt it,' said Westover, and then he lost consciousness of him again. He was rapt deep and far into the joy of his work" (18)—until social reality, the cries of Cynthia

Whitwell being tormented by Jeff, brings him back to the world.

Put into the context of realism as an aesthetic principle, this exchange is as illuminating as similar ones in Henry James's "The Real Thing." In the context of the novel it is as ambiguous as Howells's attitude toward his characters. On the face of it, West-over is asserting the superior vision of the artist not only to perceive reality but to render it, Cezanne, for example, painting Mt. St. Victoire again and again, as Westover was to do with Lion's Head. Durgin's eyes clearly see the mountain as a camera would see it. Westover's painting must have extended itself beyond that kind of "realistic" depiction as the impressionists were doing. Howells's realism was of both kinds. He practiced and was often criticized for an overly detailed depiction of scenes and analysis of actions. But he insisted that the marshaling of fact was insufficient in itself, that it must somehow capture the reality beneath the surface, particularly that of human motivation and moral choice.

The superior understanding of the true artist that gives point to his selection and particular rendering of reality is a key point in Howells's aesthetic. It becomes obvious that Westover is far from a true artist. Well toward the end of the novel, he is revealed in these blunt terms:

He was an artist, and he had always been a bohemian, but at heart he was philistine and bourgeois. His ideal was a settlement, a fixed habitation, a stated existence, a home where he could work constantly in an air of affection, and unselfishly do his part to make his home happy. It was a very simple-hearted ambition, and I do not quite know how to keep it from appearing commonplace and almost sordid; but such as it was, I must confess that it was his. (455–56)

There is little that is complimentary in the description which Howells puts into Westover's own mouth. Like the earlier scene, it has its ambiguities if one views it either in the light of Howells's principles or his social preferences. The commonplace, that corner-stone of Howellsian realism, may be sordid, philistine, and bour-geois, for all that it may be the preferred choice for art. And it may be limited and passingly dull, for all that it is the preferred choice for a decent life. In itself, this bit of characterization may be interpreted as recognizing honestly the limitations of Howells's kind of art and yet his standing by it. But taken together with the development of Westover's character and his relationship not only to Jeff Durgin but to others in the novel, particularly Cynthia Whitwell, it can be argued as having a more subtle and complex meaning.

Westover, from his first appearance, provides the main angle of vision from which we perceive Jeff Durgin, but it is difficult to believe that Howells was unaware of the peculiarly priggish in Westover. Such priggishness surely clouds Westover's moral vision as his artistic limitations cloud his aesthetic one. If we are to believe in Westover as a virtuous and true observer, we must explain away actions and statements that belie both his virtue and his fidelity as an observer. One explanation lies in the direction of recognizing a subtlety and complexity in Howells's intent and execution. Another moves toward questioning whether Howells's own moral values led him to flaws in characterization he did not detect.

However we interpret Howells's control of his material, it becomes clear that Westover and Durgin will grow further apart, both in their character and actions, as the novel proceeds. The action proper of the novel begins with Westover's return to Lion's Head after five years' absence spent studying in France. The Durgin place has now been turned into a summer hotel, Jeff has grown into manhood and Cynthia into a young woman, to become a specific object of rivalry between Westover and Durgin.

Mrs. Durgin's ambitions for her son and Cynthia's urgings get Jeff into Harvard, where the focus falls directly on Howells's first announced intention—depicting a "jay" student. Rising above any specific satirical intentions, however, is the setting forth of the raw, sensual, and amoral power which is at the center of Durgin's character. Westover's feelings toward him at the beginning can now be seen as the response of a refined and somewhat emasculate artist to the sensual and primitive in nature, the man of thought and feeling versus the man of action and passion. Westover has

recognized this characteristic early, in a description which fore-
shadows much of Durgin's conduct later in the novel: "It was
as if he were about to burst out of his clothes, not because he
wore them tight, but because there was somehow more of the
man than the citizen in him; something native, primitive, something that Westover could not find quite a word for, characterized
him physically and spiritually" (127).

Westover's difficulty in finding a word is that the word may be
"sexuality," and it lies behind the evil that Westover attributes to
him and which Howells, in other fictions, attaches to power without conscience and sensuality which threatens social conventions.

In the opposition of Westover and Durgin one can perceive war-
ring elements present in much of Howells's fiction. On the one
hand is the man of physical strength, instinct, powerful emotions,
and passion; on the other is the man of intellect, refinement, conscience, and propriety. Durgin displays most strongly the qualities
hinted at in a number of other young men: Staniford, Hubbard,
Easton, for example. Westover displays the superior refinement of
an Arbuton, a Dunham, a Halleck, or a Ford. The affection
Howells shows toward Durgin, whether inadvertent or not, may
be an endorsement of trying to escape the commonplace which
Westover seems to draw about him like a blanket for the aged
and infirm.

The conflicts in *A Landlord at Lion's Head* are importantly intensified and amplified by the women characters, Mrs. Durgin,
Cynthia Whitwell, Genevieve Vostrand, and Bessie Lynde, the latter certainly one of the two "neurotic types" Howells said he was
going to introduce into this novel. Bessie Lynde is a Boston society
woman who acquires Jeff Durgin as "my jay," but who is "keyed up
pretty sharply by nature," in contrast with Howells's usual Boston types. For much of the central portion of the story, she trembles
upon the edge of passion and just out of reach of Jeff's arms.
Their affair is broken off after this display:

He put his other large, strong hand upon her waist, and pulled her to him and kissed her. Another sort of man, no matter what he had believed of her, would have felt his act a sacrilege then and there. Jeff only knew that she had not made the faintest struggle against him; she had even trembled towards him, and he brutally exulted in the belief that he had done what she wished, whether it was what she meant or not. (336)

I do not think that it is merely the shift in attitudes toward the courting behavior of men and women from Howells's time to ours that makes Jeff's relations with Bessie Lynde such a credible part of the action. Even his more controlled courting of Genevieve Vostrand seems preferable to Westover's furtive and cold pursuit of Cynthia Whitwell. Howells uses Durgin's flirtation with Bessie while he is engaged to Cynthia as a means of emphasizing his amorality, and Cynthia is obviously too good to accept Durgin despite her qualified fondness for him. But Cynthia, her father, and Westover offer too little in the way of attractive countering moral forces. "Sanctimonious" is the word that comes most quickly to mind for both Cynthia and Westover. In Cynthia's father, a hypocritic Yankee shrewdness is brought out first in his acceptance of Durgin's behavior as it seems to win him success and later in his willingness to squeeze Durgin in the sale of his property. Westover reflects upon the "conscientious and self-applausive rapacity" with which the Yankee in Whitwell had acted.

he did not love or honor the type. . . . For a moment this seemed to him worse than Durgin's conscientious toughness, which was the antithesis of Whitwell's remorseless self-interest. For the moment this claimed Cynthia of its kind, and Westover beheld her rustic and Yankee of her father's type. If she was not that now, she would grow into that through the lapse from the personal to the ancestral which we all undergo in the process of the years. (456–57)

Despite its relatively simple plot-line and admirable characterization and tone, *The Landlord at Lion's Head* is a complex and difficult novel to interpret. In some important ways, it suggests comparison with *The Rise of Silas Lapham*. Silas's rise and fall might seem to be similar to a double pattern in the later novel: Jeff Durgin's material rise has been at the price of moral decline, and Westover's decline has been accompanied by a rise in his moral state. But such a reading would not be justified by a close reading of the novel. Durgin's and Westover's paths do somewhat cross each other, the former's ascending while the latter's declines. The crucial point can be located at the end of chapter 37, in which Westover takes on a heavy cold and Durgin comes to see him. At one point in their prolonged talk during which Westover has grudgingly accepted Durgin's care, Westover says: "Bah! . . . I'm not a woman in everything." Durgin replies: "I only meant that you're an idealist" (281).

From this point on, Westover declines in vitality, in his influence over others, and even as an artist. Durgin, on the other hand, breaks off his affair with Bessie, is rejected by Cynthia, and makes an apparently successful marriage with Genevieve Vostrand. If one wanted to point to the specific moral in this novel, one could say that the universe acknowledged Durgin's one conspicuously virtuous act (his refusal to murder the man who had whiplashed him) by burning down the old Lion's Head and providing him with the legitimate insurance money that leads to his fortune.

It may be that Howells carried out exactly what he intended. Durgin succeeds because he is just the powerful and amoral businessman who *does* succeed in a commercial society. And Westover, the effeminate and prematurely old man, is a fair portrait of the idealist-artist in American society. A sexless and sanctimonious Cynthia is just what such an artist deserves, with a shrewdly rapacious Yankee father thrown into the bargain. On the other hand, one may feel that Howells is reasserting simpler and more conventional moral verities that would have Durgin a villain and Westover a hero of sorts. Partly because of its ambiguity, partly because of the vitality of Jeff Durgin and Bessie Lynde, and partly because of a naturalistic strain that expresses some disbelief in a purposeful universe, *The Landlord at Lion's Head* is one of the most interesting of Howells's fictions.

Other Novels of the 1890s

Of the other nine novels Howells wrote during the decade of the 1890s, *The Shadow of a Dream* (1890), *An Imperative Duty* (1892), *The Quality of Mercy* (1892), and *The World of Chance* (1895) are deserving of most attention. We have already discussed the last two as part of that large group of novels dealing with economic questions. Both shed some light on questions raised about *The Landlord at Lion's Head*. The influence of environment upon a person's actions, the responsibility that the individual must take for his acts, and the attitude of the righteous to those who have fallen into sin are strong themes in *The Quality of Mercy*. An amoral universe in which one prospers or falls largely by the workings of chance was brought forward strongly in *The World of Chance*.

In *The Shadow of a Dream* Howells develops an idea he had revealed to Hamlin Garland in 1887: "What would you think of my doing a story dealing with the effect of a dream on the life of a man? I have in mind a tale . . . wherein the principal character is to be influenced by some action—I don't quite know what—through the memory of a vision which is to pursue him and have some share in the final catastrophe, whatever it may turn out to be."[2]

The story as Howells wrote it in the fall of 1889 was a short, tightly constructed study of three characters, with Basil and Isabel March acting as chorus. Howells's interest in psychic phenomena, the mysterious illness that caused Winifred's death, and his thinking back on his Ohio days were all influences in the novel. It begins with Douglas Faulkner, a past acquaintance of Basil's when he was beginning as a journalist in the West. Through Faulkner, Basil becomes acquainted with James Nevil, a college friend and now a minister, living with Faulkner and his widowed mother. Nevil is "spiritually wholesome," with a complexion "quite girlishly peachy," but Faulkner is pale, "with a sort of smokiness . . . black, straight hair . . . beautiful dark eyes . . . restlessly brilliant" (5). At that first meeting, they begin reading De Quincey (one of Howells's literary passions in Ohio) and discussing their dreams. Faulkner's dreams, so he says, are sometimes "humiliating, disgraceful, loathsome" (5).

Seven or eight years later, March meets a Dr. Wingate, who is treating Faulkner for a serious, unnamed illness. March finds the Faulkners living in a curious *ménage à trois*. Hermia, his wife, is a classically beautiful woman who nearly succumbed to illness on their wedding journey. Nevil, who seems to have no other place to go, has been in Europe with them and for the past year living in their house. Dreams and the nature of the existence of God are much of the conversations during the Marches' visit. Faulkner is deeply troubled by a recurrent dream that seems somehow connected with his illness and with the curious household relationship being maintained. At the end of part one, he suddenly dies, putting his hand on Hermia's breast and pushing her away "with a look of fierce rejection" (42).

A great deal happens in part two. Wingate knows the nature of Faulkner's dream, that in it Nevil and Hermia are in love and waiting for him to die so they can marry, but Hermia has asked not to be told the dream and he has honored her request. Nevil now has to hunt up a place of his own, leaves the church, and gets engaged. When the bride-to-be jilts him, he comes back to live with Hermia and her mother. They help him overcome his anguish, and after he has been in Europe for a year, Hermia announces their engagement. When the Marches meet her again, several years now after Faulkner's death, she has become more vital, possessing "an elastic vigor which we did not perceive at once to be moral rather than physical." That moral vigor leads her to insist that Dr. Wingate reveal to her Faulkner's dream.

In the final part, Basil learns the exact nature of Faulkner's dream through Hermia's mother, who tells him more about the apparently innocent relationship between Hermia and Nevil and who fully approves of their engagement. Hermia, however, has reached a decision. She will neither insist upon nor withdraw from the engagement; the decision must be left to Nevil. Nevil decides that Faulkner's dream is too telling an indictment of sentiments he might have inwardly entertained, and he leaves Hermia after one of the few passionate embraces in all Howells's fiction. March and he engage in a long discussion in which March takes the position of the man of science, respectful of spiritual matters but distrustful of superstitious beliefs, such as attaching great significance to Faulkner's dream. Nevil does not alter his plans to go to Europe but he does promise March that he will see Hermia again and let her hear March's argument. As they are parting at the train station, Nevil steps backward and is accidentally crushed by the train. A year later, Hermia dies and is buried by Faulkner's side.

There is a good deal of flummery in the story. Isabel is particularly tedious, and the probing into dreams and their meaning might better have gone into probing into a relationship which, even in our sophisticated and permissive age, is more than a little strange. Instead, the reader must chew on another highly refined moral choice, this time against a highly romantic, even melodramatic, setting. One must acknowledge, of course, that Howells was writing a psychological novel at the very beginning of formal psychology. In a letter of August, 1890, William James writes that he has been reading *Shadow of a Dream* and *A Hazard of New Fortunes*, "and can hardly recollect a novel that has taken hold of me like the latter." He refers to the "slighter" but "equally exquisite" *Shadow of a Dream*, and concludes: "The year which shall have witnessed the apparition of your *Hazard of New Fortunes*, of Harry's *Tragic Muse*, and of *my Psychology* will indeed be a memorable one in American Literature!!"[3]

An immediate source of ideas in the novel is the work of the French psychologist T. A. Ribot. Ribot reinforces a belief Howells also expressed in *The Landlord at Lion's Head*—that the past conditions the present, and specifically in this novel through the agency of dreams. In 1895, Howells published "True, I Talk of Dreams," a mixture of comic, whimsical, and serious observations. He speaks of a recurring dream of his own, one in which he may be dismissed from his consulship and publicly disgraced, and of many of his dreams which turn on being socially embarrassed and on being cowardly in battle. His only reference to Ribot expresses agreement with the theory that approaching disease sometimes intimates itself in dreams in advance of the disease itself. Two collections of Howells's short stories, *Questionable Shapes* (1903) and *Between the Dark and the Daylight* (1907) give further evidence of his interest in psychic phenomena.

An Imperative Duty is another short novel, surprising to most readers in that the theme this time is miscegenation. The same year, 1891, that it began serializing in *Harper's Monthly*, Mark Twain was working on *Pudd'nhead Wilson*, which is also concerned with miscegenation. Though from a liberal point of view *An Imperative Duty* is well-intentioned, it is conventional in its courting scenes and often disturbing in its treatment of race. Like *Suburban Sketches*, this novel shows a dislike for the Irish which Howells found hard to hide (they were the social class pushing into the Cambridge area where he first lived) and excessive sentimentalizing of the blacks. Howells, it has often been pointed out, openly encouraged the Negro poet, Paul Dunbar, and was among the original sponsors of the NAACP. His family was strongly antislavery, and his upbringing in southern Ohio shows him thoroughly sympathetic toward the blacks he knew there.

Nevertheless, *An Imperative Duty* must be judged on its merits, and though it may seem daring to write about a marriage between black and white in the 1890s, the handling qualifies the issue in unfortunate ways. The story is simple. Dr. Olney has returned from Europe to Boston, and Mrs. Meredith, with whom he had become acquainted while in Europe, summons him to her Boston home to help her resolve a troubling question of conscience. Her niece, a charming young woman who has already become an object of Olney's interest, is the daughter of a northern physician and a Quadroon, a woman of Creole descent who was educated in a northern convent. The moral question is whether Rhoda should go on living without being told of her true parentage. As she is being seriously pursued by a Mr. Bloomingdale, the question becomes one of possibly condoning miscegenation, though Howells defines Rhoda's trace of blackness in the most favorable way. Olney advises Mrs. Meredith to tell Rhoda and let her reveal it to her future husband if she wishes. Predictably, she rejects Bloomingdale, though Bloomingdale would not have rejected her. She is courted and won by Olney. They engage in a frank discussion of a black and white marriage, and Howells prudently takes them off the American scene and establishes them in Rome where she is "thought to look so very Italian, that you would really take her for an Italian" (101).

Intermixed with the plot is a good deal of discussion of racial and moral issues. Throughout these discussions, the substance and tone—as revealed through the characters Howells creates—are benevolent to the Negro, but sentimental, patronizing, and stereotyped. Racial characteristics are shown to have come through in Rhoda: "rich complexion of olive, with a sort of under-stain of red, and the inky blackness of her eyes and hair" (13). Her attractiveness for Olney has traces of the "happy darky" which seems to be an underlying stereotype both here and in *Suburban Sketches.* Rhoda's reaction to being told of her true parentage begins with melodramatic horror and then shifts to her sincere but inept attempts to find out what Negroes are like. One can draw one's own conclusions from a passage of exposition in which Howells describes Rhoda's peculiar charm:

It was the elder world, the beauty of antiquity, which appealed to him in the lustre and sparkle of this girl; and the remote taint of her servile and savage origin gave her a kind of fascination which refuses to let itself be put in words: it was like the grace of a limp, the occult, indefinable lovableness of a deformity, but transcending these by its allurement in infinite degree, and going for the reason of its effect deep into the mysterious places of being where the spirit and the animal meet and part in us. (89–90)

The other novels of this period seem to have been written to meet the demands of a novel a year. Yet each of them casts some light upon what Howells was trying to accomplish as an artist and reveal, in a mixture of fresh depiction and handy stereotypes, how he went about it. *The Coast of Bohemia* (1893), for example, has much to say about Howells's critical principles and attitudes toward art. The central male character here is an artist, Walter Ludlow, who suggests, more clearly than Westover did in *The Landlord at Lion's Head*, the kind of artist Howells most admires. Ludlow is clearly influenced by the French impressionists and committed to accomplishing something similar with American scenes. He finds a natural charm and beauty in rural American landscape. His chief work is "Hollyhocks," generally panned by the critics, chiefly because of the liberties he has taken with photographic realism. "Up to a certain point you are master over it, and it seems to belong absolutely to you," Ludlow comments; "but beyond that it is its own master and does what it pleases with itself" (337). The novel carries out the theme announced in the title through two central women figures, Cornelia Saunders and Charmian Maybough. Cornelia leaves Pymantoning County, Ohio, to enroll in the New York Synthesis of Art Studies, and there meets Charmian, a Park Avenue New Yorker who is trying to establish an upper-class artistic Bohemia. Both show Howells's continuing interest in the role of women in American society. "Oh," Charmian says, "if men could only be what girls would be if they were men!" (311). The love story involves Ludlow's pursuit of Cornelia, which encounters the usual misunderstandings and moral scruples before it reaches its successful end. There is something of caricature in Howells's delineation both of persons and scenes in the novel, helping a modern reader to often laugh with rather than at Howells's depiction of Bohemia seventy-five years ago, when a woman's crouching on a tiger-skin rug and smoking a cigarette were regarded as shocking behavior.

The Day of Their Wedding (serialized in 1895 and published as a novel in 1896) is a short work in which Howells put his long interest in the Shakers into fictional form. It involves two young people from the Shaker community who leave the community to be married. After spending one day in the outside world at Saratoga, New York, they decide that that is enough and return to the Shaker family to live apart. Though this might have been a penetrating psychological study, it is not that, but rather a typical bit of Howells's social realism in which the personal questions of devotion to God and the family or to personal satisfactions are debated against a swarm of contrasts between the sheltered world of the two young Shakers and the world outside.

Saratoga is also the setting for *An Open-Eyed Conspiracy* (1897). This novel and *Their Silver Wedding Journey* (1899) have the Marches as central characters. In the former, the Marches are matchmakers for Julia Gage, a typical ingenue, and Kendricks, the opportunistic journalist-literary man from *A Hazard of New Fortunes*. The complication in the love interest is that Julia is the daughter of a small-town bank president, feared to be, by Basil March, a dangerous kind of father-in-law for Kendricks to take on. Basil tells Kendricks, "I make out . . . that Papa Gage is a shrewd, practical, home-keeping business man, with an eye single to the main chance, lavish, but not generous, Philistine to the back-bone, blindly devoted to his daughter, and contemptuous of all the myriad mysteries of civilization that he doesn't understand. . . . It isn't a pleasant type, but it's ideally American" (158). Gage turns out not to be as bad as painted, and Julia simply overpowers both the Marches' scruples and her father's disapproval of a man with so little fixed income as Kendricks. Like most of Howells's novels, there are scenes here which are far better than the book as a whole. The opening scene, for example, is done extremely well, giving the reader a reminder of the December–May romance of *Indian Summer*. Basil describes his first sight of Julia Gage: "I could see two things—that she had as much beauty as grace, and that she was disappointed in me. The latter fact did not wound me, for I felt its profound impersonality. I was not wrong in myself; I was simply wrong in being an elderly man with a gray beard instead of the handsome shape and phase of youth which her own young beauty had a right to in my place. I was not only not wounded, but I was not sorry not to be that shape and phase of youth, except as I hate to disappoint any one" (3).

Their Silver Wedding Journey grew directly out of the trip the Howellses took through Germany in July–October, 1897. The Marches follow the same route from Hamburg to Carlsbad to Frankfurt, down the Rhine to Cologne, Dusseldorf, Liverpool, and home. A number of stops in between provide ample material for travel vignettes of a sophisticated kind. The cast of characters is familiar: the vulgar American capitalist abroad, the ingenue pursued by the young journalist, and various shipboard acquaintances and American tourists. The Marches hover over the on-again off-again romance of Mr. Burnamy and Miss Triscoe, who at the very end are reunited by the coincidences which Howells used, despite his realism, with great frequency.

Clemens, perhaps in response to a chiding letter from Howells accusing him of not reading him enough, made extended comments on the novel as it appeared in *Harper's Monthly* through the entire year 1899. Though he expressed greater enthusiasm with subsequent chapters, his comments on the early issues are both incisive and fair: "Is it imagination, or—Anyway I seem to get furtive & fleeting glimpses which I take to be the weariness and indolence of age; indifference to sights & things once brisk with interest; tasteless stale stuff which used to be champagne; the boredom of travel; the secret sigh behind the public smile, the private what-in-hell-did-I-come-for! But maybe that is your art" (*MT-HL*, 2: 689–90). Authorship by this time, for both Clemens and Howells, was sometimes a purely professional act.

Mention of two other full-length novels concludes this survey of Howells's fictions of this decade. *The Story of A Play* (serialized in *Scribner's*, 1897; published as a novel, 1898) sheds some light on Howells's long-held interest in the stage. James A. Herne, the actor and playwright, had proposed that he adapt *The Rise of Silas Lapham* for performance in 1897. The proposal was complicated in a number of ways. Herne had taken strong interest in *The American Claimant*, the play Howells and Twain were working on as a means of getting the further adventures of Twain's Colonel Sellers on the stage. The play under the name *Colonel Sellers as a Scientist* was produced with small success in 1887 by A. P. Burbank, who retained the rights which, in part, got in the way of Herne's later interest in producing it. Howells found these negotiations wearying, and indicative of the conflict between drama as art and as commercial enterprise. He was impressed, however, with

Herne as an actor and playwright; his review of *Margaret Fleming,* one of the first realistic American plays, called Herne "a dramatist of remarkable and almost unequalled performance" (*MT-HL,* 2:645). Nevertheless, Howells resisted Herne's proposal to adapt *Silas Lapham,* or even to make further adaptations of a dramatic version of the novel that Howells and Paul Kester had done in 1896.[4]

These and other experiences Howells had with the stage were the raw materials for the novel. The main character is Brice Maxwell, given many of the characteristics of Howells and introduced into his fiction in *A Quality of Mercy.* He has married Louise Hilary from that novel, and here the two perform much like Basil and Isabel March, with something more of jealousy and tartness in the character of Louise. Their domestic relations aside, the novel concerns itself with the difficulties Maxwell has in getting his play produced and the criticism it receives. After a first run which fails the play is produced again, this time with a femme fatale, who has already aroused Louise's personal jealousy, miscast in the lead. She is relieved of the part in time to get a more suitable actress, and the play enjoys a great success. The tone of the novel is comic, and what there is of new substance lies in the discussion of the drama and the American stage. Howells had both a liking for and a resistance to the stage, in part based on the long-established moralistic suspicions toward drama and a more modern aversion to the demands that commercial interests placed on art. "Whether he liked it or not," he has Maxwell reflect, "he was part of the thing which in its entirety meant high-kicking and toe-practice, as well as the expression of the most mystical passions of the heart" (216).

Ragged Lady (1899), which he began immediately after *The Story of A Play,* is a crowded novel, full of most of the characters and situations one might expect of Howells in 1899, but one of the worst novels he wrote. It is somewhat similar to *The Minister's Charge,* with Clem, a girl rather than Lem, the principal character. Her full name is Clementine Claxon; she is from Middlemount, Massachusetts, rustic but talented, the "ragged lady" of the title.

A wealthy bourgeois woman, Mrs. Lander, discovers her, and the reader is expected to follow her many ups and downs to a kind of commonplace success. This she finds in a second marriage, after the death of her first husband, to a minister whose previous serious interest in her had been broken off but which had survived his own marriage and death of his wife. The novel weaves in Ohio, Massachusetts, Europe, the provincial, the rich hotel-dwellers, the minister, the innocent heroine, and others, but to no great purpose or effect. If there is anything to be said for it, it may be that Howells and the world have changed much in the twenty years since *A Modern Instance*, when writing about a divorce was a daring act. Here both of the principals end up in second marriages, and another of the principal couples is divorced.

Autobiographical Works

Fiction clearly dominated Howells's writing at the peak of his powers. Among American novelists, he was also at the peak of his reputation in the public eye. "Your 84 votes place you where you belong—at the head of the gang" (*MT-HL*, 2:696), Mark Twain wrote in 1899. He was referring to a poll taken of the readers of *Literature*, in which Howells received the top number of votes for inclusion in an imagined American Academy; Twain was third with eighty. In 1908, when such an Academy was established, Howells was named its first president.

It may have been, in part, the security that comes with recognition that turned Howells to writing about himself in the 1890s. He could be sure now that his accomplishments made his life worth examining and that a public would find them interesting. Starting with *A Boy's Town* (1890), *My Year in a Log Cabin* (1893), and *My Literary Passions* (1895), Howells was to explore in detail all of his life up to his departure for Italy. He projected volumes that would continue his autobiography, but he did not bring them to a completion in the last decade of his life. The story of his first visit to New England and to literary New York appeared in the 1890s as articles in magazines, and then became the basis for *Literary Friends and Acquaintance*, published as a book in 1900. In addition, he edited a school edition of stories about Ohio, and got his father to put down his memories of Ohio at an earlier time, which Howells saw into print after his father's death.

We have discussed these works in telling the story of Howells's years in Ohio and his development as a journalist-writer.[5] They are as good a body of work as Howells ever wrote, and they constitute a set of documents highly illuminating of the American scene from 1840 to the Civil War. In addition, they give a personal and detailed look not only at American letters, but at the literature of many countries. While they primarily acquaint the world with Howells, they also do what fiction does, acquainting the reader with Howells as a representative figure, the American provincial rising to success in the centers of culture and power.

One other volume of observations came out in 1896, a collection of shorter pieces Howells had done for various periodicals, *Impressions and Experiences*. "The Country Printer," the first piece in the volume, is a valuable addition to the other materials about his boyhood in Ohio. "I Talk of Dreams," we have mentioned. "An East-Side Ramble," "New York Streets," "Glimpses of Central Park," and "Police Report" (from a visit Howells made to the Boston police station) are factual accounts of scenes also used in his fiction. "The Closing of the Hotel" turns to the many years of summer vacationing that were a part of Howells's way of life, and "Tribulations of a Cheerful Giver" takes up the subject of charity in much the same tone and depth one finds in the novels.

Literature and Life, which appeared in 1902, is a somewhat more substantial and varied collection. The personal and reminiscent pieces share the space with pieces directly concerned with literary matters. Those which add directly to our knowledge of Howells the man are partly revealed in the titles: "Worries of a Winter Walk," "Spanish Prisoners of War," "Confessions of a Summer Colonist," "Staccato Notes of a Vanished Summer," and "Last Days in a Dutch Hotel." Howells's social concerns appear throughout—for example, in the closing piece in which an Ohio

River steamer passenger observes: "But ah! and ah! where, in what
business of this hard world, is not prosperity built upon the struggle
of toiling men, who still endeavor their poor best, and writhe
and writhe under the burden of their brothers above ..." (323).

All through the 1890s, Howells was reaching back into the past.
As his living connections with that past diminished, particularly
with his father's death in 1894, but also in the inevitable passing
of other friends of his youth, so his desire to memorialize vital
aspects of his past increased. In the last twenty years of his life,
"the autobiographical urge," as he said to Mark Twain, often
overpowered him. As if he had brought together these energies
into his final decade, he was to publish in 1916 both the first
part of his autobiography, *Years of My Youth*, and one of the
strongest of his late fictions, which went back to very early Ohio,
The Leatherwood God.

Chapter Nine

Critic and Man of Letters

Howells as Critic

In the short introduction to *Literature and Life* (1902), Howells explains his need to tie life and literature closely together. "I am never quite sure of life unless I find literature in it. Unless the thing seen reveals to me an intrinsic poetry, and puts on phrases that clothe it pleasingly to the imagination, I do not much care for it; but if it will do this, I do not mind how poor or common or squalid it shows at first glance: it challenges my curiosity and keeps my sympathy" (iii). If we set that beside Howells's statement about the effect of Tolstoy's work, "the supreme art in literature had its highest effect in making me set art forever below humanity" (*MLP*, 189), we have two good touchstones for Howells's criticism.

Howells is very much a practical critic, a dealer in commonplaces here as in his fiction. What is surprising and redeeming about his criticism is that for an intensely literary man, it is so *un*literary, even *anti*literary. As his realism in fiction was a reaction against the sentimental and falsely romantic, so his commonsense criticism speaks against the self-consciously literary that measures literature chiefly by other literature, thus the new in literature always against the past. Howells honors those books which according to his measure most truly and affectingly place human life before the reader's eyes. Such a judgment is trickier than it seems and than Howells seemed to regard it; perceptions as to what life *is* differ almost as much as judgments differ as to what life *should be.* Nevertheless, Howells speaks for the common reader and for a common ground of perceived reality that makes assent and agreement about literature and life possible.

The distinction between Howells and many literary critics today is very wide and will serve to define more sharply where he stands. Some of the main distinctions are of degree—Howells grounded his criticism in the perceptions of the readers, but he would have been astounded at the probing of relationships between author and reader, text and reader, literary construct and mythical and social structures, now going on. Some are in the emphasis Howells placed on the moral effects of literature.

Five main characteristics of Howells's criticism stand out. First of all, and despite his great fondness for talking and writing about literature, criticism is a distinctly secondary function. For Howells, the obvious is both true and important: literature can exist without criticism: criticism cannot exist without literature. This alone explains much of his hostility to English critics. It was the hostility of the practicing fiction writer, dramatist, and poet to those critics who were forever holding up literary models from the past, not as encouragement to the writer creating literature now, but as ideal constructs against which the young writer will always be found wanting.

Second, literature like life is such a varied and vast assemblage of people, places, and things, actions, and relationships (and much else), that criticism which arrives at or proceeds from a set theory is likely to be misguided. The realism which Howells espoused is hardly a theoretical construct at all. It rests upon the commonest of assumptions—that readers will respond to literature as it somehow impresses them as relating to their own or others' lives. The common reader's response must be honored, Howells insists, even as one acknowledges the limitations of such a view. As theory, realism hardly goes beyond that, and as criticism becomes theoretical, it tends to attach itself to the literary matters rather than to reinforce the tie between literature and life.

Third, the critic's function is to be an engaging guide to literature more than to be a mentor. Howells's greatest contribution to criticism is probably that of bringing to the attention of the American reader, much as Pound was to do for poetry, the work of new writers writing in English and of writers, new and old, from the great body of world literature. His criticism, thus, is to be found as much in *My Literary Passions* as in *Criticism and Fiction.*

Fourth, critics, somewhat like the New Critics of recent times, are compared with natural scientists, their work to be primarily descriptive and analytical rather than judgmental. The implication is clear that the critic should be knowing in many ways, a master of languages, a student of every kind of learning, and yet one whose reading does not deny the even more vital experiences of life.

Finally, and this is both a submerged criterion in Howells's own criticism and yet one which arouses most opposition from later critics, literature has moral obligations. "Morality penetrates all things"—the words are Howells's, not Emerson's—and the emphasis upon this principle comes more from Howells's fiction than from his critical pronouncements. Theoretically, in fact, he is as suspicious of the writers of his time who bent everything to point a moral as later critics were of his own moralizing. Novelists err as they falsify the particulars and complexity of moral choice, often because they wish to propound moral views of their own. On the other hand, novelists also err who set aside, not the advocacy of specific moral behavior, but the valuing and depicting of the moral choices human beings make. Howells both supported other writers and presented characters in his fiction whose moral views were quite different from his own. In his later novels and in his own ponderings, he even questioned the idea of a moral universe and with it the idea that moral choice was really as important as he believed it to be. It would be, however, a distortion not to acknowledge Howells's almost Platonic belief in the Good and his inclining toward a critical position that valued literature somewhat in proportion as it might incline its readers to individual and social good.

Criticism and Fiction

Two sections of *Criticism and Fiction*, a collection of pieces put together from the "Editor's Study" in 1890, have provoked the most negative responses to Howells as a critic. One is the "smiling aspects" phrase in chapter 21: "Our novelists, therefore, concern themselves with the more smiling aspects of life, which are the more American..." (128). The other arises from chapters 23 and 24, which defend the American novel from the charge that it deliberately excludes from its pages "certain facts of life which are not usually talked of before young people, and especially young ladies" (147).

Though these statements can be clarified and set in context, what they imply is probably true of Howells's own fictional practices as well as consistent with his other critical comments. As to both statements, defenders of Howells have pointed out that the essays in *Criticism and Fiction* were put together, apparently in some haste, from previously published material going back to 1885.[1] The period was one in which Howells's outlook darkened considerably and in which his reading and reviewing took up many books both more tragic than his own and more frank in dealing with sexual matters. Both statements, too, are primarily observations rather than judgmental pronouncements. American life of the 1890s, for all that it embraced the violence and inequalities and injustice Howells, himself, described in *A Hazard of New Fortunes*, did allow more political freedom than was present in Russia and many other countries. The tide of immigration alone during this period testifies to an image of America, held by people around the world, consistent with Howells's observation. Whether such favorable conditions, verifiable in comparative terms with much of Europe and Asia, robbed American writers of a tragic sense, ruled out an "American" tragedy, is a more debatable question.[2] The whole passage makes a number of conjectural statements about characteristics of American writing in contrast with those of other literatures. The American short story, he believes, has reached a greater state of perfection than the short story elsewhere. American fiction seems to excel "in small pieces with three or four figures," a practice he followed until the mid-1880s and which he consciously moved away from as he attempted novels of larger scope. Though *Criticism and Fiction* is by no means a tightly constructed polemic, it does consistently follow one of its own main tenets—that the critic's primary responsibility is to describe and analyze, not to pass judgment.

Howells's temper was toward the comic, not the tragic, and that basic stance is well to keep in mind in trying to measure Howells's response to the tragic aspects of life. Though there are some works of Howells in which a reader may feel that he has been stopped short of or diverted from the tragic implications of a story, those works are not what causes even sympathetic readers to question the depths of Howells's perceptions of life. The fault, I think, is not with his attitudes toward tragedy, but with his dogged commitment to the commonplace and his determination to avoid the extremes which were most evident in melodrama, what one could argue passed for tragedy during most of Howells's lifetime. In fastening on the commonplace, he may have denied the writing of tragedy, but I think he exposed his work to a much more serious limitation: a weakness in grabbing and holding the attention of readers.

Prudishness on Howells's part is harder to explain away. The times Howells was born into placed severe restrictions, not only on the depiction of sexual relations in literature, but in life. Howells was certainly more liberal in this respect than many literate Americans, less liberal than some. In this passage as in others, one should try to separate what Howells is describing as an existing condition from what he may be supporting as an "ought." When he advises writers that they can, if they respect the conventions of the day, write about the subjects of Tolstoy and Flaubert, he is not excluding himself from that advice. Novels like *A Modern Instance* and *The Shadow of a Dream* treat of the realities of human sexual passion, albeit in a very slanting sort of way as compared with the fiction of our own time. Howells was not merely defending his own practices when he points out that cheap effects can be gained from relying upon sexual passion. When he asserts there are other passions that "have a greater part in the drama of life than the passion of love, and infinitely greater than the passion of guilty love" (157), he begins to reveal his own bias. Considering that the great majority of Howells's novels were concerned with courting and marrying, one legitimately questions the restraint with which sexual passions are handled.

But both of these matters have been given too much attention. *Criticism and Fiction* makes some admirable commonsense statements about the nature and claims of literature, which appear even more admirable at a time when academic literary criticism has become a thing in itself. Indeed, much of the thrust of Howells's criticism is against critical theorizing, criticism grounded primarily in literature and supported by a conservative academy. Quoting Burke's *Essay on the Sublime and the Beautiful*, he cites approvingly: "art can never give the rules that make an art" (7). At the center of this argument is to be found Howells's grasshopper metaphor, his belief that the scientist studying the real grasshopper is following a much better course than one who would prefer to study an artistically fashioned grasshopper. The "ideal grasshopper" is anything other than the living creature itself; it includes, according to Howells, the heroic grasshopper, the impassioned grasshopper, the good old romantic grasshopper. Much of the writing in the "Editor's Study" was directed against the sentimental tradition, and much of *Criticism and Fiction* speaks against those literary conventions and practices that stand in the way of perceiving reality.

The business of the critic, Howells wrote, is "to classify and analyze the fruits of the human mind very much as the naturalist classifies the objects of his study, rather than to praise or blame them" (30). Howells is aware, however, that classifying and analyzing literature is not exactly like classifying and analyzing physical materials. Dispassionate observation and notation are not sufficient in themselves: "When realism becomes false to itself, when it heaps up facts merely, and maps life instead of picturing it, realism will perish too" (15–16). I have an idea that when Howells uses the term "picturing," he has in mind more the impressionist painter than the photographer. It would be a mistake to think of Howells, particularly as he developed his skill, as not having an intense interest in shaping his depictions of character and event to create the effects he wants, and on ways in which surface effects give way to probing the complex reality which exists beneath surfaces.

The weakest part of Howells's criticism is a reliance on terms quite acceptable to the eighteenth century and which Howells's provincial upbringing inclined him to accept. The simple, honest, and natural[3] are the cornerstone on which Howells builds his criticism, with a surprising disregard for how much is hidden in each of these terms and how difficult it is to ascertain any embodiment of them, in literature as in life. In part, Howells failed to scrutinize these terms because he was arguing against much in art that seemed to him to be unnecessarily complex, affected, and false, and which thus separated itself from all but the connoisseur, the dilettante, and the academician. He was performing what seems to be a necessary and recurring service in art history: bringing art back to some solid relationship with the human beings who comprise its large audience. Then, too, the nineteenth century may have had a simpler conception of human verities than exists in the twentieth. Our time does not permit the kind of certitude that lies behind this pronouncement of Howells: "The time is coming, I hope, when each new author, each new artist, will be considered, not in his proportion to any other author or artist, but in his relation to the human nature, known to us all, which it is his privilege, his high duty, to interpret" (8).

Howells's Literary Passions

Howells's *Criticism and Fiction* was compiled out of the practical necessity of commenting on literature week after week.[4] *My Literary Passions* (1895) is a reminiscent work in which Howells reveals the literature to which he was drawn at various points in his life and discusses at some length those writers who influenced him most.

Goldsmith was among the very earliest of his passions and influenced him in at least two important ways. Howells, like many nineteenth-century writers in both England and America, was responsive to those who knew and appreciated the country and who viewed with regret the growth of England and America into urban-industrialized societies. (For that matter, both Turgenev and Tolstoy appealed to Howells on these grounds.) What Fairchild writes about Goldsmith could be said, with equal point, about Howells: "he suspected a causal connection between ignorance and virtue. In these respects he approaches the Noble Savage idea. But all this was in his heart. His mind, though not without some wavering, was on the side of the Enlightenment."[5] Howells's devotion to rustic virtue is more a matter of feeling than of intellect, and his mind sometimes counters it; yet his own relationship to his rustic past and a later feeling that American democracy was most perfectly exemplified in the West kept him firmly on the side of rural virtue. His passion for order and his high regard for the commonplaces of family and village life made him highly susceptible to Goldsmith's sentimental and nostalgic picturings. Like Goldsmith, he looks backward to man at the beginnings of his social organization, well beyond primitive tribal groupings but well before the village was corrupted by overrefinement and excessive civilization. It was also through Goldsmith's histories that Howells became acquainted with Greece and Rome. The ideas of the Golden Mean, of civic virtue, of a society in which individual interest could be harmonized with the common good receive their strongest reinforcement from these sources.

The earliest and greatest of Howells's literary passions was Cervantes, and that alone may be cited as inclining Howells toward or reinforcing his natural bent toward the comic. When Howells finally visited Spain in 1911,[6] he found La Mancha quite other than he had imagined it, and admits to having put it first into the map of southern Ohio and then northern Ohio. At seventy-four, he saw it in reality: "a treeless plain unrolled itself from sky to sky, clean, dull, empty" (*FST*, 168). His boyhood transposition of Cervantes's Spain to America indicates the strength of the Goldsmithian village upon him. That he dimply apprehended the tragic sadness of *Don Quixote*'s comic response to life's harsh realities becomes apparent in his further studies of Spain's history and in his Spanish travels. He is unable to explain how the "gentleness, civility, and integrity" he observes in Spain squares with the Spanish repute for "cruelty, treachery, mendacity, and every atrocity" (327). His final sentence should remind one that "the smiling aspects" phrase was not his last word on either the comedy or tragedy of American life: "I do not know," he says "how to explain the contradictions in the Spanish character. I do not know how the Americans are reputed good and just and law-abiding, although they often shoot one another, and upon mere suspicion rather often burn negroes alive" (327).

A third writer, more because of Howells's reservations toward him than because of his enthusiasms, is important to an understanding of Howells's critical tenets. His response to Thackeray reveals conflicts apparent within Howells's own practice of literature. Attracted initially by the intensely "literary" in Thackeray, it was this "literosity" he later deplored. The obvious romanticizing of a Scott could be dismissed more easily than that of Thackeray, for rising above literary posturing was the satiric unmasking of society that seems always to be a part of Howells's mature purpose. The mere clever satirist that he could be if he were but to draw upon his own bag of literary tricks was often at odds within Howells with the serious realist who could employ satire as one of his techniques. The example of Thackeray, I think, curbed Howells's own "literosity," but it may have also made him too wary of higher flights of imagination which might be mistaken for mere literary heightening.

Tolstoy's profound influences have already been noted. Howells was drawn to him both by his aesthetics and his ethics.[7] "I thought the last word in literary art had been said to me by the novels of Tourguenief, but it seemed like the first, merely, when I began to acquaint myself with the simpler methods of Tolstoy" (*MLP*, 185). He marveled at Tolstoy's simplicity, his ability to show men inwardly as well as outwardly. "Tolstoy awakens in his reader the will to be a man; not effectively, not spectacularly, but simply, really" (183).

The range of Howells's reading up to his middle years can be gathered from the many writers he singles out in addition to those discussed here: Shakespeare, Pope, Scott, Wordsworth, Tennyson, De Quincey, Macaulay, George Eliot, Charles Reade, Trollope, and Hardy, among the English; Irving, Hawthorne, Longfellow, Lowell, and Curtis among Americans; and Dante, Goethe, Heine, Goldoni, Valdés, Galdós, Verga, Björstjerne Björnson, and Zola, among European writers.

Finally, a word needs saying about some limitations revealed in Howells's avowed passions. Even the best of avowedly romantic writers receive his qualified praise. Byron, Shelley, and Keats are not the poets who provoked him into imitation; had he been fired with passion by them, he might have been a better poet than he was, but he would probably also have been a different person. His reservations toward Chaucer are more interesting, for in Chaucer's realism he should certainly have recognized a kinship. He had, in fact, great fondness for Chaucer. But, as might be expected, Chaucer arouses a response that emphasizes Howells's personal distaste for the physical. Howells's reminiscences about his early love for Chaucer and a librarian's fear of putting an unexpurgated edition in a boy's hand give way to a discussion of "lewd literature." It begins with "The streams of filth flow down through the ages in literature, which sometimes seems little better than an open sewer" (83). Though he finds Chaucer "probably safer" than other English poets of his time, he will not unqualifiedly praise him. He wrestles with his reservations, writing: "but you do get smeared with it, and the filthy thought lives with the filthy rhyme in the ear. . . ." What he gained from Chaucer was a respect for his verse and his diction, the "homelier and heartier" wording which helped keep his own writing away from "wild polysyllabic excess." His experience with Chaucer is like that with *Lazarillo de Tormes*, which, despite its being "gross in its facts" and mostly " 'unmeet for ladies,' " appealed to Howells for its "honest simplicity in its narration, a pervading humor, and a rich feeling for character" (107).

Heroines of Fiction

Heroines of Fiction (two volumes, 1900) is a less interesting book than *My Literary Passions*, though it adds a good deal to what can be said about Howells's literary preferences. It is as close as Howells ever came to academic criticism. It was written not only as the result of his long years of reviewing and writing about literature but of a short stint of public lecturing he undertook in the fall and early winter of 1899. From Grinnell College, he wrote back to Elinor: "Read *Heroes and Heroines* last night to 450 refrigerators, who afterwards many of them thawed out in individual praises. But it is not such a lecture as the *Novels* and I will read it no more" (*LIL*, 2:111). In general, he found the lecturing exhausting and vowed, except under the very best circumstances, to do it no more. But the tour did provide the notes for the heroines book, which was accepted for serialization in *Harper's Bazar* beginning May, 1900.

Viewed from our own time, Howells is to be considered remarkable for writing a book of literary criticism which focused on women writers. In his own time, Howells regretted the fact that young women provided the largest audience for fiction in America. Yet he shaped much of his fiction to that audience. *Heroines of Fiction* seems to fall under that influence to a degree that makes it impossible to tell whether it is his sense of audience or Howells's reasoned critical belief that provokes him to claim: "a novelist's power is to be tested largely by his success in dealing with feminine nature." Similarly, we cannot be sure how much Howells is expressing facts or preferences in his praise of Fanny Burney, Maria Edgeworth, and Jane Austen:

They forever dedicated it [the novel] to decency; as women they were faithful to their charge of the chaste mind; and as artists they taught the reading world to be in love with the sort of heroines who knew how not only to win the wandering hearts of men, but to keep their homes pure and inviolable. They imagined the heroine who was above all a Nice Girl; who still remains the ideal of our fiction. . . . (1:12)

His decision to confine his attention to English writers may have narrowed the broader view that the inclusion of contemporary continental writers might have provided. But one is once again faced with a gentility, if not prudery, in what he did write. As much as Howells admired the "voluntary naturalness and instructed simplicity" of the art of Defoe, he cannot discuss Defoe's heroines. For, even though Defoe had a higher morality than Fielding, Defoe was "of the day before we began to dwell in decencies" (1:2). "The topic of the best fiction of any time," he writes, "will probably be those which decent men and women talk of together in the best company..." (2:40).

Consistent with that dubious premise, Howells reserves his highest praise for the creations of Henry James. He found no other novelist James's equal in his appreciation of women and in his ability to suggest their charm. He expressed regret that James had been so identified with the single character, Daisy Miller, for he has created "more, and more finely, yet strongly, differenced heroines than any novelist of his time..." (2:164). *Heroines of Fiction* was not written as a justification of Howells's own practices, but Howells's survey of nineteenth-century fiction discloses some of the preferences which shaped his own fiction.

Man of Letters

It is impossible to even suggest the volume of Howells's contributions to American periodicals which placed him in the category of "man of letters." Though such writing occupied much of his time, early and late, he placed it in a secondary position to his fiction. He undoubtedly enjoyed the wide recognition he had inspired in being labeled the "Dean of American Letters" (Cady says the coinage "just drifted into casual use"),[8] but it came out of necessity as well as intent. One of the best essays in *Literature and Life,* among those many concerned with literary matters, is "The Man of Letters as a Man of Business." "Literature," Howells writes, "is still the hungriest of the professions" (11). The essay is a realistic assessment of how writers in the late nineteenth century made a living and the consequences to their aspirations and practices as artists. The other literary essays in this collection include: an editor's relations with young contributors, "A She Hamlet," "American Literary Centres," questions of why short stories rarely succeed in collections and how short stories differ from anecdotes and novellas, an ironic inquiry into the possibility that the "ad-smith" may be the greatest artist of the twentieth century, "The Psychology of Plagiarism," and "Puritanism in American Fiction." The last piece in the collection is a factual description of Ohio River life marked by the invasion of industry along its banks.

These collected literary essays are representative rather than inclusive of the materials which created Howells's larger reputation. The honorary degree he received from Oxford in 1904, preceding the award of a similar degree to Mark Twain in 1908, was but the most prestigious of honors bestowed upon him by this date. Perhaps his most important service as man of letters was the part he played in the careers of a number of younger American writers. Hamlin Garland's journeying to New England to meet Howells is almost a repeat of Howells's earlier trip. As Garland was one of Howells's greatest admirers and advocates, so was Howells a helpful teacher and lifelong friend. It is another interesting parallel that Garland turned his past into both fiction and nonfiction, and that his autobiographical works update Howells's descriptions of the Middle West. In 1910, he urged Garland to return to the temper and substance of *Main Traveled Roads* (1891); "You have in you greater things than you have done, and you owe the world which has welcomed you the best you have in you" (*LIL*, 2:283). *A Son of the Middle Border* (1917) came up to Howells's hopes. "So far as I know," he wrote Garland, "your book is without its like in literature. It is perfectly true to life, and beautiful with right feeling, from first to last" (*LIL*, 2:373).

It was through Garland that Howells met Stephen Crane. Howells wrote a short but detailed account of their relationship to Cora Crane, remembering that "Garland first told me of *Maggie* ... I read it and found that I did care for it immensely. I asked him to come to me, and he came to tea and stayed far into the evening. . . ."[9] When *Maggie* was published in 1896, Howells provided an introduction, as earlier he had called Crane and his novel to the public's attention in a newspaper interview. Howells was a strong advocate of Crane's great talent, and Crane was grateful for the recognition, encouragement, and friendship Howells gave him, the more remarkable for their difference in ages and even in the direction of their best work. *Maggie* remained for Howells his "first love. . . . That is better than all the Black Riders and Red Badges."[10]

Frank Norris, only a year and a half older than Crane and thirty-three years younger than Howells, might have identified him with the enemy, for the kind of "true Romance" to which Norris was drawn was not commonplace, ordinary real life. Yet Norris recognized in Howells the only American fiction writer who rose above a generally unpromising scene. Howells's review of *Mc-Teague* recognized it as new fiction, and despite the reservations he expressed toward it, the review gave Norris the greatest encouragement he had ever received. Norris's abrupt death in 1902, like Crane's in 1900, terminated a literary and personal relationship that might have done much to bring pleasure into Howells's later years.

The list of other writers whom Howells encouraged is long. He wrote to many of them, expressing an interest in their work, and he reviewed many of their works in the editorial pages he controlled. As early as 1884 Howells wrote an "open letter" to the *Century* praising E. W. Howe's *The Story of a Country Town*, which Howe had sent to him: "Consciously or unconsciously, it is a very remarkable piece of realism" (*MT-HL*, 2:492). Harold Frederic, twenty years younger than Howells, was one other writer

Howells criticized justly and with whom he became a lasting friend. He reviewed both of Frederic's early novels, *Seth's Brother's Wife* (1887) and *The Lawton Girl* (1889), and placed *The Damnation of Theron Ware* (1896) among the best of America's serious novels.

How Howells managed to do all the novelizing, essay writing, and meeting with editors and publishers and literary acquaintances and still manage a family and social life is one of the mysteries of the energy that belies his physical appearance. As a critic, though he may be faulted for a lack of precision in his terms and a lack of rigor in his methodology, he cannot be faulted in the attention he gave literature and language, past and present, and ranging from America to England and the Continent in extent. Nor can he be faulted for the grace and wit and consideration he brought to criticism. It was not only young American writers he affected at firsthand, but a much wider audience who benefited from his deanship of American letters during that twenty years or so before he began to fall from grace.

Chapter Ten
Final Decades

The Decline of Howells's Literary Reputation

After Mark Twain's death in 1910, a commemoration held on his birthday "crowded the Carnegie Hall from floor to roof with 3000 people, and a thousand left on the sidewalk, who couldn't get in" (*LIL*, 2:290). Howells had paid his tribute earlier that year in a long essay, "My Mark Twain," in which he compared his friend to all the great nineteenth-century writers he had known, and declared him "the Lincoln of our literature." Though Howells continued to be a productive writer for a decade after Mark Twain's death, it was becoming apparent that he himself belonged to the past. The uniform Library Edition of Howells's works, begun in 1911 and projected at thirty-two volumes, stopped with publication of six volumes that year.[1] In 1912, on the occasion of Howells's seventy-fifth birthday, Henry James wrote in a public letter: "You may remember perhaps, and I like to recall, how the great and admirable Taine ... greeted you as a precious painter and a sovereign witness ... your really beautiful time will come."[2] Three years later, a year before James's death, Howells wrote him: "on the whole I should say your worship was spreading among us. I am comparatively a dead cult with my statues cut down and the grass growing over them in the pale moonlight. ... I am doing my miserable memoirs, which really make me sick; but I promised to do them" (*LIL*, 2:350).

The birthday celebration to which James contributed his letter was a lavishly arranged gathering of invited notables, including

President Taft, who pleased Howells greatly by attending. The dinner was both a tribute and a promotional splurge by Harper's for their valuable literary property. At the end of the ceremonies, a figure dressed as Silas Lapham came on stage to shake Howells's hand and say, "We'll live on together." The gesture was more prophetic than it was intended to be, for *The Rise of Silas Lapham* was soon to be the only novel of Howells to have much public currency.

By the time of Howells's death, a new writer like F. Scott Fitzgerald seemed totally unaware of him. Hemingway paid homage to *Huckleberry Finn* but did not apparently even know *Silas Lapham*. Dreiser knew Howells; he wrote an interview article about him for *Success* magazine in 1898: "How He Climbed Fame's Ladder." Older men, like Dreiser and Sherwood Anderson, knew of Howells's work, but Dreiser found him as a person greater than both his writings or reputation. Sinclair Lewis, whose *Main Street* was a big novel in 1920, the year Howells died, mentioned him in his Nobel Prize speech: "Mr. Howells was one of the gentlest, sweetest, and most honest of men, but he had the code of a pious old maid whose greatest delight was to have tea at the vicarage."[3] It is ironic that Lewis's work so resembles Howells's and a further irony that Lewis's literary reputation failed to survive his own death.

The reasons for the collapse of Howells's literary reputation — for it was swift and complete enough to justify that description — are probably lodged in the complexities of social change. The works that Howells had done in the 1880s and 1890s, aimed directly at economic reform, were in tune with actual political and social reforms coming about before World War I. But the strength of these novels was overlooked, and Howells was identified with a "code," as Lewis put it, hopelessly outdated by the changes in morals and manners beginning before the war and accelerating in the 1920s.

Howells had not escaped criticism before. The harshest of it had come from the defenders of the sentimental romance. Most of the attackers were little enough known then and forgotten now;

some were offended genteel readers who applied words like "filth," "revolting," "sordid," and "vulgar" to some of Howells's novels.[4] But some criticism did point to real deficiencies of a realism that tied itself down too tightly to commonplace lines and conventional morality. An anonymous English reviewer in 1883 was being politely truthful when he wrote, "his tales are not exciting, but they are tales with a gentle current of interest in them." Nor was the same reviewer slandering Howells when he asked the question about Ben Halleck in *A Modern Instance*: "Why should so limp and boneless a being stand as the representative of the best kind of American?"[5] And it was not Sinclair Lewis or H. L. Mencken, but Ambrose Bierce in 1892, who said Howells's following was largely composed of fibrous virgins and oleaginous clergymen.[6]

For the most part, Howells remained serene in the face of criticism, early and late, partly as a matter of temperament and partly because he was too busy a writer to brood long over attacks. Though one can detect some slowing down in the very last decades of his life, the years from 1900 to 1920 were immensely productive for a man moving from the ages of sixty-three to eighty-three. He did not like growing old; "This curse of growing old!" he wrote Clemens in 1899. "The joke is all out of *that*" (*MT-HL*, 2:701). But his periods of genuine depression are few, and none kept him for long from the work he was always projecting ahead. "You are old enough to be a weary man, with paling interests," Clemens wrote to him in 1899, "but you do not show it. You do your work in the same old delicate & delicious & forceful & searching & perfect way" (*MT-HL*, 2:689).

Last Decades of Work

From 1900 on, and despite the bankruptcy and reorganization Harper's underwent that year, Howells's work was tied almost exclusively to that publishing company. Under the management of Colonel George Harvey, Howells entered into a new agreement beginning December, 1900, to edit "The Easy Chair," a department he continued until the end of his life. During the years

1898–99, he submitted a regular "American Letter" to the English periodical *Literature*, which Harper's then took over. His commitment to do a novel annually for Harper's continued on; he modified the terms to substitute fiction/travel books for novels in 1904. Both his longer and shorter pieces, fiction and nonfiction, were appearing regularly in Harper's periodicals, *Harper's Bazar* as well as *Harper's Monthly*, and in the *North American Review,* also owned by Harvey. In 1902, Harvey invited Howells to express his more controversial political and social views regularly in *Harper's Weekly*.

His association with Harper's helped tie his residence to New York during these last two decades; for a brief period just after entering into his new arrangement with Harper's as "literary advisor," he moved to lower Manhattan near the office and regularly made his appearance there. Summers he spent in upper New England; the house he bought at Kittery Point, Maine, now a W. D. Howells memorial through the gift of his grandson John N. M. Howells, became his most satisfactory place of residence until Elinor's death. Gathering materials for travel books took him abroad to England in 1904, to Italy and Paris and London in 1907, to England again in 1909, to Spain in 1911, and to England for a last trip in 1913. He returned to Ohio a number of times during these years, taking a trip down the Ohio with his brother Joseph in 1902. Once, in 1907, he and Elinor ventured a trip west as far as Duluth, which she regarded, in spite of diarrhea, "as the greatest trip of her life."[7] Earlier, he had visited the Columbian Exposition in Chicago and had gone as far west as Kansas on his lecture tour of 1899.

As full and as satisfying as these late years were, they were also years of his greatest losses. Livy Clemens died in 1904, Samuel Clemens on April 21 and Elinor Howells on May 6, 1910. Henry James died in 1916. Elinor lived long enough to see John married in 1907, and his career as a successful architect went straightforwardly ahead. Two of his sons, John N. M. and William W., both pursued successful careers, and remain in residence close to the Howells property at Kittery Point, Maine.

The many photographs we have of Howells in his later years probably helped establish his genteel image. The camera does not lie, but neither does it tell the truth. We can look at his various pictures, read the physical descriptions of him, and see him somewhat as Howells projected himself into one of his stories: "a short, stout, elderly man ... loaded down with umbrellas, bags, bundles and wraps."[8] His most distinctive facial feature was the mustache which he wore most of his adult life and which, in his later years, made him look a bit like a Teddy Roosevelt or William Howard Taft. He was of smaller stature than either, inclined to fatness, and subject to dyspeptic and liver complaints much of his late life. His manner was gentle, gracious, courtly.

But that is all one side of the description. To Mark Twain, who probably saw more of another self in Howells than anyone else, he could be pictured in a way that brought out Howells's own comic nature and which belied the official air of solid respectability. In 1901, Mark Twain sent Aldrich a picture of Abdul Hamed II, sultan of Turkey, upon which he had initialed W. D. H. The sultan is a full-bearded scowling man with a large nose and downturned eyes. Clemens wrote: "He thinks it a libel, I think it flatters. ... Compare this one with the imposter which he works into book-advertisements. They say, Notice this smile; observe this benignity; God be with you Dear People, come to your Howells when you are in trouble, Howells is your friend. This one says, Bile! give me more bile; fry me an optimist for breakfast" (*MT-HL*, 2:723).

What falling off there is in Howells's work of the last two decades is clearly in his fiction. In two letters to Aldrich in 1901 (*LIL*, 2:138, 144) he says that he hates criticism, that essaying is the enemy of the novelist, and that to write fiction is a delight. "Yet in my old age," he concludes, "I seem doomed (on a fat salary) to do criticism and essays. I am ending where I began, in a sort of journalism." Clara and Rudolf Kirk claim that "Howells' essays for the 'Easy Chair' are largely responsible for an exaggerated reputation for 'gentility' which was fastened on Howells by H. L. Mencken and other journalists of the 1920's."[9] Many of these essays are ephemeral pieces, and an idea of their nature can be gained by browsing through *Imaginary Interviews*, a collection of pieces written to an obvious journalistic design. But much of the fiction of the last twenty years carries on in an earlier Howellsian manner which may have disappointed contemporary readers hoping for strength of *A Landlord at Lion's Head* and may have caused new readers to turn away before Howells had fairly been tried.

Novels from 1900 to 1920

Of the eight to ten novels Howells wrote before he died, only two seem to hold up on their own merits: *The Son of Royal Langbrith* (1904) and *The Leatherwood God* (1916). Even enumerating the novels of these years is uncertain, for though *New Leaf Mills* (1913) is a long fiction (Howells called it "a chronicle"), it is so close to autobiography as to arouse reservations about its being called a novel; *The Flight of Pony Baker* (1902) fits the category of juvenile fiction rather than the novel; *Through the Eye of the Needle* (1907) is subtitled "a romance," and, like the earlier Altrurian romance, is not exactly a novel. What remains are *The Kentons* (1902), *Letters Home* (1903), *Miss Bellard's Inspiration* (1905), *Fennel and Rue* (1908), and *The Vacation of the Kelwyns* (1920). If one were to pick out two novels from the whole of Howells's work that best represented him as a painter of genteel domestic scenes, *The Kentons* and *The Vacation of the Kelwyns* might be good choices. Henry James called *The Kentons* "that perfectly classic illustration of your spirit and your form" (*K*, xxvi). A good critic of the American novel, Richard Chase, called *The Vacation of the Kelwyns* "quite possibly his best."[10] Both statements, I think, knowingly set aside what have come to be accepted as Howells's best works to call attention to a typical kind of Howells fiction which he wrote often and with great skill.

Both novels look backward in time, *The Kentons* to an Ohio family of the nineteenth century, *The Kelwyns* to New England in the 1870s. *The Kentons* begins with a well-managed exposition of the establishment of an Ohio family which reminds one of Howells's expertly fashioned autobiographical pieces. George Carrington has indicated the Ohio links in this novel and sees in the figure of Judge Kenton "the integrity and paternal warmth he [Howells] associated with his own father and the imposing stature of Ohio's legendary hero [Simon Kenton]" (*K*, xviii). Unfortunately, the opening scene comprises but one short chapter, and we are then swept into the conventional Howells mating and marrying story. That, indeed, seems to have been the genesis of the story, one to be called "The Discovery of Europe," whose plot was simply that of a couple who take their daughter to Europe to end an infatuation. That novel never got written in its projected form; some of the European travel material Howells used in *Their Silver Wedding Journey*. When he turned back to the original love story idea, the concept had broadened into a "pretty" notion: "how a love-affair is not merely the affair of the two young people, as we used to think, but the affair of the father and mother and brothers and sisters" (*LIL*, 2:151). What that promised was a good deal of meddling, a good deal of talk, and a happy resolution, and that is about what the novel delivers. "The stupid and stupefying cry of 'commonplace people' " (*LIL*, 2:161), which Howells said killed the book, misses the main fault; that fault is the stereotyped characterizations and actions in the novel, the warming over with only slight variations of conventional Howells fare.

We have met Mr. and Mrs. Kenton and Ellen before, in the persons of Basil and Isabel March and the ingenue who was the object of their romance-making propensities. The larger family circle of the Kentons adds little, with the single exception of Boyne, the young brother, who has enough life to help a plodding narrative along. Bittridge is a stock sentimental villain and the Reverend Mr. Hugh Breckon, who finally wins out over Ellen's refined moral scruples, is as much a stick as are most of these proper young men. All of this, with a few decorative touches from Howells's Holland trip, is handled with great skill. The best brief criticism of the novel may be that of S. Weir Mitchell, who wrote

Howells: "*The Kentons'* [*sic*] left me in a state of wonder at the art, and exasperation at the people" (*K*, xxvi).

The Vacation of the Kelwyns is essentially a long joke about the troubles of boarding in the country, troubles Howells had experienced many times. The novel was begun in the 1870s, apparently when some feckless boardinghouse keepers, like the Kites in the story, were fresh in mind. The Howellses appear as Elmer and Carry Kelwyn, and the love affair is that of Parthenope Brook and Elihu Emerance. The Kelwyns' two sons, a village drunk and his wife, some Shakers who live in the village, some tramps, a peddler, some gypsies, and a bear provide more relief from the central love story than is to be found in most Howells novels.

Howells worked first at the novel as *Children of the Summer*, put it aside for many years, worked at it again after Elinor's death, put it aside again but left it as a completed work at his death. It was published shortly after. This long period of composition may account for its episodic character and for the more barbed criticism of people and social institutions. Some of Howells's harshness to back-country meanness and poverty of intellect is mingled with the idyllic. The writing is up to Howells's high standards whether in the one vein or the other. Mrs. Kite's cooking, for example, provokes this description: "The eggs, with their discolored edges limp from standing in the pork fat, stared up dimly, sadly; the biscuits, when broken open, emitted an alkaline steam from their greenish-yellow crumb; the tea was black again" (32). The Kelwyns are caught between outrage and despair; they want to send the Kites packing, but their delicate consciences will not let them exercise their full superiority over the incapable and shiftless. Parthenope is one of Howells's more interesting women, chiefly because she seems to sum up the most that artistic parents, birth in Naples, wide reading, and talents for sketching and watercolors can do for a woman moving past her early twenties. Emerance, as is often true of Howells's young men, is not as distinctively created; in the main, he is an "experimenter," possibly a "light" man, hence Parthenope's reservations about accepting him as a mate. In the end, he does win her. Since the Kelwyns are still so involved in their own problems with the Kites, the reader is spared the usual coda in which the married couple ponders the past and future of the young folks. One long passage lends support to the novel's subtitle, "An Idyl of the Middle Eighteen-Seventies":

If it was not the first society of her ancestral city [Boston], it was society that read and thought and idealized, and was of a freedom gladder than that which has come in something like excess to the society which now neither reads nor thinks nor idealizes. If she had known it—but no girl could have known it—she was standing on the verge of that America which is now so remote in everything but time, and was even then rounding away with such girlhood as hers into the past which can hardly be recalled in any future of the world. It was sweet and dear; with its mixture of the simple and the gentle, it was nearer the Golden Age than any the race has yet known. . . . (159)

Miss Bellard's Inspiration, Letters Home, and *Fennel and Rue* can be dispatched briefly. The first is of a woman past twenty-seven who must decide about marrying a young Englishman who has taken up ranching out West. The setting is the New Hamsphire summer retreat of the Crombies, who are up to their old tricks of playing a talky chorus to love's uneven way. What is new at all in this story are the two disagreeable characters, Mr. and Mrs. Mevison, who represent the many people outside of the Crombies' own circle who seem to be separating and divorcing. The nastiness between the Mevisons gives Miss Bellard a real reason for being suspicious of marriage, though to the reader Edmund's "we ought to marry dispassionately" is already enough. They do marry and, as usual in these novels, the observing couple has the last several hundred words. *Fennel and Rue* is one of the silliest stories Howells wrote; scarcely a novel, it poses the situation of a young writer, Mr. Verrian, who is asked by a supposedly dying woman to reveal the ending of his serialized story before she dies. Upon the editor's cautious inquiry, the woman confesses she is not dying and that it was just an ill-advised trick she and a girl friend decided to play. From that tiny kernel, Howells pops a lot of corn. The author's mother is a particularly tiresome confidante, and the deceiving girl is a spiritualist of sorts whose unmasked deceit throws her into a neurotic fever. Finally, *Letters Home* (1903) is an epistolary novel in which the daughter of a rich Iowan moved to New York is pursued by a journalist-poet from Iowa and observed by a Mr. Otis Binning who writes to his married sister in Boston about it. What interest one might find is confined to the observations made about New York by the various visitors who find themselves living there. There are forty-nine letters by various correspondents beginning December 12, 1901, and ending March 12, 1902.

Compared with any of these novels, *The Son of Royal Langbrith* (1904) is a welcome return to the Howells who created Dryfoos and Jeff Durgin. Royal Langbrith's father is a credibly created business figure reminiscent of Northwick of *The Quality of Mercy*. His son, though a fitfully successful characterization, is more than a cipher, both as the protagonist who is obsessed with his father's memory and as the young man involved in the love subplot. The rather complex story establishes Royal Langbrith, the deceased founder of the Langbrith family's fortune, as a powerful offstage force. His past misdeeds are genuine enough to be convincing, and their effects come forward into the novel in the persons of those he has most victimized: his wife, his brother, and old Hawberk, who has become an opium eater. A pretender to both culture and morality, Langbrith has fathered a family by another woman and has escaped detection for his many sins during his life. Dr. Anther, a sympathetically portrayed central character, wishes to marry Langbrith's widow. She was a former mill-hand, and Langbrith's marrying beneath him has helped him rationalize his abusive treatment of her. Though she loves Anther, she cannot break out of the tyranny her son Jim, in his blind devotion to the memory of his father, holds over her. Jim is something of a playwright and spends some time in Paris with an artist friend, Falk, who plays a familiar alter ego role to the main young male character.

Through Jim's desire to commemorate his father's memory with a plaque and a public dedication, Dr. Anther, Judge Garley, and the minister Enderby are brought into a debate about whether to reveal Langbrith's true character. While they are temporizing, Jim's brother in a dyspeptic fury reveals everything to Jim. Eventually, Jim and Hope Hawberk, daughter of the man Langbrith most wronged, are married, but Dr. Anther dies without marrying Mrs. Langbrith.

In writing to Henry Blake Fuller about the novel, Howells says, "I have purposely refused several effects of tragedy that offered themselves to my hand" (*LIL*, 2:181). He probably had in mind his refusal to further visit the sins of the father upon the son and mother. Jim and Hope seem destined for a happy marriage, and the minister can see a termination of Langbrith's evil and even some good arising out of an evil past. He decides that "Royal Langbrith seemed for him a part of the vast sum of evil, not personally detachable and punishable" (*SRL*, 267). The conclusion is not necessarily a softening of the view that character cannot change and sowing evil must reap evil which is ambiguously urged in *The Landlord at Lion's Head*. Jim Langbrith does change and, for the most part, convincingly and importantly for the overall effect of the novel. The novel received generally favorable reviews and remains among the eight or ten Howells novels of most interest.

The Leatherwood God and *New Leaf Mills*

"Yes," Howells wrote to his brother Joseph in 1907, "I still hope to do *The Leatherwood God*.... It is a great scheme, and I should like the notion of making it my last great novel" (*LIL*, 2:235). It was the last novel of substance Howells was to publish—in 1916, four years before his death. Although H. L. Mencken called it "little more than a stale anecdote,"[11] other opinion has

been much more favorable. Cady may be right in calling it
"Howells' great unknown novel."[12]

The central figure of the story is Joseph Dylks, who comes to
the Leatherwood, Ohio community early in the nineteenth century
and sets himself up first as a prophet and finally as God.[13] His
attraction is particularly strong to the women of the community,
but his snorting and shouting convince no one for very long and
he is deposed, given the opportunity to leave, and dies by drowning in the river he brags he can turn into gold.

In the details which elaborate the main story, the Gillespies are
the principal characters. Nancy, some time before the story opens,
has married Dylks against the wishes of her brother David. Dylks
deserts her and in time Nancy remarries Laban Billings, of the
Leatherwood community. The reappearance of Dylks not only poses
a problem for her but for her brother's daughter Jane, who becomes
convinced of Dylks's authenticity. Matthew Braile is a crusty village
lawyer, the reasoner of the tale, who both opposes Dylks and sees
that he receives justice. The other important character in the story
is Jim Redfield, who comes close to being a stereotyped western
hero.

One of the townspeople describes Dylks's advent on the scene:

He seemed to stop, and then says he, "What shall we pray for?"
and just then there came a kind of a snort, and a big voice shouted
out, "Salvation!" and then there came another snort,—"Hooff!"—
like there was a scared horse got loose right in there among the
people; and some of 'em jumped up from their seats, and tumbled
over the benches, and some of 'em bounced off, and fell into fits,
and the women screeched and fainted, thick as flies. (8)

Dylks is chased out of hiding by Jim Redfield, who rips off a
hank of hair, scalp and all, to expose the fraudulent God. Later
Redfield is brought in as a special deputy to see that Dylks is not
harmed by the mob, for in a previous trial, Squire Braile has pro-
tected Dylks's right to his religious beliefs, as fantastical as they
are. As Dylks leaves to establish a New Jerusalem somewhere over

the hills, the novel ties up the loose ends of plot. Jim Redfield and Jane Gillespie marry. Nancy and her husband's relations are restored, and the son, Joey, witnesses Dylks's death after trying unsuccessfully to save him. Braile offers a restrained explanation about how the harsh conditions of the frontier may make people susceptible to anyone who purports to offer salvation. As a dramatization of the religious fervor and fakery and honest searching that marked the rise of such a successful prophet as Joseph Smith, martyred during the same period of time and in the same locale, the novel deserves a place with other books which attempt to understand this particular religious phenomenon.

New Leaf Mills (1913) has some of the same vigor that is effective in creating the backwoods Leatherwood community and its shouting and praying and spitting believers and blasphemers. The Powell family is the fictional family Howells created to dramatize the story of his own family's attempt to establish a Utopian community at Eureka Mills. Owen and Ann Powell draw upon characteristics of his own father and mother, but the elaborations of plot divert some attention away from an examination of the central characters. Of the minor characters, Rosy, the servant girl employed by the Powells, and Captain Bickler, who propositions her to become his mistress, are convincingly drawn. Overdale, the miller, the foul-mouthed and belligerent antagonist of the Powells, is portrayed without any attempt at either blackening or cleaning up his character. Though the work is fiction, it obviously belongs with the autobiographical works which explored Howells's Ohio past.

Howells's Short Fiction

Howells's short fiction is never likely to win a place as an important contribution to literature. Few stories are anthologized, and a thorough reading of his collected volumes of stories does not yield many stories that deserve to be. Some two dozen stories, two thirds of them written between 1895 and 1907, comprise his work as a writer of short fiction. Some of the stories do bear upon interests Howells expresses in his novels, and some have the manner of some Howells novels. The collections *Questionable Shapes* (1903), for instance, and *Between the Dark and the Daylight* (1907) contain a number of stories which collect familiar types from Howells's novels. Mr. Wanhope, a psychologist, figures often in these stories, and most of them have something to do with psychic or mentalistic experiences. One such story, "A Memory That Worked Overtime," is as trivial as a character's remembering vividly that he left a painting on a horse-car, but discovering that he had really left it at a flower shop before he ever entered the car. Another, "The Angel of the Lord," takes a more serious though not much more convincing line in telling of a married couple who choose to live in isolation in the country in order to help overcome the husband's morbid fear of dying. Overcoming that fear, he falls victim of the belief that he is being summoned by an angel of the lord. Two long stories deal with apparitions perceived by one of the characters, and a number deal with thought-transference or dream-transference. An ambitious story set in Europe, "A Sleep and a Forgetting," doubtless arises in some way from Winifred's illness. Here, the young woman has lost her memory through the death of her mother. The memory is restored when her father, who bears a marked resemblance to Howells, is attacked by a madman before her eyes. When she comes out of her swoon, her memory is restored and she marries the young doctor who has taken an interest in her case.

Another volume, *A Pair of Patient Lovers* (1901), contains the one impressive story in all the collections. This is "A Difficult Case," which Howells regarded as an unusual story. It bears a close relationship with other stories about an afterlife and with those novels in which Howells probes the questions of cosmic purpose and immortality. The central character has many of the traits of Mark Twain, who wrote Howells: "I read the Difficult Situation night before last, & got a world of evil joy out of it" (*MT-HL*, 2:719). What he must have appreciated was the unflinching disbelief of the central character in any afterlife or in any reason why he should not die. The story is really a long argument between an earnest minister of a minor religious sect and an old parishioner over the truth or untruth of an afterlife. The old parishioner, Ewbert, is presumed to be a recluse, perhaps as a result of his being disappointed in love. But, as he reveals to the minister, he has been little affected by an early broken romance, has married, had a son, outlived both, and now has a dog who provides him with decent company. He is not the least afraid of death, but for a time the minister seems to succeed in planting religious hopes in the old man's head. As he does so, the minister's own physical strength wanes until his wife insists upon taking him out of the "evil old man's" influence. When he returns, Ewbert has reverted to his materialism, takes to his bed and dies, leaving the minister to preach a funeral sermon even he does not quite understand. A passage like this indicates the temper of Howells's characterization: "Why, man, you don't suppose I *want* to live hereafter? Do you think I'm anxious to have it all over again, or *any* of it? . . . I've had enough. I want to be let alone. I don't want to do anything more, or have anything more done to me. I want to *stop*" (*PPL*, 176).

The story is an excellent one, but the distance between it and a mildly amusing but contrived story of a young man's pursuit of a piano is as far as that between the worst and best of Howells's novels. *The Daughter of the Storage* (1916) gives other examples of Howells's miscellaneous pieces in prose and verse. Howells does not appear to have often put his serious thought into the short story form, perhaps because the stories had their chief life in the magazines and were more subject to the tastes of the popular audience.

Travel Books

Howells's travel books are, with the possible exception of *Three Villages* (1884) and *A Little Swiss Sojourn* (1892), major parts of his literary work, and even these brief ones have a charm and acuteness that afford pleasure.[14] *London Films* (1905) is the first of three books Howells did about his travels in England. As with his other travel books, much of the material saw first publication as magazine pieces. This volume, he points out in the opening chapter, takes what authority it possesses from the visits of 1861 and 1865, 1882–83, 1894, 1897, and the longest in 1904.

In beginning *London Films* with observations about the English weather, Howells both risks taking an obvious tack and misleading the reader about the nature of the book. For though it is a kind of tourist guide, it is written with an acuteness of observation and phrasing uncommon to guidebooks. Unlike the real weather of the United States, Howells writes, England has "small, individual weather, offered as it were in samples of warm, cold, damp and dry, but mostly cold and damp, especially in-doors" (4). At Exeter, he finds "a bedroom grate of the capacity of a quart pot and the heating capabilities of a glowworm" (5). And who has spoken better and more economically of the peculiar force of English women?: "She looked not only authoritative; people often do with us; she looked authorized" (8).

Such observations draw a reader into the book. There is nothing startling in the contents, no grandiose design nor acute laying bare of English character. London and New York are well compared, the "shows and side-shows of state" described, the streets and tourist attractions vividly set forth. Outside London, the Henley regatta at Oxford ("Harvard Class-Day in English terms"), attracts his interest, though Howells, as sedentary in his interests as in his habits, wastes little time on the physical detail of the competition. People throughout the book interest him most, along with comparisons between England and America as to manners and attitudes, but also as to poverty and architecture and government.

Certain Delightful English Towns (1906) and *Seven English Cities* (1909) are books like *London Films.* The former begins with Plymouth, making the observation that many Americans, by virtue of their ancestry, have a consciousness of England that precedes an actual visit. Bath, to which Howells, like uncounted others, had come to take the waters, was revered by him. His fondness for eighteenth-century literature causes him to people the streets with authors of the period and the characters they created.

The essay on Oxford describes the ceremonies which accompanied the conferral of degrees (his honorary one among them, but unmentioned in the text). *Seven English Cities* turns to some of the industrial cities as well as historically important ones. Liverpool is described cursorily in the short opening chapter. The distance between rich and poor strikes him again here, where "a sort of iron squalor seemed to prevail" (5). In Manchester, he observes that railway hotels are, next to cathedrals, England's greatest wonder. Modern industry and ancient history catch Howells's attention in Sheffield. York claimed his attention for a longer visit, and at Doncaster he reveals that horse racing was his one sporting passion. Visits to the English Boston and to the two Welsh watering places fill out the book. The last chapter, "Glimpses of English Character," pays tribute to Emerson, "the best observer of England that ever was" (198).

A diversion growing out of his English visits is *The Seen and Unseen at Stratford-on-Avon* (1914), which has Shakespeare and Bacon materializing before the author at Cheltenham at a performance of *Midsummer Night's Dream*. They go on to Stratford, their conversations interspersed with descriptions of Stratford and vicinity. Howells seems to have adopted the device as a way of dealing with this most commonplace of tourist experiences. It also enabled him to pay his lifelong respects to Shakespeare, and to comment on the Bacon-Shakespeare controversy (he has Bacon himself say he did not write Shakespeare's plays). An unexpected and charming bit, undoubtedly taken from Howells's own experiences, is his describing a morning visit to a moving picture show which almost fronted the Shakespeare monument. He sat through the whole program, mostly American cowboy and Indian films, apparently one of the few adults in attendance, and enjoyed it greatly. Shakespeare in this book turns out to be a very Howellsian Shakespeare, "simple-hearted and sincere as well as wise" (26), and the wonder is that the fantasy comes off as well as it does.

There is more history woven into *Familiar Spanish Travels* (1913) than into the English books, perhaps because Howells's audience was more familiar with English history and because of his early and studiously acquired knowledge of Spain. He wrote Henry Van Dyke from Madrid, October 17, 1911: "I am here fulfilling at last the oldest dream of my life...."[15] To Henry James he sent his itinerary: San Sebastian, Burgos, Valladolid, Toledo, Cordova, Seville, Granada, Ronda, Algeciras, Gibralter, and home. The juxtaposition of his past imaginings of Spain with his present experiencing gives an unusual charm to the book, though much of it has a tourist's snap-shot quality that reflects his desire to take in as much of Spain as he could on a trip not likely to be repeated. Traveling by this time was harder on Howells—"the stopping is painful" he wrote James, "especially at the hotels of the smaller places" (*LIL*, 2:305). At Ronda, while satisfying a whim to buy a donkey's head-stall, he had a small human adventure that delighted him in the same way as had his visiting the family of the novelist A. Palacio Valdès in Madrid. The harness-maker's son had been educated at the Escuela Mann in New York, and Howells's delight was as great as his Spanish friend's in being able to say that *his* son John had been one of the architects for the Escuela Mann building.

Roman Holidays and Others (1908) is a more conventional travel book than some of Howells's earlier ones, perhaps conveying that impression because it so much dwells on the conveniences and inconveniences of travel. Most of the Italian places Howells had visited before, and his comparisons of his moods and memories of various trips add interesting personal notes to what would otherwise be a guidebook to famous sites. At times, it reveals the "whiteness" of the affluent traveler like Howells, who uses the word "darky" to describe the black entertainers whom the Welsh called "niggurs" in *English Cities*, and points out "the twinkling Japs who carried Kodaks" (69). The great works of art and architectural monuments seldom impressed him. His last stop on this trip was at Monte Carlo, where he was a dispassionate observer of gambling at the Casino.

Howells's popularity as a travel writer was such as to bring forth a short book in 1920, *Hither and Thither in Germany*, comprised of the travel portions of *Their Silver Wedding Journey*. His last periodical piece published before his death was "A Memory of San Remo," which appeared in *Harper's Monthly*, February 1920.

Letters and *Years of My Youth*

The material that went into Howells's travel books often had its first shaping in the letters Howells wrote telling others of his travels. The letters that Mildred collected for the two volumes of *Life in Letters* (1928) are but a part of the huge correspondence that accumulated during his lifetime. The letters exchanged between Howells and Clemens comprise a two-volume set in themselves, and the letters to and from Henry James and William James would, in themselves, make a splendid collection. Howells's other frequent correspondents included C.E. Norton, Thomas Bailey Aldrich, Hamlin Garland, John Hay, T. S. Perry, Howard Pyle, E. C. Stedman, Valdès, Charles Dudley Warner, his older literary friends, and members of his family. He was a full and engaging letter writer, and the collected letters, four of the six volumes now in print, as part of "A Selected Edition of W. D. Howells," should give readers a much more personal view of a complex and interesting man.

A large number of personal and literary reminiscences are among Howells's work though he did not write a full autobiography. In 1909, he proposed writing a "Literary Autobiography" as part of a proposed "Library Edition" of his works. In 1912, he began "blocking out and detailing in 'My Times and Places: an Autobiography.'"[16] From this beginning, and not without considerable struggle, *Years of My Youth* was published in 1916. He left unfilled out at his death an outline for a second volume, "Years of My Middle Life." *Years of My Youth*, which I have drawn on in the beginning chapters of this study, remains an indispensable source for anyone who takes an affectionate interest in Howells, and a revealing account of pre–Civil War life in the settled western lands. Near the end of the book, Howells writes of himself as he was when he stood ready to leave Ohio: "I was never hopeful, I was never courageous, but somehow I was dogged. I had no

journalist and a traveller . . ." (*LIL*, 2:397). The poet, journalist, traveler, grown into a novelist, critic, playwright, man of letters, husband, father, and grandfather died quietly on the morning of May 10, 1920.

Chapter Eleven

Final Appraisal

The Limitations of Howells

At the peak of his achievements in 1901, Howells read the appraisal of his talent that Henry James had made to Charles Eliot Norton thirty years before. His response is that of a man who has achieved far more than he may have thought possible in 1870, and who is yet humble about that achievement:

In a way I think their criticism very just; I have often thought my intellectual raiment was more than my intellectual body, and that I might finally be convicted, not of having nothing *on*, but of that worse nakedness of having nothing *in*. He speaks of me with my style, and such mean application as I was making of it, as seeming to him like a poor man with a diamond which he does not know what to do with; and mostly I suppose I *have* cut rather inferior window glass with it. But I am not sorry for having wrought in common, crude material so much; that is the right American stuff; and perhaps hereafter, when my din is done, if any one is curious to know what the noise was, it will be found to have proceeded from a small insect which was scraping about on the surface of our life and trying to get into its meaning for the sake of the other insects larger or smaller. That is, such has been my unconscious work; consciously, I was always, as I still am, trying to fashion a piece of literature out of the life next at hand. (*LIL*, 2:172–73)

Howells's polite and eloquent defense both reveals the firmness of his faith in American realism and fails to face the question of distance between aims and realization. The loss of wide reader interest in Howells's work after his death and the confinement of his reputation to scholars today is not because he did or did not work in "the right American stuff" or because he wrought in "common, crude material." It is more the lack of what James calls "a really *grasping* imagination." James put the matter metaphorically in his preface to *The American*:

> The balloon of experience is in fact of course tied to the earth, and under the necessity we swing, thanks to a rope of remarkable length, in the more or less commodious car of the imagination; but it is by the rope we know where we are, and from the moment that cable is cut we are at large and unrelated; we only swing apart from the globe—though remaining as exhilarated, naturally, as we like, especially when all goes well. The art of the romancer is, "for the fun of it," insidiously to cut the cable, to cut it without our detecting him.[1]

Every reader of James must make the adjustment which goes with relinquishing his grasp on this world and entering into James's special realm. The realm of Howells is earthbound; his fiction seldom soars, and when the reader becomes impatient with finding out what life was like then, he is also likely to become impatient with the questions of personal and social values which are, for Howells and ourselves, a novelist's proper, even primary, concern.

The art of fiction, James wrote, "lives upon exercise, and the very meaning of exercise is freedom. The only obligation to which in advance we may hold a novel, without incurring the accusation of being arbitrary, is that it be interesting." He did not excuse Howells or himself or other realists from this fundamental obligation. "The ways in which it is at liberty to accomplish this result (of interesting us)," he went on, "strike me as innumerable, and such as can only suffer from being marked out or fenced in by prescription."[2] Realism was for Howells something of a prescription, and his novels took on more life and interest in the mid-1880s when social and economic conditions so pressed upon him that he fully enlisted his imagination in peopling a larger canvas to address these issues of conscience and social reality. Howells describes the what and how of writing *A Hazard of New Fortunes*, "the most vital of my fictions," in a preface written twenty years after: "incidents, interests, individualities," got into the novel "which I had not known lay near.... the story began to find its way to issues nobler and larger than those of the love-affairs common to fiction.... the action passed as nearly without my conscious agency as I ever allow myself to think such things happen."[3] The bulk of Howells's fiction, however, creates the kind of judgment made by a sympathetic critic, Oscar Firkins, and without detecting its implied dispraise: "To write six novels like 'The Lady of the Aroostook' was admirable; to have written thirty would have been effeminate."[4]

Howells's Achievements

It is easy to say that Howells's loss of reputation was a result of changes in manners and morals as well as in attitudes toward art taking place in the early twentieth century. Yet his two great American counterparts, James and Twain, did not experience a similar drop from favor, even though each may have retained his hold on a different audience. Howells was very much the man in the middle; to be admired personally because he was able to maintain such a close relationship with two such different literary men; to be thought less of as a writer because, for all his literary presence, his body of fiction did not have the distinctive excellence of either.

Today Howells's work seldom arouses the intemperate responses of earlier critics. It has been given an increasingly respectful attention from academic scholars, and a handful of his novels are being kept before a wider audience in cheap reprints, largely, I suspect, read by college students in American literature classes. Out of the scholarly work devoted to Howells in the last fifty years have come some valuable recognitions: that the transition from nineteenth-century sentimentalism to the modern novel was affected by and revealed in the work of Howells; that Howells's many works accurately disclose much about American manners, tastes, morals, and values in his time and which have not been entirely disavowed by the twentieth century; and that Howells, as limited as he may appear to be, judged by some of his fiction, was an admirable and less narrow man than his earlier critics perceived.

Though it is not often remarked, Howells's reputation may suffer because of the very volume and diversity of his work which resists careful examination except by literary scholars. It can also be observed that the style that Howells's contemporaries found so admirable became more and more distant from modern American prose style. Unlike Mark Twain, he did not arrive at a vernacular which anticipated the great change which separates twentieth-century style from that of the nineteenth. Instead, he continued to write, to some degree, in the literary style of English and American predecessors who first established his sense of fitting literary expression.[5]

As a novelist, Howells wrote at least a half-dozen novels that deserve continuing general readership: *A Modern Instance, The Rise of Silas Lapham, Indian Summer, A Hazard of New Fortunes, The Landlord at Lion's Head,* and *The Leatherwood God.* Other critics might add to or substitute in this list *The Undiscovered Country, Annie Kilburn, The Quality of Mercy,* or *The Son of Royal Langbrith.* The more one extends the list, however, the more one includes novels, like *The Undiscovered Country,* which are only in part successful. If one expands the list, the obvious way is toward including novels *of a kind,* novels that illustrate specific intentions on Howells's part and which are the best representatives of other similar novels. *The Lady of the Aroostook* is such a book, illustrative of the early novels of courting and marriage, as *The Shadow of a Dream* is illustrative of Howells's interest in the psychological novel; *New Leaf Mills* is representative of works which transmute personal experience into fiction.

The distance between Howells's best novels and his poorest is great. Most of the latter were written to meet contractual obligations and most rely upon some kind of innocuous love story. Yet he is not merely the writer of one stunning work, but of a sufficient variety of estimable works to mark him as a major novelist.

Clearly, he is to be recognized for his contributions to the novel of manners. Moreover, he is the most prolific and forceful American novelist of the nineteenth century to turn the novel toward the examination of social and economic issues. In addition, he manifests an interest second only to that of Henry James in developing the novel in technical ways. Though he does not dwell upon theories of fiction in his criticism, it is clear from his work that he helped move the novel in at least three directions: one, from the small, focused character study to novels embracing a variety of representative types perceived within a complex social milieu; two, away from the dominance of an authorial voice toward the presentation of a story in an objective manner through adopting various devices of point of view; and three, away from the conventions of accepted behavior toward an examination of individual motivation and choice characterized by the psychological novel.

As a critic, Howells had more influence on American readers than any other person of his time, and this despite his avowed disaffection for criticism. Cady adds up his contributions to criticism: publication in sixty-four periodicals and nineteen newspapers; eight periodical columns, mainly literary reviews and commentary; seven volumes of criticism; and more than forty prefaces to other authors' books; altogether "substantially more than one, perhaps as much as two million of words in reviews and literary comment—virtually all of it, as was his habit, somehow contributions to criticism."[6] Cady affirms, as we have done previously in this book, the immense knowledge of language and literature that Howells brought to his criticism. By virtue of that knowledge, he helped sophisticate both the practices of writers and the responses of readers. Though the succeeding generation saw Howells as a defender of outmoded conventions and values, his position as critic in his own time was firmly with those who rejected not only romantic sentimentality but the Emersonian idealism which embodied a moralism more constricting by far than Howells's own moral bent. Currently, Howells may be at more odds with criticism than at any other time, for his criticism was never narrowly literary nor highly theoretical. As Cady has put it: "Howells believed in the culture critic, the man of letters intent upon elevating the customs, refining the language, clarifying the motives, helping to raise the quality of the life of the people."[7]

Many American writers have been good travel writers, whether describing the American scene or places abroad. Howells deserves a high place among them. His travel volumes, like his criticism, had the purpose of widening his audience's acquaintance with European as well as American culture. *Venetian Life* and *Tuscan Cities*, for all that they were early works and are now over a century old, are still useful and pleasing literary works: Although none of his works on England is as original a work as Emerson's *English Traits*, all are more than the conventional travel book.

As for Howells as a writer of poetry and short fiction, little can be said. We have noted a growth in his poetry, both in technique and in substance, but it is growth still within the conventions of nineteenth-century poetry and within what might be expected of one growing older. Most of Howells's short fiction was written after 1895, and probably he found the one-act farce a more congenial form of short work. (His only collection of early short fiction is *A Fearful Responsibility and Other Stories* [1881]; the two other stories are "Tonelli's Marriage," written during his Venetian years, and "At the Sign of the Savage," first published in 1877.) His short fiction of his later years does reflect some of his more serious concerns, though it does not show much greater mastery of technique. No one could collect a volume of Howells's short stories or his poetry and present it as a distinguished example of the form.

As with most other critical studies, this one has paid only passing attention to Howells as a dramatist. Since he wrote so many plays and remained interested in drama through so many years, some review of Howells and drama is necessary. Walter Meserve's *The Complete Plays of W. D. Howells* lists thirty-six titles, and a number of unpublished fragments and references to plays he was working on indicate further efforts. One-act plays setting up farcical and topical situations for either of two couples, the Robertses and the Campbells, were his most popular dramatic creations. All but two of the dozen he wrote were done in the 1880s. George Bernard Shaw came upon one of them, *The Garroters*, in 1895 and placed it well ahead of plays of its kind.

From 1893 to 1911, Howells wrote fourteen short plays, half of which had serious themes. His longer published plays include two comedies, an operetta, and a translation of Ippolito D'Aste's *Samson: A Tragedy in Five Acts*. In addition, he wrote adaptations of three of his own novels, *A Foregone Conclusion*, *The Rise of Silas Lapham*, and *A Hazard of New Fortunes*, only the first of which reached production. The play he and Mark Twain worked on over a number of years, *Colonel Sellers as a Scientist*, interested producers but did not reach the stage.

To the number and variety of plays Howells wrote should be added the many essays which show his continuing interest in drama, playwrights, and the theater. "Recent Italian Comedy" in 1864, helped establish him as a critic, and his defense of Ibsen and his pointing out that "Mr. Shaw is the comic analogue of the tragic Ibsen," are discerning acts of criticism at a later period. Nevertheless, his playwriting and criticism are minor achievements, even in an age that provided little support for serious American drama. The short comic plays that Howells fashioned were virtually limited to private theatricals.

When all allowances are made, and for all his sustained interest in drama, Howells cannot be brought forth as a dramatist of great skill. Walter Meserve's guarded praise says about as much as can be said: that his successes in the theater were few, that he had definite limitations as a dramatist, and that his plays only become significant in the rise of realism and in the development of American social comedy.[8]

The variety of writing Howells accomplished year by year would, in itself, earn him the title "man of letters," but his reviews and essays show a variety of interests beyond the literary. Picking at random a two-year span of writing in "The Editor's Study," 1885 to 1887, I find him touching upon Louis Agassiz, Napoleon, the Crusades, Japanese homes, Berlioz, Arctic exploration, history of California and Norway, English aristocracy, Dolly Madison,

Socrates, tramps, the Russian church, and Horatio Greenough. To be sure, a reviewer faces possibilities of this sort with every week's crop of books, but few reviewers embrace such a wide selection. This sample period has near its beginning Howells's involvement with international copyright and at its end his open letter defending the Chicago "anarchists." Throughout his life, Howells's interests and the writing which expressed it were centered in literature, but literature in a wide sense; Henry Commager in reviewing Van Wyck Brooks's *Howells* compares Brooks with Howells as a man of letters, similar in "the catholicity of his learning and the breadth of his sympathies and the depth of his understanding . . . a familiar and affectionate figure on the literary horizon, guide, interpreter, historian and symbol."[9]

The range of Howells's immense productivity and the influence it exercised are reason enough for continuing to recognize his importance. Until the 1960s, social realism as advocated and practised by Howells was the prevailing mode in American fiction. Even such an idiosyncratic novelist as Faulkner pursued that course within his preferred locale of Yoknapatawpha county. Faulkner's work is as critical of the social order of the South as Howells's was of Boston, and the moral concerns which underlay Howells's social criticism are present, and of the same kind, in Faulkner. Moreover, the fact that Howells's writing life stretched over the period between the Civil War and World War I makes his work, fiction and nonfiction, essential to an understanding of American literature and the culture from which it came during this long period.

Scholarship and Criticism

Howells is likely to retain his curious standing in American and English literary scholarship. Within American literature, he is to be regarded as a major author, though not as likely to be read as James, Twain, Hawthorne, or Melville, to mention our chief nineteenth-century fiction writers. Within the larger body of literature in English, he probably occupies a lesser position than that of George Eliot, perhaps somewhat higher than that of Trollope. In 1960 James Woodress performed the useful task of surveying four decades of Howells scholarship;[10] he proclaimed him to be a major American author, and charted the ups and downs of his reputation, observing that his reputation had been declining for at least a decade before Mencken's disposal of him in 1917. In the decade immediately after his death, his reputation continued to decline, his books to go unread. That decade, however, did see the publication of two biographies, by Firkins and Cooke, and, in 1928, Mildred Howells's collection of letters. All three are still useful. An earlier critical study, by Alexander Harvey, 1917, puzzled Howells as to what it was, and is of very little use today.[11]

The depression of the 1930s helped revive interest in Howells as a social protest novelist. Parrington's third volume of *Main Current in American Thought* (1930) and Walter Taylor's *The Economic Novel in America* (1942) gave Howells a high place in a strong current of American writing and thought. As might be expected, academic studies of Howells and his era began in the late 1930s. George Arms's dissertation on Howells's social criticism in 1939 was the first of ten dissertations in the next ten years.

Since the end of World War II, Howells scholarship has pretty much kept pace with the general expansion of academic study. Though a novel or two may get into undergraduate American literature courses and a respectable place is given Howells in all the major anthologies, his reputation as measured by the scholarly work invested in his work now outruns even his academic readership. This is attributable, in part, to the work of a first group of post–World War II scholars, and in part to the opportunities for scholarship that an author as prolific as Howells affords. At the beginning of this work stands the Gibson and Arms bibliography, an indispensable tool, and John Reeves's finding list of Howells manuscripts.

Cady's two-volume biography in 1956–58 was the first since 1924, and its combing of sources, particularly from the Ohio period, has been of use to every subsequent biographer. Other biographies since that time are by Van Wyck Brooks, Clara and Rudolf Kirk, Edward Wagenknecht, and Kenneth Lynn. Lynn's 1971 biography, subtitled "An American Life," deserves the praise given it by Alfred Kazin, "the first truly modern life." Though not confined to Howells, Everett Carter's *Howells and the Age of Realism* (1954) is still the best book on this broader subject.

Critical studies of Howells outnumber biographies, perhaps because of the difficulty of encompassing a life as long and as productive as Howells's. These include books which take in a large or central aspect of Howells's work, by Fryckstedt, Bennett, and Hough in the 1950s, Vanderbilt, Carrington, and McMurray in more recent years. Clara Kirk has done two separate studies, one of the Altrurian books (1962), and one on his relation to art. A steady production of articles continues; with the creation of a new periodical, *American Literary Realism*, in 1967, Howells is likely to attract continuing attention. Though the weight and volume of Howells studies has not yet won Howells a separate listing in the annual *American Literary Scholarship*, as it has for Mark Twain and Henry James, Howells, in the 1977 *Annual*, occupied one fourth of the space given over to nineteenth-century literature outside the discussion of individual authors.

The chief measure of Howells's academic respectability is the continuing production of the "Selected Edition of W. D. Howells," begun in the sixties under the Center for Editions of American Authors and published by Indiana University Press. As of August, 1980, seventeen of a projected thirty-two-volume set were in print with ten more ready for publication. The six volumes of letters, which should see complete publication within a few years, will give access to materials previously available only in the Houghton Library at Harvard and other research libraries.

The question raised by Edmund Wilson about the Howells edition and the whole idea of meticulously edited editions of major American authors has, in part, been answered by the financial exigencies which has caused some pulling back in the enterprise.[12] What is clearly a gain for Howells scholars and of some benefit to college and university students are the individual introductions to the Howells volumes, which are uniformly excellent and useful.

The besetting weakness of Howells scholarship (probably of all literary scholarship), particularly in periodical criticism, is the failure to consider the merits of either the Howells work being examined or of the piece itself. As with much other literary scholarship, Howells criticism is too abundantly stocked with articles which manufacture new sources for individual works or create fancied parallels with other literature or which subject an individual work or number of works to the latest fashion in exegesis or critical method. It can fairly be said that very few of the periodical pieces devoted to Howells in the past decade have anything like Howells's own breadth and sense of relevance in writing about literature.

Final Words

Howells's recognition by academic scholars has not been accompanied by a recognition within the general public. Nor is the abundance of scholarship just reviewed likely to reach the general public with any measurable effect. New writers replace old writers, and though old writers do not altogether disappear, they survive, if they survive at all, by the presence of works which somehow transcend the time in which they were written. The greatest of writers become part of a culture, and even defy American culture's ability to wear everything out at an increasing rate or to discard it for temporary or permanent oblivion. Howells's works, though some will continue to be read, are not likely to become a common cultural possession.

Two unpublished manuscripts which lie at the beginning and end of Howells's career give additional perspective to viewing his achievements and limitations. The first is *Geoffrey Winter*, a novel begun probably in 1860, and for which we have sufficient in manuscript to disclose Howells as a young romantic closer in feeling and expression to Hawthorne and Poe than to Goldsmith or Cervantes. The setting is Dulldale, Ohio; the situation the return of a former resident, vaguely described as a writer, and his mending of a broken love affair of his youth. The writer dreams about his fair cousin whom he had once loved and who leans toward him in his dream lovingly, only to push him away when he tries to embrace her. In his absence, she has married another, but the death of that husband now leaves her free to marry Geoffrey. The consummated match between a woman of passionate intensity and a man whose lack of passion is suggested by his name, Winter, anticipates other such matches in Howells's fiction. Realism is little to Howells's purpose here. Instead, he introduces a kind of apparition in the person of a young girl, Sarah, who is invited into the Winters' home as a hired girl after their marriage. She is described as young yet old, innocent yet evil, unlearned but wise, strangely attractive but repellent, and her place in the plot is certain to involve a three-way conflict of wife, husband, and child-woman. What is interesting is to see so early in Howells's career his attempting a fiction in which sexual passions seem so central, even though they are disguised in obvious romantic trappings.

At the other end of his career is *The Home-Towners*, a novel misleadingly described by most readers as being about St. Augustine, Florida, and the aged folk who gather there, exiles from their home towns. Even in its incomplete form, a typescript of some 9,300 words, the novel suggests a grappling with realities at variance with the image of an aging and outmoded novelist. Its central character is Lucius Rayburn, a journalist going south to convalesce from some kind of breakdown (Howells's subtitle for the story was "An Incident of Convalescence"). Howells's description of Rayburn's movement across the dark and bloody ground of the South is as powerful as anything he ever wrote. The hunting down and shooting of a Negro is the central event of the story's early pages, the more effectively intruded into the novel because Howells has it occur on the edges, so to speak, of the central character's consciousness. It drives Rayburn from this first place of refuge to St. Augustine, where, in time, he meets once again the boardinghouse keeper who has first taken him in. It is at this point that Howells begins to take an interest in the home-towners in St. Augustine and where the novel breaks off.

It seems likely that Howells would have knit these early events together, the starkest realities of the historical and contemporary South with the homelessness, in time and space, of aging Americans looking for a last and better home. Thus, at the very end of his career, Howells is moving beyond Ohio, Boston, and New York to embrace another expanse of American life, perhaps to confront the facts of his own homelessness.

Howells's general recognition today comes in part because of his identity with Mark Twain and Henry James, and it comes in part from a vague recognition that there was such a writer as Howells who wrote a great many books and who was a literary figure of some importance back then. As that importance can be defined, it probably gets defined in terms of some kind of fussy morality, concern for the common folk, and a strange fear of sex. Though Howells scholars are prone to resent such simple and inaccurate identifications, they might better be grateful for them, for it is in such peculiarities that Howells may continue to exist at all as a literary figure. The nineteenth century cannot be quite detached from the twentieth, though it seems to be even more remote from twentieth-century consciousness than the pre–Civil War decades or even the age of the American revolution. We may, symbolically and actually, find our grandparents more interesting, certainly more benevolent and understanding, than our parents. We find our great-great relatives sufficiently mysterious to arouse curiosity that leads to finding out about them. And though Howells by now, measured by the actual time of generations, is more than a grandfather, he still, it seems to me, is close enough to us to be father of us all. Though we grant him the importance necessary to that which produced us, we are yet reserved in both the respect and the understanding given him.

Notes and References

Chapter One

1. Throughout this volume, works by Howells are cited by abbreviations identified in the Primary section of the Bibliography.

2. W. C. Howells, *Recollections of Life in Ohio, 1813–1840* (Gainesville: Scholars' Facsimiles & Reprints, 1963), p. 95.

3. Ibid., p. 97.

4. Ibid., p. v.

5. Ibid., p. 163.

6. Frances Trollope, *Domestic Manners of the Americans* (New York: Knopf, 1949), p. 133.

7. Writers' Program of the WPA, *The Ohio Guide*, American Guide Series (New York: Oxford Univ. Press, 1940), p. 27.

8. G. Arms, R. H. Ballinger, C. K. Lohmann, and J. K. Reeves, eds., *W. D. Howells Selected Letters*, vol. 1, *1852–1872* (Boston, 1979), p. 321.

9. Mildred (*LIL*, 1: 111) writes that Henry "was a bright and normally developed boy of four when he was accidentally hit on the forehead by the bat of a playmate." Edwin H. Cady (*The Road to Realism* [Syracuse, 1956], p. 44) attributes the injury to a fall from a swing. Howells was witness to Henry's arrested development only for a brief time before he began living apart from the Ohio family, but he was keenly aware all his life of the sacrifice Henry's care entailed for Victoria and Aurelia and of the difficulty of dealing with violent behavior that arose while Henry was in the family's care. He exchanged views with his father about Henry's undergoing an operation, and X rays revealed that the condition was caused by a bone spur resulting from the early accident.

10. Edwin H. Cady, "The Neuroticism of William Dean Howells,"

Publication of the Modern Language Association 61 (March, 1946):
229–38.
    11. Cady, *The Road to Realism*, pp. 56–60.

Chapter Two

    1. Heinrich Heine, *Poems & Ballads* (New York: Hartsdale
House, 1947), pp. 100–101.
    2. *Life of Abraham Lincoln by W. D. Howells* (Bloomington:
Indiana University Press, 1960).
    3. W. D. Howells, "A Hoosier's Opinion of Walt Whitman,"
Saturday Press, August 11, 1860.
    4. Cady, *The Road to Realism*, p. 89.
    5. James Woodress, *Howells and Italy* (Durham, N. C., 1952),
p. 10.
    6. Ohio and America continued to assert their claim on Howells
during his years abroad. The death in April, 1864, of his brother
John, nine years younger than Howells, affected him greatly. "Elegy
on John Butler Howells," printed in the *Ashtabula Sentinel*, June
28, 1864, was written the morning after Howells received news of
his brother's death. He exchanged letters with his family about the
progress of the Civil War, expressing dismay at the early Union
defeats though never seeming to alter his decision to stick by his
consulate post. In an early letter, he expressed the feeling that letting
the South secede might have been the wiser course. At one point in
his stay, a possibility that his brother Joseph might be drafted raised
the advisability of Howells's coming home to take his place in the
printing business. Though he concludes his letter to his father with
a kind of literary flourish, "you have only to say come, and I come,"
the preceding paragraphs put down very plainly that Howells does not
see his future as that of returning to Ohio (*Letters*, 1:196–98).
    7. Though he turned his main energies away from poetry early,
Howells wrote and published poetry into his late years. The collection, *Stops of Various Quills* (1895) is distinctly different from the
earlier *Poems*. The titles of some poems, "Heredity," "Society," "Labor and Capital," "Equality," "Race," and "Temperament," indicate
Howells's prose concerns extending into poetry. Others take the
more conventional subjects of change, death, and the meaning of life

ing up that hill [to "Redtop," his house in Belmont] for an indefinite time to come..." (*Letters*, 3:7).

11. See Gerard M. Sweeney, "The *Medea* Howells Saw," *American Literature* 42 (March, 1970):83–89. I agree with Sweeney that "the German play is much closer, in both character delineation and theme, to *A Modern Instance*" than is Euripides' tragedy, but I think Howells was more influenced by the general theme than by specific details in either play.

12. W. Oates and E. O'Neill, Jr., eds., *The Complete Greek Drama* (New York: Random House, 1938), p. 728.

13. Howells had his share of trouble with Puritanical readers. A reader from Maine wrote the editor of the *New York Tribune*: "The whole thing from begining to end is revolting" (quoted in Everett Carter, *Howells and the Age of Realism* [Philadelphia, 1954], p. 146). This section of Carter's book, " 'Morality' in Realism," pp. 139–52, is an excellent discussion of Howells's "prudery" and the sexual morality of his age.

14. Another indication of the moral scruples of Howells's age and his response to them occurs in his reply to a letter from Professor Wilder of Cornell objecting to Howells's having in his farces and in illustrations of his stories characters who smoke: "I neither smoke, nor invent heroes, nor instruct my illustrators.... But really, if I had occasion to describe a smoking company, I should lavish pipes and cigars upon them without scruple, and should enjoy a perfectly good conscience. It is not well to confound the aesthetical and the ethical" (*Letters*, 3:257–58).

15. See *LIL*, 1:328–35, and *Letters*, 3:40–46, for a full account of the Johns Hopkins offer and refusal.

Chapter Five

1. The incident, in brief, is that Jonathan Sturges reported to Henry James that Howells had given him this advice in Whistler's garden in Paris in the summer of 1894. In James's novel, the conversation takes place between the central character, Lambert Strether, and little Bilham in book 5, part 2.

2. Both E. H. Cady and Kermit Vanderbilt make extravagant claims for *April Hopes*. I cannot agree with Vanderbilt's claim that it is "a pivotal work in the Howells canon" (*AH*, xi). Howells's exten-

sive gathering of Washington, D. C., and New York City materials probably does indicate his already-established movement to more serious social novels, but the actual use of this material argues that the novel, as it is, reverts to an earlier manner. New York survives in a single scene, Washington in a single chapter; and however trenchantly Howells contrasts Boston, New York, and Washington, that dimension of the novel is all but lost in the attention given to the central courting story.

3. Vanderbilt, *The Achievement of William Dean Howells*, p. 162, n.

Chapter Six

1. In W. D. Howells, *The Rise of Silas Lapham*, ed. W. J. Meserve (Bloomington, 1971), pp. 369–70.

2. See Graham Belcher Blackstock, "Howells's Opinions on the Religious Conflicts of his Age as Exhibited in Magazine Articles," *American Literature* 15 (November, 1943):262–78. Also in Eble, pp. 203–18.

3. See William J. Murray, "The Concept of Complicity in Howells' Fiction," *New England Quarterly* 35 (December, 1962):489–96.

4. Cady, *The Realist at War* (Syracuse, 1958), pp. 164–65.

5. Quoted in Marquis W. Childs and Douglass Cater, *Ethics in a Business Society* (New York: New American Library, 1954), pp. 137–38.

Chapter Seven

1. Everett Carter has observed that as early as 1871, in *Their Wedding Journey*, Howells "had depicted the hard fortuities of life and society and the necessity of showing the New World's ugliness" (introduction, *A Hazard of New Fortunes*, p. xiii). On November 23, 1888, Howells drafted a letter to the *New York Sun* replying to articles about his actual or supposed socialism. He recounts, as a fact, the incident in the novel of a man picking up food out of the gutter and comments: "I thought how in a truly Christian community there would have been a bureau of labor to which he could have gone for work,—not alms.... This was a piece of my 'socialism,' I suppose" (*Letters*, 3:238).

2. *Letters*, 4, 18. Citations from volumes 5 and 6 of the Howells

Letters are to the typescripts being readied for publication at the Center for the Howells Edition, University of Indiana, Bloomington.

3. "Editor's Study," *Harper's Monthly*, December 1888, p. 159.

4. In a letter to Howells generally praising *My Literary Passions*, Charles Eliot Norton had taken exception to the antithesis between "art" and "humanity." Howells replied: "Still one feels that a simple act of goodness, something done for another at the cost of one's self is the very highest thing in life. . . . It is this humanity that I set art below" (*Letters*, vol. 4, August 11, 1895).

5. Clark M. Kirk, *W. D. Howells, Traveler from Altruria 1889–1894* (New Brunswick, N. J., 1962).

6. John Tebbel, *The American Magazine: A Compact History* (New York: Hawthorne Books, 1969), p. 171.

7. Kirk, *W. D. Howells, Traveler from Altruria*, p. 18.

8. Cady, *The Realist at War*, p. 197.

9. See D. N. Rein, "Howells and the *Cosmopolitan*," *American Literature* 17 (March, 1949): 49–55. Walker was from Pittsburgh and had won and lost a fortune in iron manufacture before he entered journalism. His *Cosmopolitan* article, "Alfalfa Farming at the Foot of the Rocky Mountains" (November, 1892), described another successful venture which preceded his coming to New York in 1889 to buy the *Cosmopolitan*. Walker sought out Howells as editor for the magazine in late 1891 because he recognized Howells's importance to improving both the quality and readership of the magazine. Besides, he shared many of Howells's social ideas; "From every man according to his ability; to everyone according to his needs," appeared on the masthead in January, 1892, the beginning of Howells's short period of service. Howells accepted Walker's offer probably because it offered him a wider audience for his views and carried a salary of $15,000 a year.

10. *A Traveler from Altruria*, which came out in book form from Harper and Brothers in 1894, consisted of only the first series which had appeared under the same title in the *Cosmopolitan* from November, 1892, through October, 1893. The second series was never published under the "Letters" title. The last six of these "Letters" were extensively revised and made the first part of *Through the Eye of the Needle* in 1907. See Clara and Rudolf Kirk, eds., *The Altrurian Romances* (Bloomington, 1968), for a full account of this tangled publishing history and complete texts.

Chapter Eight

1. Lynn, *William Dean Howells: An American Life,* pp. 307, 311.
2. Hamlin Garland, "Meetings with Howells," *Bookman,* March, 1917, p. 5.
3. F. O. Matthiessen, *The James Family* (New York: Knopf, 1948), p. 508.
4. In November, 1919, an adaptation of *The Rise of Silas Lapham* by Lillian Sabine, a Washington, D.C., school teacher, was performed by the Theater Guild. Alexander Woollcott reviewed it for the *Times,* referring to it as "that fine American classic, 'The Rise of Silas Lapham,' turned into a somewhat restrained b'gosh drama." Howells was not in attendance at the premier, but his son, John, saw it and called it a "fine presentation" (John Mead Howells to Mildred Howells, November 27, 1919, and accompanying clippings, Houghton Library, Harvard University).
5. Howells's attitude toward Ohio shifted perceptibly as he grew older. His rejection of Jefferson in his twenties (his attempt at a novel in these years, *Geoffrey Winter,* is set in Dulldale) was as firm as that of any provincial who dreams of a larger life elsewhere. "Oh, how genially I come out in this ray of sunlight," he wrote Victoria on January 2, 1859 from Columbus, "after being frozen up so many years in Jefferson" (*Letters,* 1:22). On November 5, 1892, he writes to Joe about walking in Central Park: "but the Park isn't *woods.* I long for the Western woods, too" (Houghton Library, Harvard). Again on September 15, 1894, he writes Joe, "I would rather go back to Jefferson.... Here, the trail of the city is over everything" (Houghton Library, Harvard).

Chapter Nine

1. See Cady, *The Realist at War,* pp. 48–52.
2. A modern physicist, Freeman Dyson, writing about the development of the atomic and hydrogen bombs (*New Yorker,* August 13, 1979), comments on American students he observed in 1948: "They lacked the tragic sense of life which was deeply ingrained in every European of my generation. They had never lived with tragedy and had no feeling for it" ("Disturbing the Universe–II," p. 68).
3. At the beginning of *Criticism and Fiction,* Howells quotes John

Addington Symonds with approval: "Our hope with regard to the unity of taste in the future..." is that "we shall come to comprehend with more instinctive certitude what is simple, natural, and honest, welcoming with gladness all artistic products that exhibit these qualities" (pp. 1–2).

4. Edwin H. Cady, ed., *W. D. Howells as Critic*, Routledge Critics Series (London, 1973) is a large and useful compilation of Howells's critical writings from 1860 to 1911, as is Clara M. and Rudolf Kirk, eds., *Criticism and Fiction, and Other Essays by W. D. Howells* (New York, 1959), which contains other important critical essays.

5. Hoxie Neale Fairchild, *The Noble Savage, A Study in Romantic Naturalism* (New York: Columbia University Press, 1928), p. 69.

6. W. D. Howells, *Familiar Spanish Travels* (New York, 1913).

7. See Howells, "'Lyof N. Tolstoy,'" *North American Review*, December, 1908, reprinted in Cady, *Howells as Critic*, pp. 452–68, for his most complete assessment of Tolstoy and a separate piece from that published in *My Literary Passions*. The most arresting metaphor of the essay is central to specific criticism of *War and Peace*: "It is as if the story were built upon the divination of atomic activity in the moral as in the material universe where stocks [*sic*] and stones are the centres of motion as unceasing, unresting, as blind, as that of the stars in their courses, but not less guided and intended" (p. 467). See also Louis J. Budd, "William Dean Howells' Debt to Tolstoy," *American Slavic and East European Review* 9 (December 1950): 292–301.

8. Cady, *The Realist at War*, p. 223.

9. Ibid., p. 213.

10. Ibid., p. 215. Howells's lesser appreciation of *Black Riders* indicates his generally conservative stance toward poetry. He remained reserved in his recognition of Whitman all his life. In 1885 he contributed ten dollars to a fund to buy Whitman a buggy but noted that this was not to be construed as an endorsement of either his poetry or his theory of poetry. (*Letters*, 3:128). Emily Dickinson's poetry, on the other hand, received one of its most favorable reviews from Howells ("Editor's Study," *Harper's Monthly*, January, 1891), and a letter to Mabel Loomis Todd declared: "What a rare and strange spirit she was!" (*Letters*, 4, 83, December 2, 1894). Howells was aware of an outpouring of estimable poetry in the first decades of the twentieth century. The work of Frost particularly appealed to

him, but he had praise for individual works of E. A. Robinson, Masters, Aiken, and Lindsay.

Chapter Ten

1. The volumes issued were: *My Literary Passions/Criticism and Fiction, The Landlord at Lion's Head, Literature and Life, London Films/Certain Delightful English Towns, Literary Friends and Acquaintance,* and *A Hazard of New Fortunes.*

2. Henry James, "A Letter to Mr. Howells," *North American Review* 195 (1912):558–62; reprinted in Eble, p. 93.

3. In Harry E. Maule and Melville H. Cane, eds., *The Man from Main Street: A Sinclair Lewis Reader* (New York: Random House, 1952), pp. 4–17.

4. See Everett Carter, *Howells and the Age of Realism* (Philadelphia, 1950), pp. 146–47, and Cady, ed., *W. D. Howells as Critic,* pp. 147–49.

5. Anon., "American Literature in England," *Blackwood's Magazine* 133 (1883):136–61; reprinted in Eble, pp. 22 and 33.

6. Ambrose Bierce, "Dispatch from San Francisco, May 22," *Literary Digest* 4 (May, 1892):110.

7. W. D. Howells to Joseph Howells, August 18, 1907 (Houghton Library, Harvard).

8. W. D. Howells, "A Sleep and a Forgetting," in *Between the Dark and the Daylight* (New York, 1907), p. 3.

9. Clara Kirk and Rudolf Kirk, *William Dean Howells* (New York, 1962), p. 165.

10. Richard Chase, *The American Novel and Its Tradition* (Garden City, N.Y.: Doubleday, 1957), p. 177.

11. H. L. Mencken, *Smart Set* 51 (1917):267.

12. Cady, *The Realist at War,* p. 269.

13. The source of the story was Richard J. Taneyhill's "The Leatherwood God: An Account of the Appearance and Pretensions of Joseph C. Dylks in Eastern Ohio in 1828," published in a volume of the *Ohio Valley Historical Series* in 1871. Howells also told the story in his *Stories of Ohio* (1897).

14. See James L. Dean, *Howells' Travels Toward Art* (Albuquerque, 1970), for a well-done study of Howells's travel books.

15. *Letters*, vol. 6.
16. *YOMY*, apps. A–B, pp. 253–58.

Chapter Eleven

1. Henry James, *The Art of the Novel: Critical Prefaces by Henry James*, intro. Richard P. Blackmur (New York: Scribner's, 1947), pp. 33–34.
2. Lyon N. Richardson, *Henry James: Representative Selections* (New York: American Book Co., 1941), p. 81.
3. W. D. Howells, "Author's Preface," in *A Hazard of New Fortunes*, American Edition of Everyman's Library (New York, 1952), p. xxii.
4. Oscar Firkins, *William Dean Howells: A Study* (Cambridge, 1924), p. 233.
5. My comments are not meant to slight Howells's recognition of the vitality of American speech and its relation to literary expression. His intent, as he expressed it to an English clergyman in 1888, was to get back to "the utmost simplicity of expression, to disuse the *literosity* I tried so hard to acquire—to get the gait of compact, clear talk, if possible, informal and direct. It is very difficult. I should advise any beginner to study the raciest, strongest, best *spoken speech*, and let the *printed speech* alone" (*Letters*, 3:213).
6. Cady, *W. D. Howells as Critic*, p. 1.
7. Ibid., p. 2.
8. W. J. Meserve, ed., *The Complete Plays of W. D. Howells* (New York, 1966), p. xv.
9. H. S. Commager, "For Fifty Years a Literary Dynamo," *New York Times Book Review*, October 11, 1959, pp. 1, 16.
10. James Woodress, "The Dean's Comeback: Four Decades of Howells' Scholarship," in *Howells: A Century of Criticism*, ed. K. Eble (Dallas, 1962), pp. 236–47.
11. Howells wrote Thomas Sergeant Perry, August 23, 1917, about Harvey's book: "First he skies me, inordinately, and then drivels over me with talk about 'sissyism'" (*Letters*, vol. 6).
12. Edmund Wilson, "The Fruits of the MLA: *Their Wedding Journey*," *New York Review of Books*, September 26, October 10, 1968.

Selected Bibliography

PRIMARY SOURCES

A complete listing of Howells's works is to be found in William M. Gibson and George Arms, *A Bibliography of William Dean Howells*, New York: the New York Public Library, 1948. The following list of Howells's books in order of first printing includes abbreviations used in the text and identifies first editions as well as modern ones. (Page references cite the modern text wherever possible.)

1. Fiction

TWJ (1872) *Their Wedding Journey*. Bloomington: Indiana University Press, 1968.

CA (1873) *A Chance Acquaintance*. Bloomington: Indiana University Press, 1971.

FC (1875) *A Foregone Conclusion*. Boston: James R. Osgood, 1875.

LA (1879) *The Lady of the Aroostook*. Boston, Houghton, Osgood, 1879.

UC (1880) *The Undiscovered Country*. Boston: Houghton Mifflin, 1870.

FR (1881) *A Fearful Responsibility and Other Stories*. Boston: James R. Osgood, 1881.

DBP (1881) *Dr. Breen's Practice*. Boston: James R. Osgood, 1881.

MI (1882) *A Modern Instance*. Bloomington: Indiana University Press, 1977.

WR (1883) *A Woman's Reason*. Boston: James R. Osgood, 1883.

RSL (1885) *The Rise of Silas Lapham*. Bloomington: Indiana University Press, 1971.

IS (1886) *Indian Summer*. Bloomington: Indiana University Press, 1971.

MC (1887) *The Minister's Charge, or The Apprenticeship of Lemuel Barker.* Bloomington: Indiana University Press, 1978.

AH (1888) *April Hopes.* Bloomington: Indiana University Press, 1974.

AK (1889) *Annie Kilburn.* New York: Harper & Brothers, 1889.

HNF (1890) *A Hazard of New Fortunes.* Bloomington: Indiana University Press, 1976.

SD (1890) *The Shadow of a Dream* and *An Imperative Duty.*

ID (1892) Bloomington: Indiana University Press, 1970.

QM (1892) *The Quality of Mercy.* Bloomington: Indiana University Press, 1979.

WC (1893) *The World of Chance.* New York: Harper & Brothers, 1893.

CB (1893) *The Coast of Bohemia.* New York: Harper & Brothers, 1893.

TA (1894) *A Traveler from Altruria.* New York: Harper & Brothers, 1898.

DTW (1896) *The Day of their Wedding.* New York: Harper & Brothers, 1896.

P&M (1896) *A Parting and a Meeting.* New York: Harper & Brothers, 1896.

LLH (1897) *The Landlord at Lion's Head.* New York: Harper & Brothers, 1897.

OEC (1897) *An Open-Eyed Conspiracy.* New York: Harper & Brothers, 1897.

SOP (1898) *The Story of a Play.* New York: Harper & Brothers, 1898.

RL (1899) *Ragged Lady.* New York: Harper & Brothers, 1899.

SWJ (1899) *Their Silver Wedding Journey.* New York: Harper & Brothers, 1899.

PPL (1901) *A Pair of Patient Lovers.* New York: Harper & Brothers, 1901.

FPB (1902) *The Flight of Pony Baker.* New York: Harper & Brothers, 1902.

K (1902) *The Kentons.* Bloomington: Indiana University Press, 1971.

QS (1903) *Questionable Shapes.* New York: Harper & Brothers, 1903.

LH (1903) *Letters Home.* New York: Harper & Brothers, 1903.

SRL (1904) *The Son of Royal Langbrith*. Bloomington: Indiana University Press, 1969.

MBI (1905) *Miss Bellard's Inspiration*. New York: Harper & Brothers, 1905.

TEN (1907) *Through the Eye of the Needle*. New York: Harper & Brothers, 1907.

BDAD (1907) *Between the Dark and the Daylight*. New York: Harper & Brothers, 1907.

F&R (1908) *Fennel and Rue*. New York: Harper & Brothers, 1908.

NLM (1913) *New Leaf Mills*. New York: Harper & Brothers, 1913.

DS (1916) *The Daughter of the Storage*. New York: Harper & Brothers, 1916.

LG (1916) *The Leatherwood God*. Bloomington: Indiana University Press, 1976.

VK (1920) *The Vacation of the Kelwyns*. New York: Harper & Brothers, 1920.

MF (1921) *Mrs. Farrell*. New York: Harper & Brothers, 1921.

AR (1908) *The Altrurian Romances*. Bloomington: Indiana University Press, 1968.

2. Criticism

C&F (1891) *Criticism and Fiction*. New York: Harper & Brothers, 1891.

MLP (1895) *My Literary Passions*. New York: Harper & Brothers, 1895.

MIP (1867) *Modern Italian Poets*. New York: Harper & Brothers, 1887.

HOF (1901) *Heroines of Fiction*. New York: Harper & Brothers, 1901.

L&L (1902) *Literature and Life*. New York: Harper & Brothers, 1902.

II (1910) *Imaginary Interviews*. New York: Harper & Brothers, 1910.

3. Reminiscences and Autobiography

BT (1890) *A Boy's Town*. New York: Harper & Brothers, 1890.

MYLC (1893) *My Year in a Log Cabin.* New York: Harper & Brothers, 1893.

I&E (1896) *Impressions and Experiences.* New York: Harper & Brothers, 1896.

LF&A (1900) *Literary Friends and Acquaintance.* Bloomington: Indiana University Press, 1968.

MMT (1910) *My Mark Twain.* New York: Harper & Brothers, 1910.

YOMY (1916) *Years of My Youth.* New York: Harper & Brothers, 1916.

Years of My Youth and Three Essays. Bloomington: Indiana University Press, 1975.

4. Travel Books and Sketches

VL (1866) *Venetian Life.* 2 vols. Boston: Houghton Mifflin, 1885.

IJ (1867) *Italian Journeys.* New York: Hurd and Houghton, 1867.

SS (1871) *Suburban Sketches.* New York: Hurd and Houghton, 1871.

TC (1886) *Tuscan Cities.* Boston: Ticknor and Company, 1886.

LSS (1812) *A Little Swiss Sojourn.* New York: Harper & Brothers, 1892.

LF (1906) *London Films.* New York: Harper & Brothers, 1906.

CDET (1906) *Certain Delightful English Towns.* New York: Harper & Brothers, 1906.

RH (1908) *Roman Holidays and Others.* New York: Harper & Brothers, 1908.

SEC (1909) *Seven English Cities.* New York: Harper & Brothers, 1909.

FST (1913) *Familiar Spanish Travels.* New York: Harper & Brothers, 1913.

5. Poetry

PTF (1860) *Poems of Two Friends.* Columbus, Ohio: Follett and Foster, 1860.

Poems (1873) *Poems.* Boston: James R. Osgood and Company, 1873.

SVQ (1895) *Stops of Various Quills.* New York: Harper & Brothers, 1895.

6. Plays

Walter J. Meserve, ed. *The Complete Plays of W. D. Howells.* New York: New York University Press, 1960.

7. Letters and Manuscripts

LIL   *Life in Letters of William Dean Howells.* 2 vols. Edited by Mildred Howells. Garden City, N.Y.: Doubleday & Doran, 1928.

MT–HL   *Mark Twain–Howells Letters.* 2 vols. Edited by Henry Nash Smith and William M. Gibson. Cambridge: Harvard University Press, 1960.

Letters   *W. D. Howells Selected Letters.* Boston: Twayne, 1979–. Vol. 1, *1852–1872*, edited by G. Arms, R. H. Ballinger, C. K. Lohmann, and J. K. Reeves, 1979. Vol. 2, *1873–1881*, edited by G. Arms and C. K. Lohmann, 1979. Vol. 3, *1882–1891*, edited by R. C. Leitz III, R. H. Ballinger and C. K. Lohmann, 1980. Vol. 4, *1892–1901*, edited by Thomas Wortham, C. K. Lohmann and D. J. Nordloh, 1981. Vol. 5, *1902–1911*, edited by W. C. Fischer and C. K. Lohmann, 1982. Volume 6 which will complete the edition, is in manuscript at the Howells Edition Center, Indiana University, Bloomington.

G. Monteiro and B. Murphy, eds. *The Correspondence of John Hay and William Dean Howells, 1861–1905.* Boston: Twayne Publishers, 1981.

Reeves, John K. "The Literary Manuscripts of W. D. Howells." *Bulletin of the New York Public Library* 62 (June, 1958):267–363.

————. "The Literary Manuscripts of W. D. Howells. A Supplement to the Descriptive Finding List." *Bulletin of the John Rylands Library*, September, 1961.

SECONDARY SOURCES

1. Bibliographies

Blanck, Jacob. "William Dean Howells." *Bibliography of American Literature.* New Haven: Yale University Press, 1963, 4:384–448.

Eichelberger, Clayton L. *Published Comment on William Dean How-ells Through 1920: A Research Bibliography.* Boston: G. K. Hall, 1976.

Fortenberry, George. "William Dean Howells." In *Fifteen American Authors before 1900: Bibliographic Essays on Research and Criticism,* edited by Robert A. Rees and Earl N. Harbert. Madison: University of Wisconsin Press, 1971, pp. 229–44.

Gibson, William M., and Arms, George. *A Bibliography of William Dean Howells.* New York: New York Public Library, 1948. With Blanck's, still the indispensable bibliography, not to be super-seded until publication of the bibliography projected for the completion of the Howells Edition.

Halfmann, Ulrich, and Smith, Don R. "William Dean Howells: A Revised and Annotated Bibliography of Secondary Comment in Periodicals and Newspapers, 1868–1919." *American Literary Realism* 5 (Spring, 1972): 91–121.

Woodress, James, and Anderson, Stanley P. "A Bibliography of Writ-ing about William Dean Howells." *American Literary Realism,* special no. (1969):1–139.

2. Other Useful Research Materials

Carrington, George C. Jr., and Papp, Idiko de. *Plots and Characters in the Fiction of William Dean Howells.* Hamden, Conn.: Archon, 1976.

Halfmann, Ulrich. *Interviews with William Dean Howells.* Arlington: University of Texas, 1973.

3. Books about Howells's Life and Works

Baldwin, Mary A., ed. *My Mark Twain: Reminiscences and Criticism by William Dean Howells.* Baton Rouge: Louisiana State Uni-versity Press, 1967. A reprinting of the original edition but with an introduction and useful annotations.

Bennett, George N. *The Realism of William Dean Howells, 1889–1920.* Nashville, Tenn.: Vanderbilt University Press, 1973.

————. *William Dean Howells: The Development of a Novelist.* Norman: University of Oklahoma Press, 1959. Together these two books offer an overview of Howells's life and works and a detailed critical study of the later novels. Tends to argue throughout for more merit in neglected Howells novels than they probably possess.

Brooks, Van Wyck. *Howells: His Life and World.* London: J. M. Dent, 1959. Brooks's sympathy toward Howells does not keep him from giving a balanced estimate of the worth of individual novels and his place in American literature.

Cady, Edwin H. *The Road to Realism: The Early Years 1837–1885 of William Dean Howells.* Syracuse: Syracuse University Press, 1956.

————. *The Realist at War: The Mature Years 1885–1920 of William Dean Howells.* Syracuse: Syracuse University Press, 1958. Perhaps not yet the definitive biography, yet a source upon which most other biographies depend.

————, ed. *W. D. Howells as Critic.* London: Routledge & Kegan Paul, 1973. A very complete collection of Howells's criticism.

————, and Frazier, David L., eds. *The War of the Critics over William Dean Howells.* Evanston, Ill.: Row, Peterson, 1962.

Carrington, George C., Jr. *The Immense Complex Drama: The World and Art of the Howells Novel.* Columbus: Ohio State University Press, 1966. Though somewhat labored in its critical approach, this book properly and usefully focuses on Howells's art as a novelist.

Carter, Everett. *Howells and the Age of Realism.* Philadelphia: J. B. Lippincott, 1954. Still one of the best books on Howells and its larger subject.

Cooke, Delmar G. *William Dean Howells: A Critical Study.* New York: E. P. Dutton, 1922. The earliest biography, now superseded.

Dean, James L. *Howells' Travels Toward Art.* Albuquerque: University of New Mexico Press, 1970. Somewhat misleadingly titled, this is a good, close study of Howells's travel books.

Doyle, James. *Annie Howells and Achille Fréchette.* Toronto: University of Toronto Press, 1979. A useful source of information about Howells's sister and her husband, a Montreal journalist and poet.

Eble, Kenneth E., ed. *Howells: A Century of Criticism.* Dallas: Southern Methodist University Press, 1962. A careful selection of criticism to illustrate how Howells was regarded from the 1860s to 1960.

Eschholz, Paul A., ed. *Critics on William Dean Howells.* Coral Gables:

University of Miami Press, 1975. Similar to the Eble volume, but with some different and more recent selections.

Firkins, Oscar W. *William Dean Howells, A Study.* Cambridge: Harvard University Press, 1924. Best of the early biographies.

Fryckstedt, Olov W. *In Quest of America: A Study of Howells' Early Development as a Novelist.* Cambridge: Harvard University Press, 1958. Somewhat too pat in pursuing its thesis, but a careful study of Howells's developing into a particular kind of novelist.

Gibson, William M. *William D. Howells.* Minnesota Pamphlets on American Writers, no. 63. Minneapolis: University of Minnesota Press, 1967. An excellent introduction by one of the best Howells scholars.

Harvey, Alexander. *William Dean Howells: A Study of the Achievement of a Literary Artist.* New York: B. W. Huebsch, 1917. A book which baffled Howells when it first came to his attention and now a literary curiosity, only.

Hough, Robert L. *The Quiet Rebel: William Dean Howells as a Social Commentator.* Lincoln: University of Nebraska Press, 1959. Handles its limited but important subject well.

Kirk, Clara M. *W. D. Howells and Art in His Time.* New Brunswick: Rutgers University Press, 1965.

————. *W. D. Howells, Traveler from Altruria, 1889–1894.* New Brunswick: Rutgers University Press, 1962.

————, and Kirk, Rudolf. *William Dean Howells.* United States Authors Series, no. 16. New York: Twayne, 1962. These books of the Kirks, plus their introduction to the American Writers Series, *Representative Selections* (rev. ed., New York: Hill and Wang, 1961), comprise an estimable contribution to Howells scholarship.

Lynn, Kenneth S. *William Dean Howells: An American Life.* New York: Harcourt Brace Jovanovich, 1970. Balanced in its biographical scholarship and critical readings of Howells's works, deserves a high place among biographical and critical studies.

McMurray, William. *The Literary Realism of William Dean Howells.* Carbondale: Southern Illinois University Press, 1967. A study of twelve novels, largely within the framework of realism.

Vanderbilt, Kermit. *The Achievement of William Dean Howells: A Reinterpretation.* Princeton: Princeton University Press, 1968.

Essentially close readings of four novels of the 1880s, arguing for Howells's high rank as a novelist.

Wagenknecht, Edward. *William Dean Howells: The Friendly Eye.* New York: Oxford University Press, 1969. This book gains from having been written out of great admiration for the man as well as an interest in his work.

Woodress, James L. *Howells and Italy.* Durham: Duke University Press, 1952. The basic study of this important period in Howells's life.

Howells's place in American life and literature during his time is such that few books which deal with the period or with major and minor authors of that time fail to include mention of him. For that reason, I do not attempt to list the many books that one might find useful. Specific books which I have used in this study are listed in the notes. Similarly, articles about Howells are so numerous and so readily identified in the *MLA International Bibliography* as well as in the annual *American Literary Scholarship*, Lewis Leary, *Articles On American Literature Appearing in Current Periodicals*, and issues of *American Literature*, that I include only a very short list of articles below.

4. Articles

Andrews, William L. "William Dean Howells and Charles W. Chesnutt: Criticism and Race Fiction in the Age of Booker T. Washington." *American Literature* 48 (November 1976): 327-39. Takes an informed and modern view toward Howells's attitude to black writers and writing.

Atherton, Gertrude. "Why Is American Literature Bourgeois?" *North American Review* 278 (May, 1904): 771-81. Indicative of adverse criticism of Howells and others as tastes began shifting away from the past.

Bogardus, Ralph F. "A Literary Realist and the Camera: W. D. Howells and the Uses of Photography." *American Literary Realism* 10 (Summer, 1977): 231-41. A somewhat disappointing article on an interesting subject, concluding that Howells's response to photography as an analogy for realism was uncertain.

Crider, Gregory L. "William Dean Howells and the Anti-urban Tradition: A Reconsideration," *American Studies* 19 (1978): 55-

64. An informed discussion of Howells's relation to the country vs. city argument.

Dennis, Scott A. *"The World of Chance*: Howells' Hawthornian Self-Parody." *American Literature* 52 (May, 1980): 279–93. A substantial discussion of this novel somewhat apart from its place among Howells's economic novels and emphasizing what it may reveal about Howells's attitudes toward himself.

Ford, T. W. "Howells and the American Negro." *Texas Studies in Language and Literature* 5 (Winter, 1964): 530-37. Howells's attitudes toward race remain an important subject for study; this article is limited to an examination of *An Imperative Duty*.

Foster, Richard. "The Contemporaneity of Howells." *New England Quarterly* 32 (March, 1959): 54–78. A response to Lionel Trilling's consideration of Howells.

Gardner, Joseph H. "Howells: The 'Realist' as Dickensian." *Modern Fiction Studies* 16 (Autumn, 1970): Howells special Issue, 323–43. In comparing Howells and Dickens, this article sheds light on why Howells is often disappointing as a novelist.

Habegger, Alfred. "W. D. Howells and the 'American Girl.' " *Texas Quarterly* 19 (Winter, 1976): 149–56. Though much has been written on this subject, this essay contributes to an understanding of Howells's women characters and their relation to women of his time.

Kirk, Clara M. "Toward a Theory of Art: A Dialogue between William Dean Howells and C. E. Norton." *New England Quarterly* 36 (Summer, 1963): 291–319. Norton was one of Howells's closest Boston-Cambridge friends and their disagreement about idealism and realism helps define both terms.

MacMurray, William J. "The Concept of Complicity in Howells' Fiction." *New England Quarterly* 35 (December 1962): 489–96. Other articles deal with this subject, but this is a good comprehensive treatment of "complicity" as the "interactive nature of all existence and experience in which the part and the whole are continually remaking one another."

Morris, Lloyd. "Conscience in the Parlor: William Dean Howells." *American Scholar* 18 (Autumn, 1949): 407–16. Still one of the fairest, yet critical, overall assessments of Howells's place in American culture.

Munford, H. M. "The Disciple Proves Independent: Howells and

Lowell." *PMLA* 74 (Spring, 1959): 484–87. Howells's attachment to and breaking away from New England culture is well defined in his shifting relationship with Lowell.

Salomon, R. B. "Realism as Disinheritance: Twain, Howells, and James." *American Quarterly* 16 (Winter, 1964): 531–44. No one has yet tried a book which would bring these three together; this article shows how they relate to a specific important idea.

Spangler, George M. "Moral Anxiety in *A Modern Instance*." *New England Quarterly* 46 (June, 1973): 236–49. An example of an informed discussion of an important Howells novel focusing on the conflict between the author's apparent intent and the meaning which emerges from the novel.

Stein, Allen. "Marriage in Howells' Novels." *American Literature* 48 (January, 1977): 500–524. A long discussion of an important subject though too accepting in its analyses of Howells's benign view of marriage.

Sweeney, Gerard M. "The *Medea* Howells Saw." *American Literature* 42 (March, 1970): 83–89. A bit of good detective work in finding out about the melodramatic adaptation of the Greek tragedy by Franz Grillparzer which Howells saw on the Boston stage.

Trilling, Lionel. "William Dean Howells and the Roots of Modern Taste." *Partisan Review* 18 (September–October, 1951): 516–36. The recognition of Howells's stature by an important modern critic much like Howells in many respects is an important contribution to Howells criticism.

Vanderbilt, Kermit. "Howells' Studies: Past, or Passing, or to Come." *American Literary Realism* 7 (Spring, 1974): 143–53. A review article bringing the state of Howells studies up to date from the time of Woodress's 1960 survey, marred somewhat by excessive pleading for *April Hopes*.

Wilson, Edmund. "The Fruits of the MLA: *Their Wedding Journey*." *New York Review of Books* September 26, October 10, 1968. Scholarship does not often get the broad humanistic criticism it should not escape. When it does, as in Wilson's reservations about the CEAA efforts represented by this first book in the Howells edition, the scholar's reaction is too often outraged or defensive.

Woodress, James L. "The Dean's Comeback: Four Decades of Scholarship." *Texas Studies in Language and Literature* 2 (Spring, 1960): 115-23.

Index

Abdul Hamed II, Sultan of Turkey, 162
Alden, Henry Mills, 93, 118
Aldrich, Thomas Bailey, 57, 65, 83, 162, 176
American Academy of Arts and Letters, 140
American Literary Realism, 189
American Literary Scholarship, 189
Anderson, Sherwood, 159
Aristides, 119
Arms, George, 188
Atlantic Monthly, 26, 27, 31, 32, 35, 38, 39, 40, 42, *43–44*, 45, 46, 47, 57, 58, 65, 66, 67
Austen, Jane, 153

Bacon-Shakespeare controversy, 174
Baxter, Sylvester, 123
Bellamy, Edward: *Looking Backward*, 115
Belmont, Massachusetts, 44, 63, 85
Bennett, George, 189
Bierce, Ambrose, 160
Bishop, W. H., 72
Björnson, Björstjerne, 152
Boston, 31, 34, 35, 42, *43–44*, 46, 47, 54, 64, 69, 78, 81, 83, 86, 109, 192
Boston Advertiser, 35, 39, 40

Bowles, Samuel, 35
Brooks, Van Wyck: *Howells*, 187
Brown, John, 18, 31
Browning, Robert, 31
Burbank, A. P., 138
Burke, Edmund: *Essay on the Sublime and the Beautiful*, 148
Burney, Fanny, 153
Byron, George Gordon, 18, 152

Cady, Edwin, 19, 20, 54, 77, 90, 169, 184–85, 189
Cambridge, Massachusetts, 44–45, 47–48, 52, 63, 65, 98, 109, 178
Carrington, George, 189
Carter, Everett: *Howells and the Age of Realism*, 189
Cather, Willa, 72
Century, 78, 97
Cervantes, Miguel de, 17, 23, 32, 61, *150–51*
Cézanne, Paul, 126
Chase, Richard, 163
Chase, Salmon P., 34
Chaucer, Geoffrey, 18, 87, *152–53*
Cincinnati Gazette, *24–25*
Civil War, 33–34
Clemens, Olivia Langdon (Mrs. Samuel L.), 161
Clemens, Samuel L. (Mark Twain), 2, 10, 26, 33, 39, 97, 99, 112, 118, 123, 138, 140,